FRENCH EN

The P&O European Ferries Guide
to Calais, Champagne, the Ardennes
and Bruges

FRENCH ENTRÉE 7

The P&O European Ferries Guide
to Calais, Champagne, the Ardennes
and Bruges

Patricia Fenn
Diana McNair-Wilson

Quiller Press
London

Boyer Reims

First published 1988 by Quiller Press Ltd
50 Albemarle Street, London W1X 4BD

Line drawings: Ken Howard
Area maps: Paul Emra
Design and production in association with
Book Production Consultants, Cambridge

ISBN 0 907621 87 2

Printed in Great Britain by
Richard Clay (The Chaucer Press) Ltd, Bungay,
Suffolk

Contents

Notes on using the book

1 The area maps are to help the reader to find the place he wishes to visit on his own map. Each place is given a reference on the relevant area map, but they are not designed to replace a good touring map.

2 o.o.s. stands for 'out of season', Other abbreviations such as f for francs, are standard.

3 H, R and C in the margin stand for 'hotel', 'restaurant' and 'chambres d'hôte'.

4 L, M or S in the margin, in combination with 3 above, indicate the standard of the hotel or restaurant: L = Luxury, S = Simple and M is used for those in between (e.g. (H)S, (R)L, etc.).

5 The ➤ symbol means the establishment fulfils exceptionally well at least one of the author's criteria of comfort, welcome and cuisine – see also pages 26–7.

6 Credit cards: 'A' = Access, 'AE' = American Express, 'V' = Visa, 'DC' = Diners Club, and 'EC' is Eurocard.

7 ⦅🍴Ⓗ🍴⦆ means Hotel of the Year.

8 Ⓜ means market days

9 The figures above the addresses, eg 62000, are the postal codes, which should be used in all correspondence.

Author's appeal

In order to keep 'French Entrée' up to date I need all the latest information I can get on establishments listed in the guide. If you have any comments on these or any other details that might supplement my own researching I should be most grateful if you would pass them on.

Please include the name and address of establishment, date and duration of visit. Also please state if you will allow your name to be used.

Patricia Fenn,
c/o P&O European Ferries P.R. Dept.,
Channel House,
Channel View Road,
Dover, Kent.

Raisons d'Être

The idea behind this series is to cover, in depth, one particular area of France at a time, with enough detail supplied to allow the reader to decide what is right for *him*. It is not: a guide for any one income group, an objective listing, a symbolised quick reference. It is: personal, prejudiced and subjective; a description of what's on offer, with the symbols plumped out.

When the ideal is unavailable (too far, too dear, closed), an alternative may thereby be selected closest to the requirements. One man's jolly recorded pop may be another's migraine; one woman's rustic dream may be another's spider-ridden horror. You have to know these things, then *you* make the choice.

Increasingly it is becoming a reader-dictated guide. After seven years, they leave me in no doubt what they want from me. And that's the way it should be. Any ideas for improvements/ deletions are welcomed, if not always followed. For example, the idea of listing a few overnight stops around Dover drew a resounding silence, so that has gone. (Pity – I had some good ones.) Postal codes, market days, garages, are recent additions.

Certainly the guides could not continue to be valid without the constant updating that goes on with the help of readers' letters, suggesting new discoveries and keeping me posted about the fate of old ones. Keep up the good work and I will try and answer every letter personally, to say a profound thank-you.

Patricia Fenn.

Entrée to the Entrées

Categories
Old Entrée readers will know that hotels and restaurants are graded into three categories: 'L' for Luxury, 'M' for Medium, and 'S' for Simple. Value for money, with a smile, is the criterion in judging them.

'L' prices are still rather less luxurious than at home, and there are bargains to be had for those used to paying British bills for two posh beds. In France you can stay in a château for £15 a head. In this category come arrowed examples like Le Château de Ligny at Ligny-en-Cambrésis (p.98), or La Tour du Roy at Vervins (p.159). The price range nowadays is from 300f upwards for a double room.

Nipping across to France for a special celebration adds a certain extra excitement to the occasion and it's undoubtedly a good destination for pushing the boat out in more ways than one. Some well-heeled readers will only be looking for recommendations in this bracket anyway (though I think they miss a lot). The 'L' restaurants represent excellent value in that, mouthful for mouthful, franc for pound, you will probably eat better and cheaper across the Channel than at home. A meal at one of France's greatest restaurants, Boyer at Reims, at around £50, is the most expensive quoted in any Entrée to date, but just compare this with a Michelin three-star in England and it looks a bargain. For a one-night stand near Calais, La Meunerie at Teteghem (p.151) would deliciously fill the bill, with new beds to fall into if driving back to the port seemed unwise.

The **'S'** grades are the ones that need most checking, since a bad night's sleep or an uneatable meal are expensive mistakes. Letters from readers sticking to tight budgets, hung about with kids, or just appreciative of a good bargain, have been invaluable here, since in this category outward appearances can be not only deceptive but daunting. Once past the sometimes grim exterior, the contrast of a sparkling little restaurant and a warm welcome are all the more cheering.

'S' hotels will be modest but proud of it, clean, with ample hot water supplies (though you might be charged a ridiculous sum for a bath or shower) and a trying-to-please patron. They will never be on a thunderous main road, though they might have been chosen because their site is convenient for an overnight stop, when aesthetic considerations might have to bow to practicability. They may not have carpets and the lighting will be appalling. In these establishments you will have a better chance of striking up a relationship with owners or locals, but do not expect them to speak your language. Close friendships have been forged without linguistic compatibility.

The price of an 'S' double room would range from about 75f to 180f, but those in the latter group would almost certainly include a bath or shower and often more than one double bed. One-night family rooms cut down travelling costs considerably. L'Escale at Escalles (p.82) has proved its worth over many years, I liked La Touraine Champenoise at Tours-sur-Marne (p.153) and Diana fell in love with the Hôtel Roses de Picardie in St-Gobain (p.134) – all simply good.

An 'S' meal will often be taken in the hotel by weary travellers who have no wish to venture out, or in a town bistro, country auberge or Relais Routier. They can represent the best value of all; there is no equivalent in England for the 45f three-course menu, on which, if you're lucky, you can stoke up for the day. But there are pitfalls. Do not expect a D.I.Y. chef, doubling up as patron, to dish up gourmet extravaganzas. Stick to the simplest dishes. Write off the vegetables (more of this anon). Don't be tempted to make this meal your special treat. Better by far to go for the cheapest menu in a 'L' restaurant, (particularly at lunchtime when there are real bargains to be found), than the dearest in the 'S' category, which can often cost more.

In between the 'L' and the 'S' comes the **'M'** for Medium, which can be all things to all men. Harder to classify exactly, since the borders are blurred, and I am very suspicious of a Simple restaurant striving to go upmarket, or the Medium aspiring to be Luxury.

This is the bracket used by most French people, who are far more inflexible than we Brits. The honest bourgeois will spend more of his income on a weekly family blow-out than would we, and it's all part of their acknowledged rank and order to see and be seen in the best they can afford. If they are going to spend three hours over a red-faced Sunday lunch, it might as well be on a comfy chair. They wouldn't dream of descending down the social scale to eat in a Routier, though I have letters from English captains of industry, judges, naval officers, professors, who do and are proud of it. Their hotels must be classified two or three star, while the English managerial classes cheerfully put up with lino on the floor, just because it's France and fun.

M hotels cost as little as 90f for a double *simple* with only a washbasin and bidet, to 250f-ish for a room with private bath. Most of the chain hotels would come in this group and I am sure they are very practical and efficient. I do not waste space listing them because readers can find them without my help and do not need a description of plastic uniformity and manager control to know exactly what to expect.

In order to qualify as 'M', there should be adequate bedside lighting, carpeting (often up the walls too!), good furniture, sometimes a telephone and T.V. These are hotels where one would be happy to spend more than an overnight *faute-de-mieux* stop. With any luck they might still be family-run, and their owners should be friendly and helpful. My *FE4* Hotel of the Year, Les Trois Mousquetaires, see p.28, is an excellent example.

The M restaurants can be very good indeed. Here you might find a young chef who has been well trained and has decided to branch out on his own, or a self-taught, natural cook who has won a faithful local following by his reliability. Look for the French cars in the car-parks. Meals here will cost approximately between 80 and 150f.

A word of caution about some of the lowest priced menus in this category. As a catchpenny, you will often see a surprisingly cheap menu pinned up or advertised. Look carefully before committing yourself. Sometimes it will offer a choice of complete banality – shop pâté, andouillettes, ice cream – and you will be lured into paying more than you had intended in order to eat more interestingly.

You don't have to leave the port of Calais before coming across a shining example of a typical good-value restaurant in this category – Le Channel (p.51).

Another most welcome category is beginning to creep into the French Entrée vision – that of *chambres d'hôte*. These are extremely well organised in France. Based on a wide variety of accommodation, from château (the *FE6*'s Hotel of the Year is a *château chambre d'hôte*) to farmhouse, they are inspected and licenced by the State, which encourages all manner of householders to adapt their homes to B. and B. accommodation. Some provinces, like Normandy, are dotted with enticing examples. (I shudder to think how many hours of bumping down the wrong cart-track to find them will be involved in the imminent re-writing of *FE3*.) Those already listed have met with particular enthusiasm from delighted readers, who have enjoyed the experience of staying cheaply in spacious, non-cost-effective bedrooms, and meeting the often exceptionally kind families. However, because they are so varied, the vetting is even more important than usual and first-hand experiences are especially welcome.

(Unfortunately in this area there are relatively few examples of this admirable breed.)

Prices here too have risen in the short time that they have been proving their popularity. Expect to pay between 80 and 180f, more for the châteaux (though not in this book), which usually includes a better-than-average breakfast.

These limits are arbitrary and price is not always an accurate guide to the feel of the place. My contention is that most English readers will want different grades at different times. Campers who generally eat at the nearest local 'S' might well wish to mark an anniversary with an 'L'; tycoons might be only to happy to forget their expense account dinners and take their families to the cheapo.

Arrows These are the paragons, the hotels and restaurants around which it is safe to arrange a holiday. They are outstanding, in their category, for at least one (normally several) of the desiderata of comfort, welcome, good food, pleasant site. See p.26 for a list.

A Word on
Wine Sore subject. The sting in the tail to all this bargain food is the far-from-bargain wine. It comes as a nasty shock to be expected to pay more for French wine in France than in Britain. Price blocking has been blamed but I'm afraid it's probably more a case of pure commercial greed.

House wines are getting rarer by the day. When they do appear, at around 40f a bottle, they sometimes have an 80% mark-up on the bottle of plonk you might take home from the hypermarket. In more expensive restaurants the bill can easily double when appropriate wine is added. I cannot help – only warn what to expect.

Wine by the glass would be an innovation that I would much appreciate, especially at lunchtime with afternoon driving envisaged. Wine bars – *bistros à vin* – are incredibly slow to catch on. It took an Englishman to open one up in Paris (Willi's Wine Bar – recommended!) and it has been an outstanding success, but provincial towns do not seem to have got the message. The alternative is a small glass of the cheapest, no-choice, gut-rot in a seedy bar; few restaurants that I have found have agreed to serve a single glass with a meal. French chauvinist eating and drinking habits die hard.

A Campaign It grieves me inexpressibly to note the disappearance of fresh veg. from French menus. With the neighbouring market stalls groaning with covetable fresh produce, the restaurants have the cheek to dish up khaki tinned beans and frites. It's an insidious process, paralysing imaginative vegetable cooking. Where are the well-chosen, lovingly-prepared individual vegetable accessories that used to complement each dish? The best one can hope for nowadays, even in expensive restaurants, is a portion-controlled standardised side dish of the same selection for everybody.

If every French Entrée reader, and especially those who write to me about this very phenomenon, were to ask specifically for fresh veg. and make offensive grumbling noises if he didn't get them, it might be one small step for posterity.

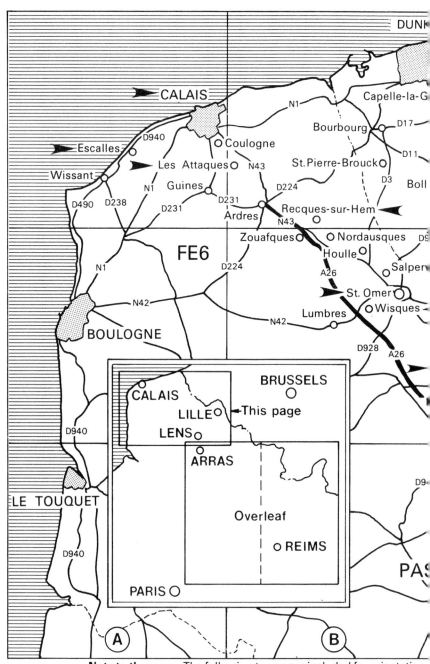

DUNK

CALAIS

Capelle-la-G

Escalles

Bourbourg

D17

Wissant

Coulogne

St. Pierre-Brouck

D11

Les Attaques

N43

Boll

Guines

D224

D231

D3

Ardres

Recques-sur-Hem

N43

Zouafques

Nordausques

D9

Houlle

Salper

St. Omer

Wisques

Lumbres

N42

D928

A26

BOULOGNE

FE6

N42

N1

D490

D238

D231

N1

D224

A26

CALAIS

BRUSSELS

LILLE ← This page

LENS

ARRAS

D9

Overleaf

LE TOUQUET

REIMS

D940

PAS

PARIS

(A)   (B)

Note to the maps: The following towns are included for orientation purposes only, they are not dealt with in this guide: Arras, Boulogne Charleroi, Dunkerque, Lens, Le Touquet, Lille, Mons, Paris, Roubaix

12

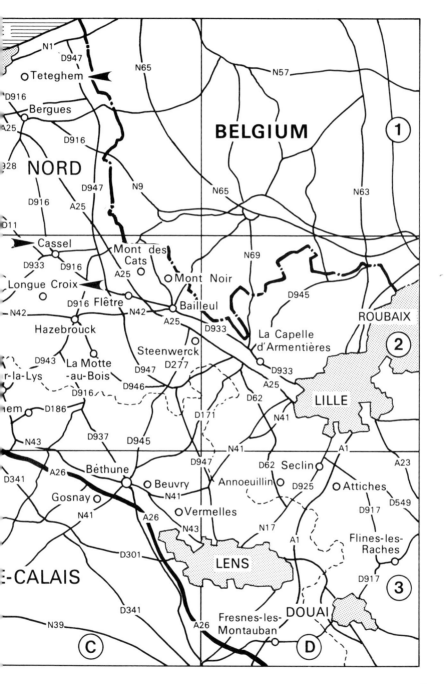

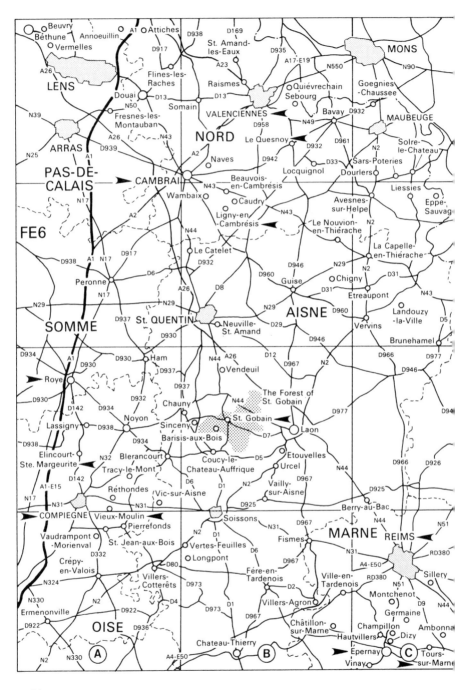

14

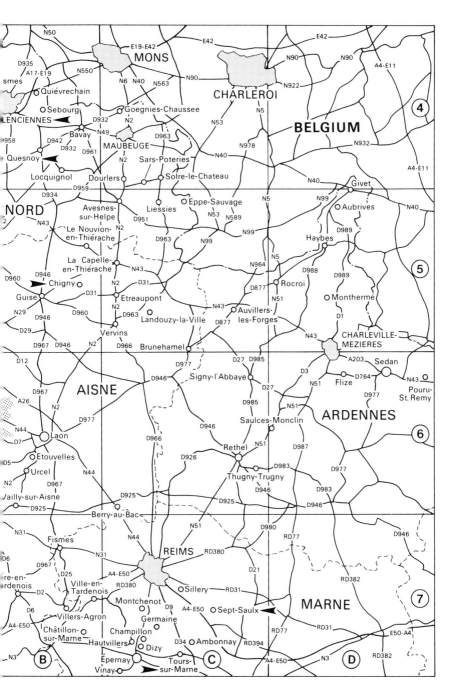

15

Tips for Beginners

Maps and Guides

Good maps are essential and I must stress that those in the front of this book are intended only as an indication of where to find the entries. They should be used in conjunction with the appropriate Michelin maps: 236 covers the whole of the North, Flanders, Artois, Picardy, down as far as Compiègne; 53 goes further west, Arras to Charleville-Mézières; 56 covers Paris to Reims. The green Michelin guides *Champagne* and *Flandres, Artois, Picardie* are essential for more detail on individual sightseeing.

The red Michelin, apart from all its other virtues, has useful town maps. It's a bit slow to spot a newcomer though, unlike its rival Gault-Millau, now also in English, though I prefer the French version. This gives more specific detail but has less comprehensive coverage and is strongly biassed in favour of *la nouvelle cuisine* (its authors did invent the label in the first place); it is useless for the really basic hotels and restaurants.

Logis de France do a good guide to their hotels, obtainable at the French Government Tourist Bureau at 178 Piccadilly. This is the place to go for general advice, free maps and brochures and details of the admirable gîtes system, which provides simple self-catering accommodation in farmhouses and cottages. We have stayed in gîtes all over France and found them invariably reliable and cheap, and often more comfortable and interesting than hotels, but you have to be quick off the mark to book the best in peak season.

Booking

Sunday lunch is the Meal of the Week, when several generations settle down together to enjoy an orgy of eating, drinking, conversation and baby-worship that can well last till teatime. You should certainly book then and on fête days. Make tactical plans and lie low, or it could be a crêpe and a bed in the car. French public holidays are as follows:

New Year's Day	France's National Day, 14 July
Easter Sunday and Monday	The Assumption, 15 August
Labour Day, 1 May	All Saints' Day, 1 November
VE Day, 8 May	Armistice Day, 11 November
Ascension Day	Christmas Day.
Whit Sunday and Monday	

If you wish to book ahead and do not speak French, try and find someone who does to make a preliminary telephone call. If necessary, write in English and let them sort it out, but make sure when you get the confirmatory letter that you understand what you've booked. Many hotels nowadays will ask for a deposit. My method is to send them an English cheque; they then either subtract the equivalent from the bill or return the cheque.

Make good use of the local tourist bureaux, where you will find English spoken. Let them do the booking for you if you have problems. This is the place to pick up maps and brochures.

Getting Off to a Good Start

I know that many of my readers living some distance from the appropriate Channel port might need an overnight stop in this country en route. There's a lot to be said for starting off on the adventure of a trip abroad bright-eyed and bushy-tailed after a good night's sleep. However, as English hotels tend to be disproportionately expensive, this can add an unwarranted tax on the budget, especially on a family holiday. My suggestion is to make for the English equivalent of the *chambres d'hôte*, which I and many a reader so much admire. The rise and rise of the b. and b. is a phenomenon heartily to be encouraged. If your image of the landlady is of carpet slippers, boiled cabbage and spartan loo, think again. Nowadays the lady of the house is quite likely to be a bank manager's wife, dishing up sustaining breakfasts and often evening meals too, and your bathroom may well be en suite.

The definitive guide to these worthy establishments and to small hotels and inns is *Staying off the Beaten Track* by Elizabeth Gundrey. It costs £6.50 from bookshops or from Explore Britain, Alston, Cumbria, and is the nearest thing I know to French Entrée this side of the Channel, with every entry personally vetted by Elizabeth herself. There are several ideas listed within easy reach of Dover, and a stay here would get the holiday off to a fine start. Similarly French readers will find this guide a splendid 'English Entrée'.

How to get there

The obvious gateway to most destinations featured in *FE7* is Calais. P&O European Ferries offer a round-the-clock service from Dover with up to 15 return crossings a day. Two of the ships on this route are the largest ever built for the short-sea service – *Pride of Dover* and *Pride of Calais*. Twice the size of existing vessels, they operate at 22 knots and cruise across in just 75 minutes. Capacity is 650 cars and 2,300 passengers – and facilities are equally impressive with three restaurants, three bars and a duty-free shopping complex.

If you're heading for Bruges, you can take your pick from a host of day and night sailings on various routes . . . from Dover or Felixstowe to Zeebrugge with P&OEF; or from Dover to Ostend with the company's Belgian partner, Regie Voor Maritiem

Transport. Osten options include RMT's Jetfoil service if you are travelling without your car.

Look out for the special low-season fares on all routes as well as short-break bargains – you can travel for half-price on trips up to 60 hours and there are also big savings on 5-day Mini-breaks.

Apart from car ferry services, P&OEF offer a comprehensive range of day trips, short breaks and holidays with accommodation and Channel crossings included in the price. Several of the hotels reviewed in *FE7* are available in the company's 'Continental Weekender' and 'Motor Away' brochures. For further information on car ferry bookings ring Dover (0304) 203388. For short breaks and holidays ring 0304 214422 or write to P&O European Ferries (Holidays), Freepost No. 1, Dover, Kent CT16 3BR.

Closing Times The markets, like the rest of the town, snap shut abruptly for lunch. I regularly get caught out by not shopping early enough; if it's going to be a picnic lunch, the decision has to be made in good time. From 12 p.m. to 2.30, and sometimes 3, not a cat stirs. At the other end of the day it's a joy to find shops open until 7 p.m. Mondays tend to be almost as dead as Sundays and it's likely to prove a grave disappointment to allocate that as a shopping day.

It does not pay to be casual about the weekly closure (*fermeture hebdomodaire*) of the restaurants. It is an excellent idea to ensure that not every restaurant in the same town is closed at the same time, but do check before you venture. Thwarted tastebuds are guaranteed if you make a special journey only to find the smug little notice on the door. 'Sun. p.m. and Mon.' are the most common and often it will take a good deal of perseverance to find a possibility open then.

Changing Money

Everyone has their pet method, from going round all the banks to get a few centimes advantage, to playing it the easy and very expensive way of getting the hotel to do it. It depends on how much is involved and how keen a dealer you are as to how much trouble is worth it. I change mine on the boat, where I have always found the rate to be very fair. If you get caught outside booking hours, the *bureaux de change* stay open late.

Telephoning

Most of the public telephones in France actually work. You put your 1f piece in the slot and watch it roll down for starters, then as many more pieces as you estimate you will need. If it's too much, out it all comes at the conclusion of conversation.

To dial U.K. from France: 19, wait for tone, 44, then STD code minus 0, then number.

Inter-departmental: Province to Province: Dial just 8 figures (e.g. 21.33.92.92.)

Province to Paris: Dial 16, then 1, then 4 followed by 7 figures (e.g. 16.1.4X.XX.XX.XX)

Paris to Province: Dial 16, then the 8 figures

Please note that all numbers you refer to should be 8 figures only (e.g. 21.86.80.48 not (21) 86.80.48).

To dial France from U.K.: 010, pause, 33, 8-figure code.

Emergencies: Fire 18; Police 17; Operator 13; Directory Enquiries 12.

Markets

We Brits go to France to sleep cheaply, eat well and to shop. The markets are more than just a utility – they are part and parcel of the French scene, and everyone loves them. Take your time strolling round the colour and hubbub, and experience the pleasure of buying from someone who knows and cares about his wares. The man selling you a kitchen knife will be an expert on knives and will want to know what you need it for; the cheesemonger will choose for you a cheese ready for eating today or in a couple of days' time, back home. Trust them. Choose for yourself the ripest peach, the perfect tomato, and buy as little as you need and no more, so that you can buy fresh again tomorrow. Stock up on herbs and spices, pulses and dried fruits, soap scented with natural oils, honey from local bees, slices of farmers' wives' terrines – every village a veritable Fortnums on market day. The day of the market in the nearest town is listed in most entries – (**M**).

Take with You   Soap (only the grander hotels supply it) and a decent towel if you're heading for the S group and can't stand the handkerchief-sized baldies. If self-catering, take tea, orange juice, breakfast cereals, biscuits, Marmite, marmalade – all either expensive, or difficult to locate, or horrible.

Bring Home   Beer is a Best Buy and the allowance is so liberal that you can let it reach the parts of the car that other purchases fail to reach, i.e.: load up. Coffee is much cheaper; cheeses are an obvious choice if the pong is socially acceptable. If, like me, you have a weakness for *crème fraîche* and resent paying double at home, you can rely on it staying fresh for a week, so long as its not confined to a hot car. I buy fresh fish if I see a boat coming in while I'm homeward bound, and early expensive vegetables like asparagus, artichokes, mange-touts and the wonderful fat flavoursome tomatoes. Electric goods are often cheaper, Le Creuset pans, glassware. Jancis Robinson's notes on p.181 will help choose the best bargain of all – the wine.

Breakfasts   A sore point. The best will serve buttery croissants, hot fresh bread, home-made preserves, a slab of slightly salted butter, lots of strong coffee and fresh hot milk, with fresh orange juice if you're lucky. The worst – and at a price of between 15 and 40f this is an outrage – will be stale bread, a foil-wrapped butter pat, plastic jam, a cup of weak coffee and cold sterilised milk. Synthetic orange juice can add another 10f to the bill. If you land in an hotel like this, get out of bed and go to the café next door.

Tipping   Lots of readers, used to the outstretched British hand, worry about this. Needlessly – 's.t.c.' should mean what it says – all service and taxes included. The only exception perhaps is to leave the small change in the saucer at a bar.

Garages and Parking   Considerably older and wiser since I started travelling so often, I now have sympathy with readers who insist on a garage. I have to tell you that my locked car has been twice broken into and once stolen altogether (recovered three weeks later with £2,000 worth of damage). The latter disaster was from a well-lit street outside a very grand hotel, so my experience is altogether different from that of a reader who advises street parking after having all his belongings pinched from a car in an underground car-park. I can only advise removing any valued belongings, however tiresome that may be, and taking out adequate insurance.

What Next? The long-delayed *FE8 – The Loire* is now being researched. It is a mighty and utterly delightful project and cannot be rushed. I hope to have it buttoned up by September 1988, so publication will probably be early '89. I already have a file of readers' ideas. More please. *FE3 – Normandy* is being completely re-written, so any comments on that area are also particularly welcome.

Thanks To stalwart, intrepid, tireless, indefatigable Diana McNair-Wilson, without whom this book could never have been written and to Moët et Chandon for unique hospitality.

Calais, the Pas-de-Calais, the autoroutes, Champagne, the Ardennes, Bruges

Number 7 may seem at first glance a hotchpotch of a book. The area it covers is wide, varied, and important to the British traveller in many different ways.

It starts off in France's first passenger port, **Calais**, follows the new autoroute down to within 30km of Paris, swings east to the unique Champagne area, on to the Belgian border via the remote and undiscovered Ardennes, and diverts into Belgium to prise out its pearl – Bruges.

The intention has been to cover in some detail the whole of North-Eastern France, to link up with the sister book, *FE6*, which uses Boulogne as its port of entry and reports on the area west of the autoroute. Bruges is included here because it is almost a sovereign state, easily disassociated from the rest of its country; there are no plans at present to write a book on Belgium and, with easy access from either Calais or Zeebrugge, it seemed unthinkable not to find space somewhere for such a uniquely fascinating city.

The **Pas-de-Calais** has been researched and written about by me and other guiders so often that you would think there is nothing new to say. Not so. Not only have there been many management changes since I researched *FE4*, but I am pleased to say there are new discoveries revealed here for the first time. My Hotel of the Year, Le Château de Cocove at Rêcques-sur-Hem, see p.114, is one of them; I foresee it becoming everyone's favourite even before the next update is due.

This is an area anxiously hovering on the verge of dramatic changes. Forecasts of the effects of the Chunnel and of the final stages of the A 26 have been made but no-one knows with any degree of certainty how the inponderables will influence lives, country, and style of this transit area. However disturbing or rewarding these changes may prove to be, I find it difficult to believe that the unexpectedly rural areas not far from the port will change their character just because more cars and juggernauts thunder so near, or because more labour is employed in the area. Villages just off the N 43 after Ardres – Rêcques-sur-Hem is an example, or Zouafques or Licques – are centuries away from Chunnelling, and I suspect will continue to be; the forests of Guines and Tournehem will continue to shelter picnickers and game, the monosyllabic rivers – the Aa, the Hem and the Slack – will sprout no tourist caffs on their banks.

The Pas-de-Calais has accepted vast numbers of foreigners for generations and has still managed to keep some treasures to itself. One of my favourite modest restaurants, the Restaurant de la Gare at Les Attaques, only 9 km from Calais, lies amid a network of canals, along whose roadsides you are likely to meet nothing more frenetic than a battered deux-chevaux, driven by a hunched-up farmer in hurry. If you're of a mind you can bump along the waters' edge all the way to the ferry. There's another silent watery world that few hell-bent tourists are likely to discover north and east of St-Omer, past the marais, where low Flemish-style cottages line the canals and the pace slows down to that of the barges.

The northern section of the A 26 at the moment is the emptiest autoroute I know. You can drive down to Arras, King of the Road, with only a scattering of lorries to worry about. Easy stop-offs either side of the A 26 down to its almost-complete section to Laon are indicated. From there to Reims the N 44 is an unpleasant heavily congested route. If time allows, far better explore the delightful country to its west, following, perhaps, the D 967.

Champagne is a unique area, whose cellars are visited by thousands of tourists every year. I cannot claim it is generally beautiful countryside or that its grey villages are the most appealing, and I would not suggest a long stay here, but I found it improved with further acquaintance and in any case the city of Reims and the cellars of Épernay should be on every discerning traveller's itinerary, if only for a few days. The *gastronome* will certainly have his rewards.

Then on to the **Ardennes**, which I reluctantly allocated to Diana to research. She found, as I knew she would, one of the least-appreciated, most rewarding regions of France waiting for her. The Ardennes is a tourist area without, they would say, enough tourists. The little inns in charming sleepy villages set in deep forests, on the steep hillsides, by the rivers, are never spoiled like their more fortunate counterparts nearer the ports by too-easy custom. They know they must woo their customer and, having attracted him, give him pleasure and the incentive to stay and return. The 'S' hotels and restaurants in this area are probably the best bargains in the book (but there is plenty of more upmarket accommodation and restaurants too). The whole region deserves a mighty arrow to direct new pioneers towards its delights.

Bruges I kept for myself. Again, a stay of two or three days would be about right to get a taste of this enchanting city that has everything – good hotels, good food and a lotta history – and once the taste has been acquired, the appetite will demand future similar treats. Ideal for a winter break, but obviously even better when the street cafés are lively and the canals glitter.

Towards **Paris**. The autoroute was the eastern border of *FE6* and so for ideas from there to the coast you will have to buy that too! Diana explored to the east and found an enormous variety of historic towns, and the royal forests of Compiègne, Ermenonville, Retz, and, particularly, St-Gobain, which have become amongst her favourite destinations. Neither she nor I could face Lille. It is so vast a conglomeration that the prospect of a worthwhile assessment daunted us both. I doubt if few tourists willingly get embroiled and I'm sure the businessmen get well entertained, so please forgive the cowardly omission. Surprisingly though, Diana did find much of interest in Valenciennes and the Lillois outskirts.

I hope that *FE7* will help a wide range of travellers: those who use Calais for a day's shopping, those who have only time for a weekend near the port, those en route to Paris, those who plan a few days of special interest in Bruges or Champagne, and those who have time to explore a wonderfully unspoiled slice of the real France – the Ardennes.

SPECIAL RECOMMENDATIONS

The hotels and restaurants marked by an arrow ➤ have been selected for the following reasons:–

Aire-sur-la-Lys. *Hostellerie des Trois Mousquetaires* (HR)M. Long-standing unfailing excellence. Good food, comfortable accommodation.

Les Attaques. *Restaurant de la Gare* (R)S. Best 'S' meal in the Pas-de-Calais.

Calais. *Hôtel Meurice* (H)M. Best Calais Hotel.
George V (HR)M. Welcome newcomer, with good food.
Hôtel Windsor (H)S. Reliable, convenient, inexpensive.
Le Channel (R)M. Consistent high standards in all price brackets.

Cambrai. *Hôtel Beatus* (H)M. Comfortable, quiet.

Cassel. *Le Sauvage* (R)L. Skilful use of regional ingredients.

Chigny. *Mlles Piette*(C). Top value *chambre d'hôte*.

Compiègne. *Hostellerie du Royal Lieu* (H)M(R)L. Quiet, strategic position, good food and comfort.

Élincourt-Ste-Marguerite. *Château de Bellinglise* (HR)L. Supreme luxury.

Épernay. *Les Berceaux* (HR)M. Comprehensive service, friendly management.

Escalles. *L'Escale* (HR)S. Reliable good value.

Ligny-en-Cambrésis. *Le Château de Ligny* (HR)L. Perfect luxury in interesting setting.

Longue Croix. *Auberge du Longue Croix* (R)M. Excellent cooking in unusual situation.

Le Quesnoy. *Hostellerie du Parc* (HR)M. Charming setting, regional cooking.

Rêcques-sur-Hem. *Le Château de Cocove.* HOTEL OF THE YEAR.

Reims. *Hôtel Crystal* (HR)M. Lots of character, central position.
Boyer (HR)L. In a class of his own.
Le Florence (R)L. Excellent food, up-and-coming.
La Champagnière (R)M. Pretty, good value.
Le St Nicaise (R)S. Honest bistro cooking.
L'Impromptu (R)S. Good value, fun.

Roye. *La Flamiche* (R)L–M. The best table in the Somme.
Le Florentin (R)M. Good-value, regional cooking.

St-Gobain. *Hôtel Roses de Picardie* (H)S. Good value, attractive setting.
Restaurant du Parc (R)M. Good food in pleasant surroundings.

St-Omer. *St Louis* (H)M(R)S. Reliable good value.
Le Cygne (R)M. Pleasant setting, best in town.

Sept-Saulx. *Le Cheval Blanc* (H)M(R)L. Quiet; excellent cooking.

Signy-L'Abbaye. *Auberge de l'Abbaye* (HR)M Good value, good welcome.

Teteghem. *La Meunerie* (R)L. Best cooking in the Nord.

Tours-sur-Marne. *La Touraine Champenoise* (HR)S. Good value in popular tourist area.
Valenciennes. *L'Alberoi* (R)L. The ultimate in station buffets.
Vervins. *La Tour du Roy* (HR)L. Interesting setting, outstanding food.
Vieux Moulin. *Auberge du Daguet* (R)M. Good food, delightful setting.
Wisques. *La Sapinière* (HR)S. Quiet, well-situated, good simple food.

Bruges. *Hotel Prinsenhof* (H)L. Tasteful luxury.
Pandhotel (H)M. Comfortable, central.
Hotel Adornes (H)M. Quiet, comfortable.
Hotel Aragon (H)M. Helpful owners, convenient.
Portinari (H)M. Central yet quiet, comfortable.
De Karmeliet (R)M–L. Interesting cooking
Maximiliaan Van Oosterich (R)M. Good food in tourist centre.
Sint Joris (R)S. Good simple cooking in central square.

The following hotels are featured in the **P&O European Ferries 'Continental Weekenders'** brochure and/or the company's **'Motor Away'** holidays brochure and can be booked at inclusive rates including Channel crossings. (See page 18 for details on how to obtain a brochure.)
Bollezéele: *Hostellerie St.-Louis*
Calais: *Hôtel Georges V*
Calais: *Meurice*
Cambrai: *Hôtel Beatus*
Douai: *La Terrasse*
Laon: *La Bannière de France*
Recques-sur-Hem: *Le Château de Cocove* (HOTEL OF THE YEAR)
St.-Omer: *La Bretagne*
St.-Quentin: *Hôtel de la Paix et Albert.*

Map 2C   **AIRE-SUR-LA-LYS** (Pas de Calais) 58 km SE of Calais; 19 km SE of St-Omer

62120
(M) *Fri.*

This little town stands at the confluence of four rivers, the Lys, the Melde, the Laquette and the Mardyck, and at the junction of four canals. Surrounded as it is by all this water and the greenery of fields and trees, it is hard to believe, on a sunny day, the dark northern skies ever frown on the red roof-tops of Aire-sur-la-Lys.

The vast Grande Place is bordered by 18th-century houses, many of them decorated with Corinthian pillars; and an Hôtel de Ville, richly ornamented with the coat of arms of the city and a splendid Renaissance balcony.

The church of St-Jacques, completed at the end of the 17th century, is a noble pile, but hardly as interesting as the fine Collégiale St-Pierre of roughly the same date. This Collégiale is considered one of the finest examples of the Flamboyant and Renaissance styles in Flanders: it shelters the miraculous child-virgin statue of Notre-Dame Pannetière, which dates from the 15th century and is the object of a pilgrimage.

Elsewhere, little streets cut at angles off the Grande Place and there are other squares to explore. The main street runs behind the Grande Place, which is sheltered from its traffic by those lovely 18th-century houses.

➤ **Hostellerie des Trois Mousquetaires**
(HR)M
Château de la Redoute
21.39.01.11
Rest. closed Sun. p.m.; hotel & rest. Mon.; 20/12–20/1.
AE, EC, V

My only reservation about making the Hostellerie Hotel of the Year for *FE4* was the problem of getting a reservation! Those readers who persevered reaped their reward. Ne'er a cross word about food, comfort or hospitality. Even the breakfast, that Achilles heel of many an otherwise favourite hotel, is excellent, with home-made jam triumphing over the usual placcy pots. The Hostellerie is a shining example of an establishment that has not been spoiled by lavish publicity and should be doubly commended for keeping up its very high standards.

What makes the Hostellerie des Trois Mousquetaires such a very sought-after hotel? First and foremost, I put the service. As soon as weary, travel-worn guests arrive at this charming little, late-19th-century château, a maid appears to carry their cases up to their rooms (almost unheard of today in France) and returns to them, before they descend, with a glass of fruit juice. Atmosphere is quiet and leisured, like that of a well-run country house. There are 12 comfortably furnished bedrooms in the little château itself (170–350f), 2 apartments in the gate-house (230f and 300f) and 15 more bedrooms are planned in an extension that should be open by June 1988. *La famille* Venet (who come originally from Lille) need the extra room: it must be frustrating constantly to turn disappointed guests away. Weekends are usually booked for weeks ahead; even during the week it is often hard to find a place.

Most English visitors are happy to sample Philippe's bargain 65f menu. While enjoying the home-made terrines and quiches regularly seved as an entrée, they can watch him at work behind a glass screen turning the grilled meat that constitutes the main course. The local French, many of whom are welcomed by Madame Venet as friends and regulars, tend to indulge more in the à la carte dishes, like sweetbreads braised in champagne, duck with raspberries, frogs'

Les Trois Mousquetaires

legs and calves' sweetbreads feuilleté. Whichever way you play it, it's all very good news indeed.

Madame does the lovely flower arrangements that decorate the drawing-room and dining-room. Monsieur (senior) loves gardening, and escapes, when possible, to his three hectares of well-tended land. There are white chairs and tables, ready for an aperitif, set beside a little lake; and white ducks swimming in the Lys behind the house. Unbeatable in its price range in the whole district. If you can get in, you shouldn't miss the opportunity.

Arrowed again on every account.

Europ'Hôtel
(H)S
21.39.04.32
AE, EC, V

A comfortable old house in the Grande Place. Large bedrooms (100–150f) with surprisingly good-sized bathrooms; very attractive, classical, flowered wallpaper on the stairs and along the corridors.

Downstairs, there is a small, jolly bar where the respectable old men of Aire sit and gossip over small cups of coffee and tall glasses of Pernod. Monsieur works at his desk to one side, rising from his accounts from time to time to serve behind the bar, and only too willing to suggest eating-places in the quiet streets around. Parking on the Grande Place.

Map 3D/4A   ANNOEULLIN (Nord) 85 km SE of Calais, 18 km S of Lille

59112
 Tues.

Exit Carvin from A 1.

Le Charolais
(R)M
9 r. J.-B. Le Bas
20.85.69.40
Closed Sun.
p.m.; Tues.
p.m.; Mon.;
Aug.
Dinner by
reservation
only
AE, V

A delightful small restaurant in the village street, just past the Place
de la Mairie. A refreshing atmosphere of youth in the dining-room,
which is furnished with cheerful pink tablecloths and pretty curtains.
M. and Mme Buffetaub, who have run the restaurant for five years,
are indeed very young and so are their two helpers. None the less
they produce a competent and experienced cuisine that many of
their seniors would be proud to emulate.

The restaurant specialises in dishes from the Dordogne and above
all, of course, in the splendid Charolais meat that always seem to
have the edge on other species of beef. Menus start at 72f. Service a
little slow. On the day we lunched there, there were so many people
(including families with children and a baby in a push-chair) that I
could only admire Madame for keeping her cool while moving
gracefully around the crowded tables.

We ate mussels and shrimps cooked with sorrel, followed by a
Charolais entrecôte, served with a bubbling-hot marrow bone.
Young daughter's verdict: *'Delicious!'* Certainly a restaurant to which
we would both like to return.

Map 1B   ARDRES (Pas-de-Calais) 17 km SE of Calais

62610
 Mon.,
Thur.

Turn off the N 43 to find this strikingly pretty and tranquil little town,
fortified in mediaeval times; the triangle of its steeply sloping,
cobbled Place d'Armes is surrounded with time-warped houses,
roofs awry; worn grey steps lead up to the 17th-century Carmelite
chapel. Avenues of lime trees lend unusual character, a large lake
well-equipped with pedalos and pleasant cafés (try *La Frégate* for
omelettes and frites on the terrace) is an added attraction, and all so
near to Calais, bang on the main route south.

So far so good, as generations of English travellers have
considered, but herein might lie a snag, since there have been signs
that the Ardres hoteliers have not hesitated to take advantage of the
easy trade. The more modest and friendly became less welcoming
and more immodest, the Grand Hôtel Clément got grander in prices
and attitude as well as name. Old devotees began to write expressing
disenchantment. It takes time for a situation like this to settle down
and become assimilated. Just about now, I think the customers have
cottoned on sufficiently to say 'Enough', and the hoteliers have
realised that the worm might well turn, if not bite the hand that used
to feed it! A reassessment therefore:

Grand Hôtel
Clément
(R)L(H)M
9 Esplanade du
Mar. Leclerc
21.82.25.25

Son Francis, after a spell with the mighty Georges Blanc, has taken
over the kitchen here in this nice old Relais de Silence, run by the
Coolen family for many years. His cooking is in the modern idiom
and many readers feel its sophistication and expense do not accord
well with the rustic ambience. Menus are 100, 180 and 290f and wine
is equally pricey.

Grand Hotel Clement.

Closed Mon.;
Tues. lunch
o.o.s.; 15/1–15/2
CB, AE, DC, EC
Parking

Rooms are much more in keeping with expectations and cost 200–340f. Breakfast is generally applauded.

Le Relais
(HR)M
Bvd C. Senleck
21.35.42.00
Closed Tues.; 1/
1–5/2
AE, EC, V
Parking

Turn right as you approach the town on to the D 231 to find this picture-book little auberge immediately on your right. For years it was the kind of country-pretty, simple lodging, run by a friendly family, that we all hope to find in France; then it went through a bad patch and has changed hands recently.

When I revisited it was still simply furnished and had kept the rustic character of its beamed dining-room and log-fired reception area, but there is no doubt that the new owners have plans to upgrade the whole enterprise, and will then probably up their prices, currently a modest 133–220f for a double room, most with showers, two with baths. Good luck to them if they get it right – the bedrooms could do with a face lift, and it may well prove to provide the comfortable medium-priced accommodation and good food that we used to expect from the Clément. But it's early days and the pitfalls are obvious. Currently menus are 59f, 110f and 164.50f and cuvée de Relais is 32f.

Le Relais

Double room in annexe of simple rustic hotel. Room very warm, with central heating left on all night in chilly April. Toilet en suite in space that must once have been cupboard. Room 200f, breakfast 33f in bar of main hotel, with very good coffee and excellent fresh bread with fresh pot of butter. Dinner: as usual in Northern France, the 72f menu was very plain. We chose the 102.50f menu – good smoked salmon crêpes, unusual duck and haricots with mushrooms, chicken with tasty sauce, twelve choices of cheese, usual sweets – selected and enjoyed large chocolate mousse.' – Quentin Grey.

La Bonne Auberge
(HR)S
*Rte de Guines,
Brêmes*
21.35.41.09
*Closed Sun.;
Mon. o.o.s; 15/
12–15/1*

1 km W of Ardres on a sharp bend on the D 231.

I like this best of the three old-timer Ardres possibilities, mainly because it hasn't changed much and still achieves, without fuss or pretension, what it sets out to do – i.e. offer simple accommodation and food with a smile.

There have been mild grumbles in the past – some of the rooms on the road can be noisy and bathrooms are few – but what has never been refuted is the warmth of Mme Désmoulins' welcome.

The seven bedrooms are pretty and pristine, and good value at 100f or 120f. One has a shower. The food is honest and copious. The

54.50f menu offered onion tart/terrine-maison/soup; roast pork/tripes/omelette, and desserts. Others are 78f and 123f and a bottle of cuvée de la Bonne Auberge costs 35f. Tables in the garden in fine weather.

Map 1B   **LES ATTAQUES** (Pas-de-Calais) 8 km SE of Calais

62730

Few blinkered travellers on the N 43 bother to deviate. Their loss, because a turn either side, but especially south and westwards, brings swift reward. A mere 8 km from the Calais sprawl and it's another world from the port commercialisation. Here is canal-land, its flatness enlivened by the occasional barge, locks, bridges and towpaths. I often use the minor road at the side of the Attaques bridge to take me all the way back into the heart of Calais, avoiding the lorries and G.B.s. You can see them speeding along in parallel, fretful bumper to bumper. It probably takes me ten minutes longer and shakes up the liver a bit, but allows me to arrive at the ferry in a better humour than that of the usual traffic-light frustration.

► **Restaurant de la Gare**
(R)S
Rte d'Ardres
21.82.22.28
Closed Mon.;
eves.
Parking

Signposted from the route nationale. You cross over the bridge and there it is, as the name implies, by the station, with easy parking and light years away from many road pull-ups. It is regrettably rare in this area to find such an unequivocally French restaurant dedicated to serving high quality food to locals rather than tourists. Because it lies a little off the main route in a generally unexplored region, it is still known only to the fortunate few who live nearby or happen to have stumbled upon it, and its prices reflect this limitation.

Francis Rambaut is a butcher by trade, so this is primarily the place to go for home-made terrines, foie gras, rillettes, and of course meat, but, wanting something lightish on my last visit, I did have some immaculately fresh langoustines in an attractive salad.

Their *menu conseillé* has to change every day because some of the locals eat there regularly and rely on its variety. It costs 36f. A typical sequence might be a gratin of seafood, sauté of rabbit, apple cake or a good cheese selection, washed down with house wine at 5.30f a small pichet.

The next price up – 52f – has more choice; say a generous platter of smoked Ardennes ham and one of the patron's entrecôtes. For 96.50f you get five courses of more sophisticated fare – the duck becomes magret and the steak Rossini; but it's the cheaper menus that are the prime cause for congratulation here.

At present there are three rooms, functioning according to demand – canny lorry drivers stoking up/wedding celebrations. Not smart, but spotless and agreeable. There is talk of opening in the evenings (which would be good news) and building on an extension (which might be bad).

'*The welcome was extra friendly, although the restaurant was busy and we had not booked. We chose and enjoyed the 53f menu. A seafood entrée, hot and topped with melted cheese, was delicious, as was the entrecôte. We had cheese in preference to the tart, and good coffee. The house wine was extremely good value.*'

Undoubted arrow for best 'S' meal in the area.

Rest de la Gare Attaques

Map 3D/4A   **ATTICHES** (Nord) 84 km SE of Calais; 20 km S of Lille

---

59710
(M) *Wed.*

Exit Seclin from the A 1.

**La Taverne de
la Toison d'Or**
(R)M
*21 r. Henri
Dhennin
20.32.96.93
Closed Sun.
p.m.
No credit cards*

Follow the minor road from Attiches for 3 km in the direction of
Phalempin.
   Five hundred years ago, Phillippe le Bon fought a battle here.
Centuries before, it was on the route taken by the Knights on their
way to and from the Crusades: indeed 'Le Toison d'Or' means the
Golden Fleece, and this is the theme that M. Matthies has chosen for
his charming, country-style restaurant. It was originally a late-18th-
century farm but was operating, until this energetic patron bought it
six years ago, as a small factory making beer.
   The building that is now the restaurant started life as stables and
was later used to store the hops and barrels. Hard to realise that the
conversion into this fine, open dining-room was done entirely by M.
Matthies himself, whose artistic hands are apparently as capable of
manual work as they are of dealing with his imaginative cuisine. He
moved concrete loading piers, built a fireplace and even forged the
wheel-shaped, wrought-iron fittings that are suspended from an
unusual, barrel-shaped, brick ceiling – a ceiling so unusual that the
house is classified a listed building. On the walls, Monsieur has
placed carved wooden light fittings in the shape of heraldic shields.
In winter the leaping log fire makes the dining-room a welcoming

place in which to eat (à la carte only). In summer guests may eat out in the garden as well. A lengthy meal and a good wine should come to about 200f. Playing it more carefully there is St-Jacques aux poireaux (55f); steak with marrow bone and morilles (wild mushrooms) 75–95f.

| Map 5D | **AUBRIVES** (Ardennes) 248 km SE of Calais |

| 08320 | 8km SW of Givet on the N 51. |

La Debette
(HR)S
24.41.64.72
Closed Sun.
p.m.; Mon.
lunch; 20/12–
12/1
AE, EC, V

A good hotel and restaurant in a large, quiet village on the Meuse, the sort of village where nothing seems to happen very much. Above are the densely forested hills of the Ardennes, plentifully stocked with wild boar, deer and other game – so these are on the menu during the hunting season.

Twenty rooms (100–180f) are a little shabby: worn carpets and the colours of the decoration fighting hard amongst themselves. But Mme Michel is warm and friendly and speaks a little schoolgirl English. Her clientele in the spotlessly clean dining-room seemed solidly local – an excellent recommendation. Menus (48, 75 and 135f). 75f menu included beignets de scampi, caille aux petits raisins, cheese and dessert. Wide windows, hung with attractive flowered curtains, overlook grass, fruit trees and roses.

| Map 5C | **AUVILLERS-LES-FORGES** (Ardennes) 240 km SE of Calais |

| 08260 | 31 km W of Charleville-Mézières; on the D 877. S of the N 39 Cambrai–Charleville. |

**Hostellerie
Lenoir**
(HR)M
24.36.30.11;
24.54.30.11
Closed Fri.;
Jan.–Feb.
AE, DC, EC, V

A most attractive, family-run Logis with a celebrated patron-chef in a quiet village street; designated a 'Relais de Silence'.

Many are the honours and accolades bestowed on the estimable M. Lenoir: Diplôme d'Honneur Grand Palais CNIT Paris, Le Sommelier du Nord and so on, and *so on* . . .; He has lived all his life in this house (it was a café when his parents had it) and was born in the room above the bar. A very pretty dining-room, with pink tablecloths and lots of flowers, opens on to a courtyard. Menus: 110f, 190f are mouth-watering: 'mousse de pigeon au foie gras; soufflé de Sandre'. And the menu is translated into English, too: 'poached egg, topped with dill-marinated salmon; steamed fillets of sole served with crispy vegetables, bean sprouts and soya sauce – with local pleurotes as an accompaniment'. Bedrooms (135–260f) are lovely, as one might expect. There's river and wooded hill country to the north-east and those fascinating Thiérache churches to the west. Makes for a totally indulgent, special stop.

| Map 5C | **AVESNES-SUR-HELPE** (Nord) 184 km NE of Calais; 18 km S of Maubeuge |

| 59440
(M) Fri. | A picturesque little agricultural town, fortified by Vauban, on the N 2, 33 km N of Vervins, 58 km E of Cambrai by the N 43, D 934, D 962. |

The centre is charming. There are old houses dominated by the imposing square tower of the collegiate St Nicolas, built between the 13th and 16th centuries, and some attractive little shops.

La Grignotière
(R)S
Av. de la Gare
27.61.10.70
Closed Mon.;
Tues. p.m.
AE, DC, EC, V

M. and Mme Muller have owned La Grignotière for the last nine years and run it with warmth and enthusiasm. It is on the main road, near the station. Inside are white tablecloths covered with pink lace cloths, brown tiled floor, tall walls decorated with copper and pewter and the head of an old wild boar. And all lovely and cool on a very hot day.

Menus (56–85f) specialise in fish. 56f menu includes les rillettes de Mans; le langue de boeuf Ravigote (cooked with onions); cheese or crème caramel.

La Cremaillère
(R)M
26 pl. Général
Leclerc
27.61.02.30
Closed Mon.
p.m.; Tues; 5/
1–19/1; 1/7–15/
7
AE, DC, EC, V

A quiet restaurant in an old house on the Place opposite the church of St-Nicolas. A long dining-room with a tiled floor, a certain amount of copper gleaming on the walls, stained glass panels on doors that divide the restaurant from the kitchen.

It is an excellent little restaurant that deserves a large clientele but was sadly empty when we visited it one Friday night in early July. Food was beautifully presented and served with much grace by friendly Mme LeLaurain. On the 80f menu, we ate two different sorts of terrine as starters, followed by pork for one of us and chicken for the other, and finished with a splendid gâteau marbled with cream and strawberries.

Altogether, a noteworthy stop that must suffer from the doldrums that seem to affect the tourist trade in parts of Northern France. So, please rectify in future!

Map 2C | **BAILLEUL** (Nord) 76 km SE of Calais

59270
(M) *Tues.*

Exits 10, 11, 12 from A 25.

The town was almost totally destroyed during the last great German offensive of the First World War. At the time of its liberation, June 1918, only a few of its houses were left standing. It was subsequently beautifully rebuilt in neo-Flemish style, only to suffer, within the next two decades, the terrible bombardment of 1940. It is hard now to believe that the golden, weathered church and the proud houses on the Grande Place (where on Tuesdays there is a big country market) rose again from those ruins.

The origins of the fine belfry date from the 12th century; in places, its walls are over one metre thick. The weathercock at the summit of the tower is in the form of the Poitevine fairy Mélusine. Similar weathercocks are found all over Flanders: legend has it that the fairy, far away from the castle and family, keep sentinel over these little towns, on the lookout for fire, or to warn of the approach of enemies.

The church of St-Vaast, rebuilt in 1932, has some fine stained-glass windows that trace, among other events in Bailleul's history, a visit to the town in the 16th century by the Emperor Charles V (it was then part of the Spanish Empire); the uprising against the Hapsburgs; and the tragic years of the First World War.

A la Pomme d'Or
(HR)M
27 r. d'Ypres
28.43.11.01
Closed Mon.
and Tues. p.m.;
Aug.
A, DC, V

Well, M. Dennnequin, you certainly have changed things around since we were last here, three years ago. Then there was one elegant dining-room with expensive menus, and an entrance café with dishes in the lower price range.

First and foremost, this amiable proprietor sat down and had a good hard think about economics. Having noticed that the rise in inflation was frightening tourists away from the establishments of many of his competitors, he decided to do away with set menus, level all his prices, and cater for a more popular market. The result is that his restaurants consistently do a roaring trade, he told me, while those of his competitors (a touch of smugness here) are 'a little empty'. Dishes are suggested, rather charmingly, by apple-shaped placards pinned to the walls: rillettes d'oie 19f; crêpes aux fruits de mer 23f.

The bedrooms (80–230f) are as clean as ever and were shown to us with great pride. But, alas for conventional tastes, M. Dennequin has invested in the most extreme of modern décor: panoramic views of forest glades (or was it sunlit beaches?) run down entire walls. There is a double bed, set almost flush with the floor, that incorporates in its surrounds knobs for operating the T.V., lights, etc.

Map 6B

BARISIS-AUX-BOIS (Aisne) 236 km SE of Calais

02700

14 km SE of Chauny, by the D 1, D 7, D 53; 5 km SW of St-Gobain.

Auberge de Bernagousse
(R)S
23.39.39.63
Closed Mon.
p.m.; Tues.
V

Mme Maroigner of the Hôtel Roses de Picardie, St Gobain, recommended the Auberge de Bernagousse, and her husband led me there in his car in the morning. They often send families there who are staying at their hotel – it's cheaper, they said, than going to a formal restaurant.

The led me from the D 1 to the D 53 just north of Coucy-le-Château, to pass through Verneuil-s.-Coucy: the Auberge is signposted up a narrow road leading to a forest glade, just before the village of Barisis.

All this area of the Forêt de St Gobain-Coucy is honeycombed with limestone caverns. In the Middle Ages they were greatly enlarged when stone was removed to build the great château at Coucy. Before the First World War people lived in them. Between 1914 and 1918 the German line ran through this peaceful place; the extensive cavern that tunnels below the ground beside the parking for the Auberge was used as a field hospital and taken and retaken seven times during the course of the war. During the last war, the Germans used the caverns as a munitions depot (notice the railway tracks running across the rides into the trees); here were stored torpedoes and the V1s and V2s with which they bombarded England. Today hundreds of mushrooms are grown commercially in the humid atmosphere. By tradition, this clearing has always been a place of hospitality: the name Bernagousse derives from 'Nagousse', a friend of the Irish missionary St Gobain, who ran an eating-place for the people working in the forest.

Monsieur makes a welcoming host, and is a mine of information on the area. His menus include a wide choice of dishes at remarkably reasonable prices: sauté de veau (33f); ½ langouste mayonnaise (50f); confit de canard (46f); fromage de chèvre grillé (25f). It makes for a charming and unusual eating-place.

Map 4B	**BAVAY** (Nord) 157 km SE of Calais

59570
(M) Fri.

21 Km E of Valenciénnes on the N 49.

In Roman times, Bavay was one of the most important cities in the North of France. The rectilinear plan imposed in those days is still traceable in the layout of the streets. Eight Roman roads radiated from Bavay, that which ran towards Cologne being the most frequented. Much of this old Roman settlement was uncovered subsequent to the terrible bombing of 17 May 1940. You can still see the marks left by the passage of foot traffic and the ruts of the chariot wheels in the monumental Forum (open every day from 9 a.m. to noon and from 2 p.m. to 5 p.m. except Tuesday and Sunday, 2 p.m.– 6 p.m.) that is situated in a quiet street off the Grande Place.

Near the Forum is the Musée gallo-romain, a modern building that, with the help of an audio-visual presentation, traces the earliest history of this ancient town.

The Grande Place is dominated by a statue of Queen Brunehaut. Engraved on the pedestal on which she stands are the names of seven of those old Roman roads. Behind her is the Hôtel de Ville (which houses the Syndicat d'Initiative): its classic 18th-century granite façade contrasts strangely with its belfry, which is built out of brick.

There are two celebrated restaurants in Bavay. The **Carrefour de Paris**, Porte de Gommeries, 27.63.12.58, is built at the crossing of two Roman roads. When we visited it in April 1987, it was a closed for extensive renovations, so we would be happy to hear if it still lives up to its considerable reputation. The other is the **Bagacum**, in a quiet street off the road that runs towards Avesnes and Helpe.

Bagacum
(R)M
R. d'Audignies
27.66.87.00
Closed Sun.
p.m. Mon.; first
3 weeks in July;
first 15 days in
Jan.
All credit cards

A very popular restaurant and (while the Carrefour de Paris was closed for renovations) *the* eating-place of Bavay. It is housed in a one-hundred-year-old converted barn: high ceilings with exposed beams, stuffed birds perched on ledges of brick walls, stained wood mangers, and ducks and geese (either models, or in pictures) *everywhere*. These latter are the particular obsession of Pierre Lesne, who has owned the restaurant for the last six years. He is extremely enthusiastic about his cuisine, travelling 250 km to shop in the great Rungis market outside Paris or, almost as far in another direction, to buy fish from the boats that put into Boulogne. His specialities are his fish dishes – le filet de sole Bagacum au saumon fumé et au confit de poireaux (70f à la carte) and, not surprisingly, goose or duck-related recipes – le foie gras de canard Landais macéré à l'Armagnac (75f); les aiguillettes de canard au miel et au vinaigre d'hydromel (honey products are a speciality of Bavay and its surrounding countryside) (68f).

Menus at 80f and 130f usually include the above dishes, although Monsieur changes his menus every three months. Charming dining areas: white tablecloths over dark green, and a gallery with more tables upstairs.

Map 5B	**BEAUVOIS-EN-CAMBRÉSIS** (Nord) 158 km SE of Calais; 9 km SE of Cambrai

59157
 Thur.

La Buissonnière
(R)M
92 r. Watremez
27.85.29.97
Closed Sun.
p.m.; Mon.;
Aug.
V

It should have been a memorable Sunday lunch. There were all the right ingredients: a renowned restaurant, a chef who is a member of les Toques Blanches du Hainaut, a peaceful setting in a quiet village on the Cambrai–Le Cateau road, an elegant and well-furnished dining-room. Imagine, then, our disappointment to find that the service was slow; the food, when it arrived, was good but unexceptional; and the cool, blonde Mme Drubay had clearly little regard for 'the English'. She was, in fact, one of the least friendly restaurateurs that we came across, although affable enough to other (French) guests in the three-quarters empty room.

Well, Madame, I was not so keen on you either – or on the 16f you charged for an unremarkable glass of white wine. Menus: 80f (weekdays); 160f (Saturday evening and Sunday).

Map 1C	**BERGUES** (Nord) 40 km E of Calais

59380
 Mon.

2 km from the A 25, exit Bergues.

One of the most popular suggestions in *FE4* was this little Flemish town. Readers have found it a convenient distance from the port for overnight stops in either direction, and it is just large enough to offer a choice of accommodation and food. I sent Diana off to record her impressions, but first, readers' views:

Au Tonnelier: *'We agree with your comments. We used it for our first night in France. Very comfortable room with shower at 190f. The mid-range menu at 73f. was well worth the drive from Calais. Breakfast at 16f, with both butter and jam served on dishes.'* – P. T. Jones.

'We were very impressed with Au Tonnelier – very pretty hotel and restaurant; on the 62f menu we enjoyed soup, veal and dessert. The restaurant was full of lively French families of all ages and I feel your description of 'solid burghers' is perhaps a little ungenerous. The Manageress was most interested to read the entry in your guide, although she told us that she has now redecorated the bedrooms and improved various facilities.' – Miss A. J. Marden.

Hôtel du Commerce: *'Three of us had a double room and breakfast for 200f. We found the reception friendly and the accommodation very comfortable. Au Tonnelier being closed, we had a wonderful dinner at **Auberge du Cornet d'Or**. The only set menu was 105f but it* *was truly worth every centime and we quite liked being the only foreigners around.'* – Eileen McNeal.

These are typical of most letters on my file, but it is only fair to let one mild dissenter have his say:

Au Tonnelier: *'Hotel and restaurant are spic and span but run in that infuriatingly condescending manner which makes guests feel uncomfortable throughout their stay. Madame Duclerq and her sister (?), the chef, are in firm command. Though we were ordered to appear for dinner at 7.30 p.m. it was over an hour before any food appeared and even longer before wine was produced. When we wanted an after-dinner stroll round the town square we were told "Don't you want to go to bed?" – at 10.30 p.m.! and were only reluctantly let out..'* (No name, in case he wants to go back!)

Here is what Diana found:

What a haven is the ancient Flemish town of Bergues, especially if one has battled with autoroute traffic on the homeward run. It still seems to be dreaming (in spite of the grievous destruction of 1940) within its mediaeval walls, the golden-yellow brick of the fortifications reflected in the tranquil moat that encircles much of the town. In the quiet Grande Place, the clean lines of the tall belfry, of 16th-century origin and one of the most beautiful in Flanders, rise proudly towards the sky. It was burned in 1940 and dynamited by the Germans in 1944. The new tower, built after the war in that lovely sandstone by the architect Gelis, follows closely on the lines of the original with a certain simplification in the decoration. Its carillon of fifty bells plays one tune on the hour and another at the half-hour: some of the most famous – and possibly the most tuneful – chimes in Northern France.

Elsewhere, the orderly streets retain characteristics of 16th- and 17th-century Flemish architecture: old gable-ends, sculptured keys over the window, decorated dormer-windows . . . In summer, the window-boxes on these elegant houses are ablaze with geraniums: those to the north of the town casting spectacular images into the Canal de la Colme.

Hôtel du Commerce
(H)S
28.68.60.37
Closed 25/6-13/7

Small, spotlessly clean and well-maintained hotel on the Grande Place. A large bar on one side has an entrance separate to that of the hotel itself. Bedrooms cost from 90f (washbasin and bidet only) to 150f with bath and W.C. Tiled loo and shower (5f) in corridor. Plenty of room to park in the square outside, opposite the church. The friendly proprietors receive, they told us, *'Beaucoup des Anglais'* and seem very pleased to do so.

Au Tonnelier
(HR)S–M
R. du Mont-de-Piété
Closed 1/1–20/1; 20/8–8/9
EC, V
Parking

Tonnelier means cooper: barrels were once made in this 1679 house that stands in a quiet street off the Grande Place, just round the corner from the Hôtel du Commerce. The three DeClerq sisters run this small hotel (12 bedrooms) and restaurant that has been in their family for the past 84 years. Bedrooms in the old section cost from 95f; W.C. and bath (16f) in the corridor. Bedrooms in the newer part have bath etc. en suite (190f). The sisters have extensively renovated the bedrooms over the last five years, and plans are now afoot to redecorate the stairs and corridors. They are extremely proud of their reputation for 'good, old fashioned cooking'. Menus cost 52f, 73f and 95f. Specialities include lapin aux pruneaux (on the three-course 52f menu), cassolette dunkerquois (four-course 73f menu), lotte a l'Américaine and filet de veau à l'ancienne (five-course 93f menu). Free and locked parking in central courtyard.

Au Cornet d'Or
(R)L
26 r. Espagnole
28.68.66.27
Closed Sun.
p.m.; Mon; end
of June–middle
of July
V

Michelin accords Au Cornet d'Or two knives and forks. I would like to bestow on the restaurant all the accolades at my disposal, not least because, having ordered one menu between myself and my young daughter, we were brought portions large enough to satisfy two of the best of gourmand trencherpeople. Apart from this, the food is delicious and exceptionally well-presented. Michèle and Brigitte Tasserit have evolved a *nouvelle cuisine* that is very much stamped with their own particular style.

For that memorable shared meal we ate mussels in cream sauce as an 'apéritif' (compliments of the house); smoked salmon rolled around a tartare filling and decorated with a tomato 'rose'; rosettes of beef arranged like petals on the plate; bland fromage de Bergues and strong fromage de Vieux Lille, followed by raspberry sorbet served in raspberry coulis (130f). All this in elegant surroundings: tall-backed, brocade-covered chairs set around white tablecloths and pink napkins. Draped green curtains half divide the dining-room, giving the tables a quiet, cosy, intimate atmosphere.

Map 6C | **BERRY-AU-BAC** (Aisne) 301 km SE of Calais

02190
Guignicourt

19 km S of Reims by the N 44.

La Côte 108
(R)M–L
23.79.95.04
Closed Sun.
p.m.; Mon.; 20/
12–1/2
AE, CB, DC

A useful main-road stop between Reims and Épernay, but popular with the locals as well as with travellers. The oddly-named (any ideas?) restaurant is in a substantially elegant house with mock rustic dining-room and terrace.

Lots of good fish and regional dishes win patron Serge Courville a Michelin star. His mainly traditional cooking is supplemented by a magnificent cellar.

The cheapest menu at 105f is recommended; carte prices can be alarming.

Map 3C/4A | **BÉTHUNE** (Pas-de-Calais) 83 km SE of Calais.

62400
Ⓜ *Mon.*

Not my favourite town, with the Grande Place a sad and windswept space, littered with blowing débris; I include it because of its proximity to the autoroute and possible convenience for an overnight stop, but hurry on by if at all possible.

The two World Wars caused terrible destruction to this ancient town, fortified by Vauban. All the houses on the Grande Place were rebuilt in traditional Flemish style after 1918. The Germans occupied the town during the last war and, when they left, fired the 1 km from the station to the Place.

Miraculously, the 15th-century belfry, which stands alone (the oldest in the Pas-de-Calais) among the parked cars, largely escaped the devastation on the 1940s. Climb the long staircase to the gallery at the top: from here, there is a splendid view of Béthune and its straggling suburbs, on to the fertile farmland of the flat plain and, in the distance, are the spoil heaps of the coalfield.

Le Vieux Beffroi
(HR)M
Grande Place
21.68.15.00
AE, DC, EC, V

A tall, 1930s house on the Grande Place. Very friendly, cheerful proprietors; a lift to the good-sized and clean bedrooms (100–220f); restaurant (menus: 65–97f; and à la carte), and breakfast (including orange juice) taken in the large, café-like room by the entrance. Tables and chairs on the paving outside, well frequented by locals.

Map 3C   **BEUVRY-LÈS-BÉTHUNE** (Pas-de-Calais) 87 km SE of Calais

---

62660
Beuvry
Ⓜ *Fri.*

4 km W of Béthune on the N 41.

Hôtel France II
(HR)M
21.57.34.34
All credit cards

Used to be known as *the* hotel of the region. Now, alas for M. Amic and his son, the recently opened **Chartreuse du Val St Esprit** at Gosnay is rapidly poaching that coveted accolade.

The hotel is set in peaceful parkland. There are ponds and marshes with duck and moorhen, goats, chickens, and an old spoil heap – fast reverting to nature – on the horizon.

Rather dull bedrooms (284f) include T.V. and minibar as well as all the expected conveniences. In the restaurant, Duc de Luignes, the menus are from 80–120f and specialise in foie gras and fish. La famille Amic have been here for 17 years and, from 1987 onwards, it strikes me that they are going to have to pull their socks up.

Map 6A   **BLÉRANCOURT** (Aisne) 230 km SE of Calais; 35 km NE of Compiègne

---

02300
Chauny

From the N31 Compiègne–Soissons road, at Trosly-Breuil take the D 335 and the D 935.

Hostellerie le Griffon
(HR)M
Château de Blérancourt
23.39.60.11
Closed Sun. p.m.; Mon.; 24/ 12–30/12
AE, DC, EC, V

A famous hotel and restaurant built into the outer walls of the 17th-century castle of the Dukes of Gesvres, which was abandoned during the Revolution. The bedrooms (170–220f) we did not see, as everyone was busy preparing lunch. The large dining-room looked very inviting. It overlooks the castle ruins, and there is a big terrace, covered with a canvas roof, where meals are served during the summer. Menus 140f and 180f.

Map 1B　　　　**BOLLEZÉELE** (Nord) 47 km SE of Calais

59470
Wormhout
(M) *Wed.*

The direct route is the N 1 to Gravelines, then the D 11, from whence the Hostellerie is clearly marked on the D 226, but a more interesting approach for those wishing to get a taste of the strange, flat, canal-dissected territory is to turn off the N 43 at Bayenghem-les-Eperlecques and follow the D 221 and D 226. Bollezéele is a village of neat little Flemish-style houses and few shops. The three-naved church of St Wandrille was built in 1606 on much earlier foundations.

Hostellerie St-Louis
(HR)M
478 r. de l'Eglise
28.68.81.83
Closed Sun. p.m.; Mon.
A, V
Parking

The Hostellerie has filled a gap in the hotel scene in this barren area and become very popular with tour operators and guidebook writers alike, since I wrote about it in *FE4*. There is the prevailing feeling that it just misses being very good indeed for reasons hard to pin down, but I think the following letter sums up the general view of readers who have stayed there recently:

'We stayed at the St Louis largely on your recommendation. The family were indeed friendly and helpful. Your comments on the bedrooms were right – you can have too much of brown – but the bathrooms were supplied with tons of really hot water at the highest pressure we have ever encountered in France. A hiccup in the heating system was dealt with, with extreme promptness. It was very comfortable and peaceful.

'Primarily we went to France for the food. We had two dinners and Sunday lunch at the Hostellerie. The restaurant was choc-a-bloc for Saturday dinner and Sunday lunch, mainly with locals who were clearly enjoying themselves. If we had one disappointment it was the absolute unchangingness of the menu at all three meals (same pudding each time), so that with a limited choice of entrée and main dish, it proved difficult at our final meal to try something different. That said, the cooking was excellent, the service friendly and helpful; the wine list was particularly extensive on clarets. Coffee was delicious. Ideal for an overnight stop, but probably less suitable for an extended stay.' – Kenneth Savage.

Diana's recent updating:
The Hostellerie St Louis is set back from the D 11 just before it runs into the village. Built in 1760 as a private house, it was bequeathed to the village at the end of the 19th century by its old, blind and unmarried owner for use as a home for the elderly. Both the exterior and the interior have considerable character. Green lawns and plenty of parking space front the house. Within, there is a small ante-room furnished with reproduction period furniture and a big marble fireplace – the sort of room conducive to interesting, whispered conversation and perhaps a *coupe maison* (champagne and blackberry liqueur). On the other side of the house is a large and imaginatively furnished dining-room. The old chapel attached to the house is used for conferences. In 1985 *FE4* had mixed feelings over the restaurant, finding the chef's approach to his cuisine somewhat undisciplined while acknowledging that he brought imagination and individuality to his craft. Since those days young M. Philippe Dubreucq (who speaks English), finding himself at a 'crossroads' in his art, as he put it, has apparently taken the right path and

subsequently many culinary bouquets have been bestowed upon him.

Menus are from 90–250f. Specialities include cassolettes des mers sauce Gilamesh and assiette de ris de veau et rognons.

On the staircase is a large, stained-glass window portraying St Louis standing under an oak tree: a touch of 19th-century whimsy. Bedrooms (220f) are labelled in *cardboard* (hardly less eccentric) with the names of regions: 'Île de France', 'Languedoc', 'Provence' and so on. They are good sized, each with its own bathroom and, as the hotel is a Relais de Silence, at least one should be guaranteed a good night's sleep.

Map 1B	**BOURBOURG** (Nord) 28 km E of Calais

59630
 Tues.

The simplest way to arrive at Bourboug is to take the N 1 to Gravelines, and then the D 11, but for those with time and inclination to explore the flat Flemish pastureland of the area, a little map-reading, following perhaps the canals, would be much more interesting.

Rarely visited by tourists, Bourbourg is a sizeable town of many squares, with an impressive town hall and an old church topped with a delightful carillon.

La Gueulardière
(R)M
4 pl. Hôtel de Ville
28.22.20.97
Closed Mon.
AE, V

This popular restaurant has had a facelift and the cheap *brasserie* part has gone. Now it's all upmarket brick pillars, the statutory 'made-it' tapestry chairs, smart pink tablecloths. Time will tell if this is good news, since the prices have rocketed accordingly, but in any case it's a very agreeable and comfortable refuge, particularly on a bad day, when a prolonged lunch seems indicated.

The waitresses are friendly and helpful and there are one or two original touches to the menus, like the 'sélection du chef' cheeses, which are slices of four different varieties, two of them local, served with a fanned apple quarter sprinkled with walnuts – a far better idea than the often battered cheeseboard, of too many varieties, not all of them in good nick. But the desserts are disappointing – soggy tarte aux fraises – which at this price level is not good enough. Menus at 110f and 155f.

Map 5C	**BRUNEHAMEL** (Aisne) 122km SE of Calais

02360

49 km W of Charleville-Mézières; 12 km S of the N 43 (Cambrai–Charleville-Mézières) on the D 977.

Hôtel de la Hure
(HR)S
23.97.60.14
Closed Aug.

If only the autoroutes hadn't taken the tourist traffic away from sleepy villages such as Brunehamel! Establishments like this excellent little hotel must find it increasingly hard to survive. Mme Lepointe hardly ever has any tourists, nowadays, she told me, except for a local man who stayed here a month. It is such a pity, for there are her nice, clean bedrooms (53–70f) all ready, and delicious food on the menus (40 and 60f).

On the 40f menu we ate tartelette aux fromages; côte de porc, garniture de légumes; cheese; and drank iced water from a pitcher. Lots of room to park in the Place across the way, and little traffic except for the occasional tractor, and a herd of black and white cows finding their own way home along the street.

Map 1A	**CALAIS**

62100

(M) *Wed.,
Thur., Sat.*

SHOPPING

Easing the queues at the Continent is the new Mammouth, 3 km to the west, clearly marked from both the N 1 and the coast road. It is altogether brighter, fresher, better than its tired predecessor, with excellent cheese counter, fresh local fish, good charcuterie and, with an eye to the main reason for its existence, an outstanding booze section. Prices may be a franc or two higher than at the Continent, but pay them willingly. Open every day from 9 a.m. to 9 p.m. The Continent is open Mon.–Sat. 9 a.m.–10 p.m.

For those who prefer to take their shopping with a breath of French air, there's usually easy parking in the pl. d'Armes and most of the interesting food shops are in the r. Royale which leads off it, its continuation the bvd Jacquard and a left turn into the bvd La Fayette.

Calais

On a corner of the square is the **Maison du Fromage**, lacking Philippe Olivier's charm and dedication, but stocking 200 different cheeses, including northern locals like Maroilles, Boule d'Avesnes and le Dauphin, plus of course farmhouse butter and crème fraîche. **Le Fin Bec** in the bvd Lafayette is a smaller, classier cheese specialist, with time and inclination to advise.

Back on the square, the Nicolas concessionaire **Au Gourmet** supermarket makes it a short hump to the car for last-minute duty-frees. With more time to choose, make for the **Caves St-Pierrre**, behind the pl. Crêvecoeur, except on Thursdays and Saturday, when the markets make parking nearby problematical.

Calais' weakness/speciality is chocolates and pâtisserie. In the bvd Lafayette is the **Ducard** establishment, where M. Ducard practises his dying craft as a *maître chocolatier*. No commission is too fantastic for him to conjure up in chocolate or spun sugar, from pinnacled châteaux to portraits of loved ones. His everyday chocolates are superb too, and the aromas of chocolate and roasting almonds from his workroom add to the temptation. At Easter time the eggs overflow into the little salon de thé but usually this is a good stop for a cup of Earl Grey and a pastry.

Mme Ducard runs another, larger tea shop, just off the pl. d'Armes. Her **Fraîche Saveur**, with an unexpected garden behind, does light lunches as well as teas, home-made ices and her husband's pastries and chocs. **Caprice**, on the pl. d'Armes, with tables outside and on the little lawn behind, is another teatime alternative. Outhiers and Leonidas in the r. Royale also have a sophisticated selection, but M. Ducard says only his are truly home-made.

For a picnic baguette make for **J. C. Delahaye** in the r. des Thermes off the other side of the square; he makes fantasy pastries too, including 'Calaisienne', a layered coffee meringue.

Blondel, bvd Lafayette, is the best fishmonger in town, but better still buy from the stalls on the quays; their range and timing is unpredictable, depending on what the last boat brought in, but fresh mussels and flapping plaice at least are certainties.

Good *charcutiers* are **Patrick and Stephanie** in the bvd Lafayette and **Davelu** and **Bellynck** in the r. Royale. **Gastronomie du Sud-Ouest** specialises in brandied fruits, tinned pâtes, nut oils and Fauchon preserves. For presents and clothes around the pl. d'Armes and down the r. Royale, look out for **Etchola** on the square, a bizarre overflowing Aladdin's Cave of a shop. On the other side, in the r. de la Paix, is **Élégance Enfant**, the best children's clothes temptation. Turn into the r. Royale to find **René Classe**, for fine porcelain and crystal; **Descamps** now has branches in England, but this one I find particularly irresistible for gorgeously thick towels and bed linen. You have to have the right shaped square pillows though to buy the lovely pillow cases. Look out for their sales.

This is the classiest area for shops and there are some distinctly upmarket labels, like Lacoste at **Sprint**, and Rodier at **Monsieur**. **La Madrague** has some expensive presents, but also some cheap jokey ones a little different from English ideas.

After the Tourist Office it all gets a bit seedy, around the railway station, and becomes the bvd Jacquard. Two department stores,

Printemps and **Prisunic**, are here. **Coraline** would tempt the younger female shopper, with some exceptionally pretty merchandise.

In the bvd Lafayette, after the busy pl. Albert 1er, is the intriguing mix of the chic and not-so-chic that lend character and piquancy to French shopping. On the corner is Calais' classiest men's shop, **Port Royale** , with labels like Lanvin and Louis Féraud, next door to the nostalgic **Henry Martin**, displaying serried rows of buttoned caps, berets, boaters and Sherlock Holmes hats. **Cactus**, in complete contrast, is a trendy boutique.

Cupillard is a kitchenware shop for serious cooks, with a full range of Le Creuset pans. **Jean-Pierre Fusil** is another shop with few English equivalents, selling knives, pistols and guns. On the other

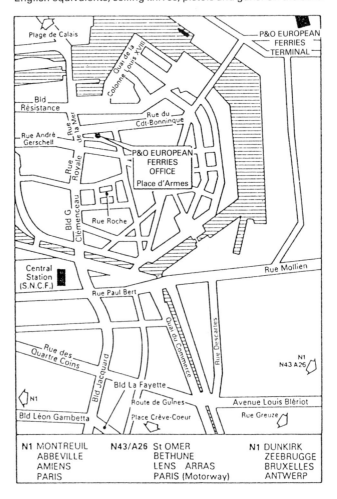

N1 MONTREUIL	N43/A26 St OMER	N1 DUNKIRK
ABBEVILLE	BETHUNE	ZEEBRUGGE
AMIENS	LENS ARRAS	BRUXELLES
PARIS	PARIS (Motorway)	ANTWERP

side of the boulevard is **Marose** for smell-now, buy-later perfumerie.

Vegetable and fruit shops are thin on the ground. **Pierre-et-Beatrice** in the bvd des Alliés, near the lighthouse, is the nearest to the terminal, probably the freshest, and has some interesting possibilities to bring home, like fresh herbs and those winey Charantais melons which never seem to taste so sweet when bought in England.

For freshly ground coffee go to **Cafféa** in the r. Royale, or stock up in the quantities of vacuum-packed Arabica at the hypermarkets – both are particularly good buys.

HOTELS

Meurice
(H)M–L
5 r. Roche
21.34..57.03
AE, DC, V
Parking

Calais' top hotel still, after many years. Augustin Meurice first opened its doors in 1772, to care for passengers off the Paris stage-coach. It was the first of a string of Meurice hotels along the road inland from Calais, culminating in the prestigious Hôtel Meurice in Paris.

Drive up to this post-war reincarnation and first impressions are more of an institution than a luxury hotel, but once inside it all starts getting palatial, with sweeping marble staircase and lots of gilt echoing the hotel's 18th-century origins. Vast salon, lots of deep armchairs, flock wallpapers, glossiest mags, make it a calm other-world haven, which would guarantee a restful stay.

The bedrooms come in two styles – Directoire plush and modern plastic. You might almost be in two different hotels. I much prefer the former, especially as, being older, they are more spacious. No. 18 has lots of lovely non-cost-effective space, with lobby, loo, and bathroom all separate. Remarkable value for 240f. Others start at 190f.

Last time I stayed breakfast was a placcy let-down, and the service was not three-star, but otherwise Meurice is way ahead of the others, and arrowed accordingly. Allow time for getting the car out of the creepy garage.

Georges V
(HR)M
36 r. Royale
21.97.68.00
AE, DC, EC, V
Parking

Currently making a determined bid to be Calais' second upmarket hotel and restaurant, under the same direction as the Bretagne in St-Omer (see p. 135). The Beauvalots have certainly transformed the hotel; it is now functionally modern, if a shade boring, and all 45 rooms have private bathrooms, double glazing, and colour T.V. so that not a single episode of *East Enders* need be missed.

If you like eating and sleeping under one roof, in Calais it has to be at the Georges V. See under 'Restaurants'.

Double rooms cost 180–210f. Good car-park.

Le Richelieu
(H)M
17 r. Richelieu
21.34.61.60
AE, EC, V

In a quiet side street off the r. Royale, opposite the public gardens and with lots of flowers in its own window-boxes.

The rooms, if simple, are comfortable and clean and some have balconies overlooking the park, but there are only two with baths and four with showers. Since they all include breakfast for two, the prices are good value and the management is friendly. 169–159f.

Bellevue
(H)M
Pl. d'Armes
21.34.53.75
V
Garage

Another Calais hotel bent on improving itself. Ever since Gault-Millau gave it the thumbs-up, it's gone decidedly upmarket, with complete refurbishment in the carpet-up-the-walls style. Some of the rooms have small balconies from which to watch the goings-on of the compats in the Place; all have English T.V. to watch goings-on back home. With bar, videos, lift, it is functional and efficient (if somewhat lacking in charm), which apparently is what most travellers want in a transit town like Calais, and not at all bad value, at 100–230f, in English money if you wish.

La Sole Meunière
(H)M
53 r. de la Mer
21.34.36.08
V

Strangely no feedback on this one, which I find difficult to understand, because it's the only hotel in Calais with sea views, has friendly patrons, M. and Mme Trouart, and is well furnished, with a fountain in the salon, no less. Rooms are 180–240f. Reports particularly welcome.

➤ **Hôtel Windsor**
(H)S
2 r. Cdt Bonningue
21.34.59.40
AE, DC, EC, V

This little hotel, convenient for the ferry, on the approach road to the pl. d'Armes, wins more plaudits than any other, due largely to the friendliness of the owners, M. and Mme Privat (other hoteliers please note). They speak English and Italian.

There are only fifteen rooms, all of them clean and comfortable; two have baths, at 205f; eight have showers, at 180f; and the rest are *simple* at 130f. Oh yes, and one with three beds, sleeping four people, which costs 304f but is always booked well ahead. All these prices include breakfast, so the bargain is obvious.

Convenient, friendly, well-situated, reasonable prices, lock-up garage = an arrow.

'We agree with your readers that the Windsor is a nice little hotel, very convenient for the ferry and shops. We have stayed there several times and have always found M. and Mme Privat most helpful and pleasant. It is the only hotel we have found where one is offered extra coffee at breakfast.' – Mary Wilson.

RESTAURANTS

➤ **Le Channel**
(R)M
3 bvd de la Résistance
21.34.42.30
Closed Sun. p.m.; Tues.; 1/ 6–10/6, 20/12– 15/1
AE, DC, EC, V

No diminution of the invariable high standards that have made it a French and English favourite at all levels for the ten years since M. and Mme Crespo took over. Only the decor has changed this year – the high-backed tapestry chairs, standard fittings for solidly respectable French restaurants of 'un certain standing', have given way to lighter, rose-coloured velvet versions. The comfort and service are as welcoming as ever.

The 62f (not Sundays) menu is remarkable for quality and quantity: a platter of fine slices of smoked haddock, colour naturally cream not hectic saffron, surrounds a well-dressed salad of frisée and radicchio. Then freshest Calaisien cod, served with a spicy coral sauce and a timbale of rice; a cheeseboard loyally supporting La Maison des Fromages, with regional cheeses in due season, and a choice of desserts – usually six or seven tarts, strawberry, bilberry, almond – and a chocolate gâteau, regrettably garnished with glacé cherries.

Most popular with the Brits is the next price up, at 95f, which features a platter of langoustines with good mayonnaise, a

Boullonais sole, or salmon 'au verjus du Perigord' (wine vinegar).

The Perigord menu, at 118f, is best reserved for hefty winter appetites – foie gras de canard, gésiers aux cêpes, navarin d'oie, and for a whole wet afternoon, the Menu Gourmand at 210f includes a bottle of wine and six courses of multi-national multi-regional dishes (M. Crespo is Spanish, lived in Perigord and Lourdes.)

The Crespos are wine buffs and their list is well chosen and interesting. Réserve de la Maison costs 40f.

Arrowed once more for absolute reliability, testified by numerous readers' letters, and outstanding value. Calais should be proud of Le Channel.

Georges V
(HR)M
36 r. Royale
21.97.68.00
Closed Sat.
lunch; sun.
p.m.; 24/12–6/1
CB, AE, DC

Sylvie Beauvalot, an artist as well as chef, has decorated the Georges, the 'restaurant gastronomique' in bizarre mediaeval style, defined by the odd heraldic banner and piece of chain mail. Divided at waist height is Le Petit Georges, already very popular for its good-value 59.90f menu – three courses of the like of croustade of seafood, medaillions of pork with pepper sauce, fish lasagne, gigôt of lamb.

For serious eaters, the 130f menu offers a dozen oysters or a terrine of scallops, then a panaché of fish with mushrooms, or stuffed quails, and a good cheeseboard with local cheeses like Mont des Cats represented.

The ambitious carte includes langoustine and duck foie gras salad; veal kidneys and sweetbreads on a bed of fresh noodles, turbot and monkfish feuilleté with a langoustine sauce.

The service is outstandingly efficient and helplful, and I think the Georges V deserves Calais' second arrow as an interesting new alternative to the Channel. See under 'Hotels'.

Le Detroit
(R)S–M
7 bvd de la
Résistance
21.34.43.10
Closed Fri.

Bright, airy cheerful decor, with a sunny rear garden, Le Detroit would fill the bill for a summer lunch. It profits from the overflow from its better-known neighbour, Le Channel, but several readers have liked it well enough, in its own right, to write commending the 60f menu.

Coq d'Or
(R)S
31 pl. d'Armes
21.34.79.05
Closed Wed.
AE, V

Recommending the Coq d'Or should carry some insurance policy for the guidewriter. It goes up and down faster than a choppy crossing. When it's up (and that is currently, which is why it's featured) the value is excellent, and takes no account of the easy custom inherent in its position on the pl. d'Armes. 40f buys three simple courses of good quality. The bits and bobs of lacy tablecloths, real napkins, good glasses are encouraging in a restaurant in this price bracket, and the service, on my last visit at least, was efficient and friendly. But there have been spasmodic unfavourable reports, which cancel out the arrow for this year. Be prepared to eat surrounded by fellow countrymen.

L'Arnaque
(R)S
6 r. des Quatre
Coins

For years I've plodded down Calais' unfrequented grim back streets, convinced that somewhere, away from the tourist belt, I would find a little gem, undiscovered by fellow hacks, patronised only by the Calaisien cognoscenti. I found Le Moulin à Poivre, which proved to

21.34.60.53
Closed Sun.
AE, V

be far too expensive for what's on offer; I found l'Assiette (see below), which meets the bill but is always full, and I found l'Arnaque. I wrote about it in *FE4* but oddly enough drew no response from readers whatsoever. Which made me think that perhaps I was on the wrong track and visitors to Calais, on transit or on foot, cannot be bothered with the less obvious. And with Le Channel around, who can blame them? However, I shall persist, for those who want a change, hit the town on a Tuesday, when Le Channel is closed, find themselves at the far end of the bvd Jacquard when hunger pangs strike, or just prefer to eat with the French.

The r. des Quatre Coins is almost the last turning on the right off the boulevard, and l'Arnaque is the very French-looking house a few doors down on the right. It's had a recent face-lift and reorganisation and now there are two dining-rooms, one freshly painted green and white and the other awaiting treatment. High ceilings, panelling and greenery give it a domestic rather than commercial feel.

At lunchtime it gets full with local office workers, tucking into the dish of the day (not Sats.). On my last visit it was a substantial sauté of lamb, served with a buttery baked potato (unusual in France) for 30f (36f with wine). If this arrangement happens to suit, it is top value.

49f buys three courses; the next one up at 75f is the most popular with the Brits, offering more variety, and 169f offers five courses, but personally I would go for the bargains. House plonk is 40f a litre.

Dominique Richard-Multeau, the patron, is friendly, helpful, likes the English and speaks enough of their language to explain the menus, which he courageously refuses to have translated.

Côte d'Argent
(R) M
Parking de la
Plage
34.68.07
Closed Mon. in
summer, dinner
in winter
AE, V
Parking

The town's most upmarket fish restaurant; the Calais businessmen eat here, which is usually a good sign, but my reactions have been akin to:

'A convenient place to eat because of the easy parking. The 85f menu, which appears not to change daily, provided excellent moules gratinées, fresh cod, cheese and dessert. Wine list uninspired but adequate. Lunch for two, with drink, came to 257f. I would use it again but it certainly does not "vaut un detour".'

La Sirène
(R)S
r. de la Mer

Another fishy restaurant, which might come in useful if all that was required was a plateful of moules or some other simple dish. They do serve lunch later than any other restaurant that I quizzed, so could be friends in need.

La Goulue
(R)S
r. de la Mer
Closed Wed.

Meat-eaters should cross the road from La Sirène to this little bistro, decorated in Parisien *fin-de-siècle* style, which continues to offer good-value steak and better-than-average frites. With salad, they cost 50f.

L'Assiette
(R)S
2 pl. de Suède

The nearest restaurant to the port, and yet somehow still relatively tripper-free. The regular clientele appear to be locals – many of them friends of the moustachioed M. Bonnet, judging by the way he takes

21.34.15.10
Closed Mon.
p.m.; Sun.; 2
weeks in Aug.

a swig from their wine and orders them about. (But then he did the same to me, so perhaps it's par for the course.) No menu, which some might find off-putting since there is no guarantee of what the bill is to be; M. Bonnot asks you what you fancy, and if the ingredients were available in the market that day, that is what you may well get.

I got tomatoes stuffed with crab (next table's moules farcies looked good) and sole meunière (they had steak au poivre), which cost me 65f with house plonk but it was unclear who paid for that.

Unconventional, full of atmosphere; you'll like it or hate it. I like it.

La Duchesse
(R)L
44 r. du Duc de
Guise
21.97.59.69
Closed Sat.
lunch

Not my kind of restaurant, but everyone else I've asked approved so I include it, with reservations. La Duchesse used to be a tea-room but has now gone very smart. I find the plush decor over-the-top, and I wasn't very happy about the mayonnaise on my langoustines, but it's certainly very comfortable and quiet – a welcome respite from the beer and skittles round the corner in the main street.

The cooking is very ambitious, with dishes like ris de veau frais aux trois couleurs, chausson farci au crabe, on the carte. The cheapest menu is 98f and the wine list, of 220 appellations, understandably pricey. Allow at least 200f for three courses.

Le Touquets
(R)S
51 r. Royale
21.34.64.18
Open 12 p.m. to
2 am daily

A Calais institution, unbeatable in its class, for cheap cheerful noisy non-stop value. Stick to the front section, away from the garish casino bit, and fill up the kids on menus at 44f inclusive of wine. Don't underestimate the idea of one well-cooked dish from the carte either, if it's quality rather than quantity you're after.

Fraîche Saveur
(R)S
3 r. André
Gerschell
21.96.89.71

Sad news here– Mme Ducard tells me that she is going to have to sell her delightful little restaurant/shop. French Entrée readers have liked what she offers as much as I do, and patronised her establishment regularly during the season, but the Calaisiens have failed to appreciate the style, and business for the rest of the year has not justified the expenditure. So I can only say make the most of the Fraîche Saveur while you can.

It is, as its name implies, fresh and bright and cheerful, with a welcome little garden at the rear of the green and white restaurant. The incomparable Ducard chocolates, pastries and home-made ice creams are on sale, to eat or to take away, with a range of light snacks and lunch dishes at very reasonable prices. Perhaps they are too reasonable. Quiche Lorraine 8.50f, fresh artichoke soup 6.50f, salmon with dill 17.50f, rabbit with wild mushrooms 49f, sea bass with shrimp sauce 42f, are examples of what's on offer and there is a commendable *suggestion de ce jour*. Wine, served only with food, is available by the glass. Open every day. Black mark, Calais, for letting this one go.

A welcome new discovery for me in Calais has been an agreeable bar. It's been there all the time, but I always assumed, as no doubt readers do too, that it was reserved for the yacht club members, as it is situated overlooking the marina. You aim for the beach, then turn left towards the yachts, and it is situated in the tower on the quay, simply called the Yacht Club Bar. Henri Ravisse, esteemed Chairman of the Chambre de Commerce and lifelong Calais devotee, pointed it out to me, and I agree with him that it is much the most agreeable place in the town to have a quiet drink in pleasant surroundings (unless you like the beer-swilling celebratory atmosphere of most of the bars in the town). Here you sit high above the basin, and can watch the ferries' progress, all far removed from fellow countrymen who have not yet caught on. They do light snack meals too at lunchtime.

Map 4B	**CAMBRAI** (Nord) 149 km SE of Calais

59400
(M) *daily
except Mon.*

1 km from the A 2.
 The centre of the rich cereal lands of the Cambrésis. Cambrai suffered as badly as any town could in the fierce fighting of the First World War. The Hindenburg Line – a line of blockades, barbed-wire, cannon and machine-gun posts – ran through its centre. In 1917, armoured tanks were used in battle for the first time by the British,

under the command of General Byng; the breach they made in the Line lasted for ten days, until the German Army received reinforcements and the battle turned again.

Old photographs of those war days decorate many a hotel and restaurant. There is the famous one of the British officers playing a piano in the Grande Place with the jagged ruins of the 18th-century Hôtel de Ville (since restored) in the background. Another shows smoke drifting across the 16th-century wooden Maison Espagnole (which now houses the Syndicat d'Initiative): it miraculously survived while houses on either side were totally destroyed.

Leave your car in the pl. Aristide-Briand and explore Cambrai on foot. It is a cheerful town, with attractive shops and a wealth of little restaurants. Louis Blériot, one of the earliest aviators, was born in the r. Sadi-Carnot: a plaque on the wall is inscribed with the date of his birth. The church of St-Géry is probably Cambrai's most celebrated monument: among other treasures in it, is a painting by Rubens of Christ being placed in the Tomb, described in the 19th century as 'one of the most beautiful Rubens in France and, without doubt, one of the master's greatest works of art.'

In the r. de l'Épée is the Musée Municipale (open every day, except Tuesday, from 10 a.m.– 12 p.m. and from 2–5 p.m., closed January and February). It houses some really marvellous treasures: portraits by Velasquez, paintings from the Flemish school of the 16th and 17th centuries; works by Matisse and Utrillo; 16th-century tapestries; bronzes from Gallo-Roman times; pottery and jewels from the Merovingian era . . .

By car, trace the remnants of the ancient gates and walls that once fortified the town. It is a sobering thought that, out of the devastation of the wars, so many things were conserved and so much has risen again.

Leave the N 44 at Masnières and drive on along narrow country roads, through Crêvecoeur-sur-l'Escaut and Les-Rues-des-Vignes (a corruption from the Latin *Vallis Cellae* or the 'Cell in the Valley') for a picnic by the 12th-century Cistercian abbey or Notre-Dame de Vaucelles. Entry to this vast, decaying red-brick abbey complex (destroyed during the Revolution and the First World War) is limited to the last Sunday of each month from April to September; 3–6 p.m.

Hôtel Beatus
(H)M
718 av. de Paris
27.81.45.70/71
AE, DC, EC, V
Parking

Follow the N 44 1.5 km from the centre of Cambrai in the direction of St-Quentin. This splendid whitewashed hotel stands beyond a large chestnut tree, cypresses and flowering fruit trees in its own garden, well set back from the road. Proprietors are the Corczynski family (of Polish extraction), who also own the little café near the entrance. Twenty-six lovely bedrooms furnished in the style of Louis XV and Louis XVI: the best look straight out on to the garden and they cost from 190–245f.

Next door is the hospital, once the site of a vast château, that was destroyed during the war and the land on which it stood bequeathed to the city by the owner.

Arrowed for comfort and quiet situation.

Hostellerie du Château de la Motte Fénelon
(HR)M
Square du Château
27.83.61.38
Rest. closed Sun. p.m.
V

Leave Cambrai by the Valenciennes road, turn second left beyond a bridge and follow the narrow street that leads to the hotel grounds. In the early 19th century the land belonged to a wealthy laundryman who had drained the surrounding marshes to use as drying-fields for his thriving industry. Moving quickly up the social scale, he married into the Cambrai nobility and built this magnificent house surrounded by 8 hectares of parkland. During the wars, it was occupied and looted by the Germans. Restoration to its former glory started in 1973, and the hotel was opened in 1974.

There are 7 modern-style bedrooms in the château (260f) and 22 motel rooms in the park (240f). Decoration and furnishing in the château are excellent: white paint, moulding picked out in gold leaf, parquet floors with good rugs, reproduction period furniture, marble fireplaces and lovely chintz curtains in the tall windows. Downstairs in the cellars (used by the Germans as a shelter) is the restaurant Les Douves. Here circular tables are covered with white cloths and decorated with dried flower arrangements. Two elegant dining-rooms on the first floor. Menus, also printed in English, are 135 and 185f. 135f menu includes salade de lapéreau, papillote de saumon et rascasse, tables des douceurs (desserts). Breakfast 25f. An elegant and tranquil place in which to stay.

Le Mouton Blanc
(HR)M
22 r. d'Alsace-Lorraine
27.82.30.16
Rest. closed Sun. p.m.; Mon.
V

Hotel and restaurant near Cambrai station. Parking in front of the hotel or outside the station. Charming bedrooms (115–250f), all recently redecorated in pretty colours: blues, pinks, and so on, the shades picked out in the pillowcases on the comfortable beds.

The young patronne has run the hotel, dining-room and nearby self-service restaurant for the last year with the help of her father and brother. There is an attractive air of vitality about the place which reflects her enthusiasm. The 1916 dining-room, decorated with wood in the Flemish style, has been 'lightened' a trifle – fresh white paint, attractive chairs and tables – to bring it into the 1980s. Menus (80–180f) are imaginative. The self-service restaurant, just round the corner, shares the hotel kitchen. Well up the gastronomic scale itself, this large cheerful room offers such dishes as pot-au-feu; boeuf bourguignon; les oeufs au plat, façon Portugaise; delicious fruit tarts etc; all set out enticingly on the counter.

If all this industry continues in such an efficient way, Madame's reputation (already high) will be a force to be reckoned with.

A l'Escargot
(R)M
10 r. Général de Gaulle
27.81.24.54
Closed Mon.
AE, EC, V

Another chic Cambrai restaurant close by the main square where, incidentally, parking is metered; leave your car in one of the side streets. One dining-room in a charming, well-lit room downstairs by the entrance, another on an upper floor.

90f menu includes a quarter carafe of red wine, mineral water or beer. Delicacies include regional dishes such as boudin aux pommes, coquille de poisson gratinée, andouillettes de Cambrai. Pièce de résistance is half a langouste grilled over real charcoal (none of your gas-fired and heated briquette contraptions here!) in the converted fireplace. Menus at 90f and 140f.

Aux Arcades
(R)M
12 r. du
Maréchal-de-
Lattre-de-
Tassigny
27.81.30.80
Closed Wed.
p.m.; Thur.
p.m.
AE, DC, EC, V

Lively Marcel Dessailly, formerly owner of Aux Arcades, has retired from the administrative side of the restaurant in favour of his son and young M. Fresnay. M. Dessailly, senior, now concentrates on his cuisine – a craft he has been perfecting over the last 47 years.

A meal à la carte in the *brasserie* at the entrance, accompanied, traditionally, by a glass of beer, would come to 70–100f. More elaborate menus (78f, 98f and 160f) are served in the two big upstairs dining-rooms. On the 78f menu are terrine au poivre vert, épaule de veau farcie . . . Ambience is elegant and relaxing.

Le Crabe
Tambour
(R)M
52 r. Cantimpré
27.83.10.18
Closed Sun.
p.m.; Mon.;
first 3 weeks of
August, one
week in
February
V

There is room, surprisingly, to seat one hundred people in this little, early 1900s building on the busy street that runs on towards Arras. Usually room to park on the pavement outside.

During the war, it was a café. M. and Mme Robinet bought the place five years ago and swiftly earned themselves a name for their classical cuisine. Small dining-room downstairs is furnished *au style rustique*: copper pans hanging on rough-cast, white-painted walls, old pictures, doll sitting in antique push-chair. Another dining-room upstairs, reached by a ladder staircase. The Robinets specialise in fish: petite salade de haddock; feuilleté d'oeufs brouillés au saumon fumé; ragoût de St Jacques et langoustines au Champagne. Meat dishes include côtes de veau Franc Comtoise poêlé (veal with gruyère and eggs on top). Menus at 95f and 135f.

Le Petit Chef
(R)M
1 r. des Docks
27.81.47.46
Closed Sun.
p.m.; Mon.
p.m.; between
Christmas and
New Year, and
2 weeks in July
V

M. Dessailly (a son of Marcel Dessailly of Aux Arcades) is the chef here – his father ran the restaurant for 17 years and it was from him that he learned his craft. It is beside the St Quentin canal and is a favourite stop for boats moving along this waterway.

There is a cosy, café atmosphere in the entrance/dining-room: cheerful red-and-white tablecloths and a bar. In the inner dining-room, the atmosphere is more formal: lacy tablecloths and potted plants. Between October and April, specialities are couscous and andouille chaud. Lots of regional dishes at all times. 103f menu and carte.

Map 5C

LA CAPELLE EN THIÉRACHE (Aisne) 269 km SE of Calais; 16 km S of Avesnes

---

Hôtel
Restaurant de
la Thiérache
(HR)S
16 av. du
Général de
Gaulle
Closed 14/2–28/
2
EC, V

A post-war house, entered through an arch that fronts the busy N 2 and at the further end of a courtyard. Good-sized bedrooms (95–170f), slightly shabby but with good furniture, and everywhere spotlessly clean.

The large dining-room (menus 45f, 55f, 80f and 135f and à la carte) is cheerfully furnished. Artificial flowers everywhere, plain walls, flowered wallpaper on the ceiling and plates on shelves. 80f menu (served at sparklingly white-clothed tables) includes a dozen snails, confit de canard maison aux champignons, cheese and dessert.

Plenty of room to park outside. Set back from the road like this, guests should enjoy a quiet night, without a diversion from their main route.

Map 1C	**CAPELLE-LA-GRANDE** (Nord) 43 km NE of Calais, 9 km S of Dunkerque

---

59140
Dunkerque

Turn off the A 25 at the Bergues exit, direction Dunkerque Centre.

Le Bois de Chêne
(R)M
48 r. de Bergues
28.64.21.80
Closed Sun. p.m.; Sat.; 2 weeks Aug.

Christian Vandeneeckhoutte is a great exponent of local dishes, served, in his little restaurant in the dreary Dunkerque outskirts, at moderate prices. His 70f menu is a bargain. He has researched regional recipes in danger of dying out, thanks to the dictates of *nouvelle cuisine* and the chippies. Among his specialities is a definitive potjevleisch dunkerquois, a terrine of rabbit, veal and chicken. Ice creams are home-made and ingredients are local wherever possible. A possible arrow, after a few more reports.

Map 2C	**CASSEL** (Nord) 50 km SE of Calais

59670
(M) *Thurs.*

32 km NE of St-Omer by the D 933, or junction A 25 Steenvoorde.
Probably the most interesting excursion to make from Calais, but pick a clear day, when you can see for ever, or at least as far as the sea, 30 km away.

The town is built on the slopes of Mont Cassel, a green hill that has been fortified since time immemorial. Normans, Flemish, French, Spanish and English all fought to hold it. Romans camped here and engineered seven roads from Cassel towards the coast or to connect up with their other strongholds. In the First World War, Maréchal Foch, Commander-in-Chief of the Armies of the North, and the English General Rumer stayed in Cassel, whence they directed the Battle of Flanders. There is a huge equestrian statue of Foch, honorary citizen of the town, set in an 'English garden' at the summit of the hill (178m). Behind him stands a windmill that was reconstructed from the once-famous 16th-century mill burned in 1911. It commemorates the 29 working windmills that stood on the hill's grassy slopes at the beginning off this century.

Cassel's fine, triangular-shaped Grande Place, one of the largest in Flanders, shows little sign now of the bombardment and devastating fires that the town suffered in 1940. There are coats of arms over doorways that lead into secluded courtyards; weathered rooftops that might have existed since mediaeval times. Don't miss a visit to the Renaissance museum in the Hôtel de la Noble Cour. Among earlier memorabilia of Cassel's history is the office where Foch worked and where he spent 'the most distressing hours of his life': those between 23 October 1914 and 21 June 1915. Open every afternoon between Easter and October.

**L'Hôtel de
Schoëbeque**
(HR)M
32 r. Foch
28.42.42.67
Closed Mon.;
Feb.
DC EC, V
Parking

This fine 18th-century building in a narrow street off the Grande Place was once the home of a M. Paul Lehglé, seigneur of Schoëbeque and Deputy-General of coastal Flanders, who, like many another aristocrat, fell to the guillotine during the French Revolution. It is celebrated today as having been the headquarters of Maréchal Foch in the months between October 1914 and June 1915; from here he directed operations in the Battle of l'Yser, returning often during the long drawn-out Flanders campaign. George V and the Prince of Wales stayed at the Schoëbeque in 1917, Field-Marshall Haig, in 1916, 1917, 1919. It was also visited during those war years by Albert I, King of the Belgians, and by Prince Edward, Duke of Connaught. One wonders if the nine tall, elegant bedrooms (185f with bath) and the salon with its old, mellow panelling have changed much since those days. Certainly, the whole place retains an agreeable atmosphere of days-gone-by.

However, if the hotel side of the establishment is all a little faded and creaking, the restaurant itself presents a delightful vitality. Young M. Potisek is hard at it before a roaring wood-fire, cutting up the carcase of a lamb with deft butcher's strokes, grilling the joints over iron bars, stirring the sauces and, in between, helping his guests to more wine, while the plates are ready warming on the hearth. Dishes are eventually presented with a beaming smile and guests' faces scrutinised to judge their reactions.

Not feeling particularly hungry the day we went there for lunch, I merely ate grilled crevettes roses, sauce à l'ail (36f); while my daughter set about the children's menu: a man-sized steak grilled over that wood-fire, braised celery and French fries (*how* can potatoes that look like chips, taste so infinitely better than the British version? (25f). The inevitable ice-cream to folllow cost 14f.

No set menus, but those à la carte prices were hardly ruinous. For example: poulet grillé, beurre d'estragon (48f); côte de porc aux herbes (42f); mousse au chocolat (18f).

Parking is in the small courtyard by the front door beyond a rather grand and embellished entrance.

► **Le Sauvage**
(R)L
Grande Place
28.42.40.88
Closed Wed.;
Sun. p.m.;
Tues. p.m.
AE, DC, EC, V

A truly stunning view over the flat Flanders plain from the summer dining-room of this old Flemish inn. In winter the smaller dining-room, cheered by a log fire, is used, but still ask to see the view across the courtyard, with the lights of St-Omer flickering away far below.

By some computer quirk, in 1986 Michelin listed Le Sauvage, with its 'trois fouchettes', under Carteret in the Manche, whose inhabitants by now must be feeling pretty savage themselves at being asked for directions to the restaurant 200 miles away. Poor M. Decaestecker, to whom this was a very serious omission indeed, remonstrated and was promised amends in the 1987 guide, but found to his horror that he was left out altogether. Perhaps the '88 version will offer him a rosette to compensate. Clever Gault-Millau think he's worth two toques, the high score of 16/20 and their 'Lauriers du Terroir' for good regional cooking, and I only hope that their approval will be enough to keep him going – it would be a terrible loss to the area if the lack of publicity – essential to a restaurant of this calibre – should force him out of business.

I think he gets better and better, but, make no mistake, this could be an expensive meal – say 300f on the carte, with temptation from a wonderful wine list of 600 fine wines. The 100f 'Menu Rustique' is the one to go for, so long as the dish of the day suits you; the next one up at 195f has seven courses and M. Decaestecker's *dégustations* are meals rather than tasters.

His Belgian origins are somewhat in conflict with modern cooking. He has no doubt *heard* of *nouvelle cuisine* but its influences here are hardly discernible. He serves a coarse purée of carrots and one of cabbage, but then, wavering, adds a portion of traditional carrot slices and a hefty cabbage leaf wrapped around some home-made noodles, to hedge his bets.

On the cheapest menu, one dark and dirty night when appetite was keenest, I ate langoustines, cooked in cider with a kick of the juniper-flavoured genièvre, from Houlle, to make it rich not cloying. The sauce was too good to leave – home-made brown rolls made mopping up a double pleasure. The terracotta sauce of a sauté de cabriau (roe-deer) was richly sticky and mildly spiced with curry – hardly a Flemish flavour but an interesting and effective combination. An alternative might have been casserole of hare, or chicken from Licques stuffed with pigs trotters, no lightweights, any of them. Pousses d'houblon (hop shots) are used as garnishes, stuffed in omelettes, or in feuilletés.

The carte offers more regional specialities, like potjevleisch Cassellois, a terrine of rabbit, veal and chicken. Desserts include beignets de cramiques; M. Decaestecker relates that these go back to the time when his thrifty grandparents used to prepare some biscuits – cramiques – for their return from early mass. Whatever were left were fried in batter and used for lunch.

To find a chef so dedicated to his region and so ready to exploit its produce must earn an arrow.

| Map 5B | **LE CATELET** (Aisne) 170 km SE of Calais; 21 km S of Cambrai |

02420

On the N 44, 9 km from the A 26 Masnières exit.

Restaurant de la Croix d'Or (R)M
23.66.21.71
Closed Sun. p.m.; Mon.; two weeks at beginning of Jan.; 15/8–9/9
EC, V

An old Relais de Poste that featured in the Guide Michelin as La Croix d'Or as long ago as 1935. In the centuries of Spanish domination, this little village stood on the frontier line between the Kingdom of France and the Spanish Empire. The old castle (of which little now remains) was one of the border fortresses.

M. Capelle (senior) ran the restaurant for 25 years while his wife did the cooking. Ten years ago he handed over to his son but still takes an active part in the management. The family takes great pride in their fresh food: fish from the boats at Étaples and vegetables from the great Rungis market.

Menus (90–160f) specialise in fish. There is a dining-room large enough to seat up to 40 people, with a paved floor, an old oak buffet and attractive pink tablecloths. Lots of geraniums in the window-boxes, and plenty of room to park in a large space across the road.

Monsieur is an intelligent man to talk to, with a fund of local knowledge.

Map 5B | **CAUDRY** (Nord) 160 km SE of Calais

59540
(M) *Tues.,*
Fri., Sun.

2 km from Beauvois-en-Cambrésis, off the N 43 Cambrai–Le Cateau road.

Caudry is a small, linen-manufacturing town that developed in the 19th century. When Jackie Kennedy was received at the Vatican, she wore a veil made in Caudry. An 1840 church, remarkable chiefly for a shrine to St-Maxellende, virgin and martyr, who was born in Caudry and perished in St-Souplet in 670.

Nouvel Hôtel
(H)S (R)S–M
5 r. St-Quentin
27.85.12.48
Rest. closed
Sun.; hotel cl.
one week mid-
Aug.
AE, EC, V
Parking

A cosy hotel with a very friendly patronne: Mme Happe. Upstairs a little shabby: linoleum on the staircase and landing. Cheerful bedrooms (115–225f), breakfast included; those in the upper price range have big bathrooms, and the best rooms overlook the little Place.

A large dining-room with old-fashioned buffet and white table-cloths. 52f menu proposed: quiche lorraine or andouillette de Cambrai; côte de porc charcutière; cheese and dessert. The more adventurous 80f menu included terrine de faisan and truite flambé Normande. An unpretentious hotel with a reasonable restaurant. Parking in the courtyard at the back.

Map 7C | **CHAMPILLON** (Marne) 32 km SE of Calais

51160
Ay

5 km N of Épernay on the N51.

Royal Champagne Marne.

Royal **Champagne** (HR)L *26.51.11.51* *AC, CN, DC, EC* *Parking*	Beautifully situated on the slopes of the Montagne de Reims, above the Épernay vineyards, this Relais et Châteaux hotel houses its guests in little bungalows, whose individual terraces take full advantage of the view. They are not particularly large nor luxurious but chintzily comfortable. 480–800f. The restaurant is more plush, with wrap-around picture windows. It has a Michelin star and would cost 350f à la carte or 280f on the menu, with a lighter lunchtime version at 200f. As you might expect, since it is owned by Moët et Chandon, the list of champagnes is mightily impressive.

Map 2D   **LA CHAPELLE D'ARMENTIÈRES** (Nord) 88 km SE of Calais

59280	Take exit 8 from the A 25 in the direction of Fleurbaix, then follow signs for La Chapelle d'Armentières.
	    During the First World War, the front line ran through the flat farmland that surrounds this village north-west of Lille. Like so much of northern France it dates mostly from those post-war days.
	    Coming from Armentières, turn right off the southern end of the busy main street for the r. Omer Ollivier and the restaurant La Ferme d'Averdoingt. It is on the left of the road, 1½ km outside the village, just before the bridge that spans the A 25.

Restaurant la **Ferme** **d'Averdoingt** (R)M *199 bis, r. Omer* *Ollivier* *20.35.30.64* *Closed Sun.,* *p.m.; Mon.* *AE, EC, V* *Parking*	Cheerful M. Lucien Bara took over from his predecessor, a renowned chef, two years ago and has swiftlly earned himself a reputation for his cuisine. Guests arriving for lunch were met with beaming smiles and enthusiastic greetings from the owner. Menus 85f and 120f. A la carte menu with some really tempting dishes: brochette de langoustines (at 98f the most expensive item) and nougat glacé au grand Marnier (25f). The restaurant itself (two dining-rooms) is a modern, red-brick extension built on to (and well in keeping with) a typical Flemish farm.

Map 5D   **CHARLEVILLE-MÉZIÈRES** (Ardennes) 271 km SE of Calais

08100
(M) *Tues.,*
Thur., Sat.
	119 km E of St-Quentin, 22 km NW of Sedan.
	    Situated on the river Meuse, originally two towns – Charleville *and* Mézières – but today united into a sprawling whole.
	    The poet Rimbaud was born in Charleville: visit the museum that commemorates his life and houses examples of folklore from the district. Above the town rises le Mont Olympe – hardly Olympic by Grecian standards. It was so named during the centuries of the Crusades.

Auberge de la **Forest** (R)M *Montcy-Notre-* *Dame*	'La Forest' is, in fact, a French name. This charming restaurant on the D 1 just outside Charleville-Mézières, direction Nouzonville, is named after the forested area that surrounds it. The dining-room is large with brown cloths over white cloths on the tables and a view through the windows of those lovely trees.

24.33.37.55
Closed Sun.
p.m.; Mon.
EC, V

55f menu offers coquille de poisson mayonnaise, sauté de veau marengo, salad and dessert. Very friendly Mme Baudlet speaks good English: the menu, she told us, changes every day. Menus: 55f, 90f, and 115f.

**Restaurant
Mont-Olympe**
(R)M
r. Paquis
24.33.20.77
Closed Sun.
p.m.; Mon. p.m.
o.o.s.
AE, EC, V

M. Laurent, or 'François I' (as he likes to call himself, being the first chef to serve *fruits de mer* in the Ardennes), runs this admirable restaurant situated on a terrace at the foot of le Mont Olympe.

Somewhere on the hill above are the vestiges of an old Crusader castle of which today only a few stones remain. The house, built in 1910, and its grounds belonged to an architect until Monsieur acquired it. It is much favoured by the birds of passage who moor their motor-boats and yachts on the river Meuse below. *Menu touristique* at 78f seemed an excellent bargain: *kir* as an aperitif, a choice between five or six *entrées* and four *plats*, followed by dessert and accompanied by a quarter of vin de pays. Other menus at 65f, 145f. Children's menu at 40f.

Map 7B

CHÂTEAU-THIERRY (Aisne) 343 km SE of Calais; 41 km S of Soissons

---

02400
Ⓜ Tues.,
Fri.

On the D 1 2 km S of the A 4.

Built in the valley of the Marne, the old town centre of Château-Thierry is remarkable for the vestiges of its 14th-century fortress and as the birthplace of the 17th-century story-teller Jean de la Fontaine. The house where the latter was born is now a museum dedicated to his work; there are some magnificent editions of his fables with illustrations by 18th and 19th-century artists (visits: 10 a.m.– 12 p.m., 2–6 p.m). Just south of the Grande Place (where the Syndicat d'Initiative is situated) is La Tour Balham, once part of a fort built in the 12th century by the Comtes de Champagne, which became, in the 16th century, the home of Jean Balham, grain merchant. Today it shelters a branch of Monoprix.

**Auberge Jean
de la Fontaine**
(R)M
10 r. des Filoirs
23.83.63.89
Closed Sun.
p.m.; Mon.
DC, EC, V

Coming from the south, this elegant restaurant is in a side-street on the right of the main street just before it crosses the river Marne.

Jacques Chène and Guy Giraud are the owners. It is obviously a favourite lunching-place with local businessmen. A menu 'pour nos clients pressés' (110f, weekdays only) is provided, no doubt with these gentlemen in mind. However, in spite of this, we found the service slow, the waiters highly talented in the art of avoiding their customers' eyes. Another menu 'léger et savoureux' (140f) offered some tantalising dishes. We tried the à la carte menu: 'la terrine de ris de veau et ses frivolités au foie gras' (60f) and 'rouelle de gigôt d'agneau grillé au beurre de thym' (68f), and thoroughly enjoyed it.

Verdict: a worthwhile eating-place, but hopeless if you are in a hurry.

**Hôtel et Motel
de la Girafe**

A good find – follow the main boulevard west to a roundabout with a Shell garage: La Girafe is just across the road.

(H)S
Pl. Aristide
Briand
23.83.02.06
Always open
EC, V

Monsieur René Baduel has lived in this 200-year-old hotel for 60 years (it belonged to his parents before him) and, judging by the energy shown by his five-year-old grandson who proudly helped show us around, its future is assured for another couple of generations or so. Ninteen rooms altogether, in the hotel, its annexe and motel building (90–180f): all very simple with rather dull furniture and decoration, but clean.

Monsieur speaks excellent English, having lived in Camden Town, London, for some years. He makes a kind and friendly host.

Hôtel Île de France
(HR)M
23.69.10.12
Closed 24/12-
30/12
AE, DC, EC, V

A large hotel (56 bedrooms), well set back from the D 1 Soissons road, about 3 km outside Château-Thierry. Mme Renet has been here 15 years and is a friendly person, as indeed were all the other staff we met. Bedrooms (130–280f) were perhaps the most interesting side of the hotel: clear, fresh colours and very clean. The lounge and the large dining-room looked a little dull, but the menus (50–185f) seemed imaginative.

On the 50f menu were maquereau au vin blanc, feuilles de vignes; poulet Basquaise; dessert. A good-value hotel, which should prove quiet at night.

Map 7B

CHÂTILLON-SUR-MARNE (Marne) 230 km SE of Calais; 23 km W of Épernay

---

 Wed.

On the D 23 N of the N 2.

An ancient little town, dominated by the massive statue of Urbain II, the Pope who initiated the First Crusade, and surrounded by hill slopes covered with vineyards, with a view over the river Marne.

La Porte Oubliée
(R)S
26.58.37.58
Closed Mon.
EC, V

A small restaurant that enjoys a considerable local reputation. The two dining-rooms are cramped and rather scruffy, with red tablecloths and black walls. But then one shouldn't always go by appearances: and certainly not in this case. Both dining-rooms were crowded, with Madame dashing hither and thither. Seems the curious name is taken from a well-known local legend, but we hadn't the heart to stop la patronne in mid-stride to ask her the story. Please find out – we'd love to know!

Menus 60f, 90f and 120f. On the 60f menu were champignons à la Grêcque, poulet au four, pommes frites, cheese/dessert.

Map 6B

CHAUNY (Aisne) 229 km SE of Calais; 21 km S of St-Quentin

02300
 Tues.,
Fri.

Hôtel de la Gare
(HR)S–M
23.52.11.91
DC, EC, V

Nothing of interest goes on in Chauny that we could see, but it's a useful stopping-off place, none the less. Take the D 338 off the D 1 and follow the signs to the station for this good-value hotel. Bedrooms (72–116f) are, by and large, rather shabby with old-fashioned furniture. In contrast, the dining-room is sparklingly fresh and clean with pretty, pinky-orange tablecloths and a wood-fire in winter. Jolly café-entrance, well patronised by locals (a good sign by any account). Menus at 50f, 90f and 160f. 90f menu looked intriguing: terrine de lapin, osso bucco à la Milanaise, cheese, dessert. Helpful staff. Parking on the pavement outside the hotel or in the station car-park.

| Map 5B | **CHIGNY** (Aisne) 245 km SE of Paris |

02120
Guise

12 km W of Etreaupont by the D 31 and D 26.

Nothing much happens in the little village of Chigny. It is surrounded by fields and reached by narrow, winding lanes. There are strings of sausages hanging in a window of a red-brick house where only the sign outside suggests that it might belong to a butcher; the carcase of a pig, tied to a ladder is propped up against a wall. Chigny is a village of little, old cottages, typical of the Thiérache: some of them date from past centuries, many of them built just after the First World War.

L'Espérance
(CR)S
23.60.21.15
EC, V

The *chambres d'hôte* belonging to M. Hubert Camus are attached to a little inn that was a farm in the early 19th century. He converted the barn next door eight years ago and, in it, built these cheerful bedrooms (99f, bed and breakfast). All very clean and fresh: exposed beams, shower and loo on the landing.

In the main building, there is a small restaurant, and a bar (well patronised by locals). Simple 42f menu includes tomato salad, côte de porc, boeuf braisé aux haricots, tarte aux pommes.

Lots of room to park out front, and a gîte, that sleeps another five people, down at the bottom of the garden.

➤ **Mlles Piette**
(C)
23.60.22.04

A red-brick 1765 Thiérache farmhouse with white doors and shutters near the village hall. The sisters, who live in a modern, white-washed house next door, have done all the decoration themselves – and, in impeccable taste it is, too. The upstairs of the farmhouse, once the granary, has been converted into five bedrooms, all beautifully done up (much of the wallpaper is, in fact, English) and furnished with antiques; one of the beds has a lovely, old, white, family bed-cover. Washbasins in all the rooms, and modern bathroom and loo in the corridor. Exposed beams and rafters here and there, ornaments, steps down into some of the rooms and a general atmosphere of an old-fashioned country house.

And such good value – bed and breakfast for two people costs 114f; two of the rooms have three beds (145f). I liked the Mlle Piette that I met: she was busy painting the wall of her own garden, ready, no doubt, for the season that lay ahead. I can imagine that she wouldn't rest until everything was little short of perfect.

Arrowed for top-value *chambre d'hôte* accommodation.

| Map 6A | **COMPIÈGNE** (Oise) 258 km SE of Calais |

60200
(M) *Wed.,*
Sat.

9 km E of the A 1.

When the Germans came to Compiègne in 1942, they found a town that had largely escaped the ravages of the war. To please their Chief-of-Staff, shortly to inspect the scene, they committed what must surely be the ultimate act of vandalism: they burned all the buildings between the station and the town hall, the object being to present him with evidence of a subjugated community.

There is little about Compiègne today to remind one of those days. Although you have only to go the Clairière de l'Armistice to see a replica of the railway carriage in which the First World War came to an end (the original was burned on the Reichstagplatz in Berlin in the last war) or read the memorial set into the wall, near the Tour Jeanne d'Arc, that marks the spot from where 48,000 French men and women were deported to the concentration camps, to remember the part that Compiègne played not so long ago. Miraculously, none of the town's chief monuments were destroyed and it is a place of considerable interest to the tourist.

'My greatest delight in Compiègne,' wrote Robert Louis Stevenson, 'is the Town Hall.' This 15th-century Gothic masterpiece is considered one of the most beautiful pieces of civic architecture in the North of France. Next door is the Musée de la Figurine Historique, which contains 85,000 model soldiers illustrating military history throughout the ages: my favourites were the very life-like ones made by Abbé Ducoin in the 1960s. Not far from the Tour Jeanne d'Arc is the Musée Vivenel, a fascinating collection of ceramics and local crafts that illustrates the connection between the progress of civilisation and the development of art.

The château of Compiègne is the third royal palace of France: there were only three capable of housing the whole court. The present building dates from the time of Louis XV and much of the interior decoration was done under Louis XVI. Here Napoleon III married the 17-year-old Marie-Louise of Austria: it was in order that she should have plenty of space in which to ride, that the great avenue was cut from the palace into the Forest of Compiègne.

But the most brilliant period in the château's history came under Napoleon III when, for 18 years, he made it his autumn residence. Privileged house parties came to Compiègne by special train: alongside members of the aristocracy were Pasteur, Verdi, Dumas and the architect Viollet-le-Duc (see Pierrefonds).

Visit the museum-like appartments (10–11.15 a.m. and 1–4.15 p.m.) and try to people it with those ghosts. La Musée de la Voiture (in the old kitchen yard) is a splendid collection covering a wide field, from horse-drawn vehicles, bicycles and Bolée's first steam coach to the railway carriage designed for Napoleon III by Viollet-le-Duc and used when the Emperor travelled from Paris to Compiègne.

**Hôtel de
Flandre**
(H)M
*1 quai de la
Republique*

A good, old-established hotel on the north bank of the river near the station. The original was built in the time of Louis XIV: it was reconstructed in classical style after the Second World War. Bedrooms (160f and 230f, including breakfast) are rather drably furnished, but spacious. Go for those at the back. M. Doulmet speaks

44.83.24.06/40
All credit cards

exellent English and is a mine of information on the sights and restaurants in the town, and, indeed, for miles around. Parking in the street outside, which we considered risky: make sure you leave no valuables in your car.

From the A 1 take Exit 10 in the direction of Compiègne-Sud and Reims.

► **L'Hostellerie du Royal-Lieu**
(H)M (R)L
9 r. de Senlis
44.20.10.24
All credit cards

A lovely hotel on the Paris road just outside the town. Behind it is a large and peaceful garden and, beyond that, the cool glades of the forest trees – once, as the name implies, the King's hunting area.

Bedrooms are quite charming, each one individually decorated in the sort of excellent taste that drives me wild with envy. Three of them are en suite with 'boudoir' – so bring along that favoured child! Not expensive (if you take into account a British equivalent), but still in the slightly upper price range at 275–385f. Menus *are* pricey: 180–230f. However, as Mme Bonachi is unlikely to lean on you to eat on the premises, there are lots of alternatives in Compiègne itself, no distance away. The dining-room overlooks that leafy garden; in fine weather, there are tables and chairs set out on the terrace for apertifs.

'A very pleasant hotel, with comfortable and convenient bedrooms in a wing behind the main building, and so very quiet. Rooms are much better value than most. Food and service are very good and there is a good wine list, but the mark-up on Burgundy wines is excessive, even by French standards; Bordeaux wines are much more reasonable.' – David Hallifax.

Arrowed for quiet site in strategic position, comfort and good food.

Le Bistrot de Flandre
(R)M
2 r. d'Amiens
44.83.26.35
Closed 20/12–15/1
AE, EC, V

Although the address is different, Le Bistrot de Flandre is actually next door to l'Hôtel de Flandre. At one time, it was the hotel dining-room; now, the concession is owned by M. Chudant who runs a lively restaurant, popular with tourists and locals alike.

On the 65f menu we ate: assiette de jardinier (salad), épaule d'agneau farcie, a good variety of local cheese and tarte aux fruits. Helpings were generous and the service swift and friendly.

Hôtel de Harlay
(H)M
3 r. de Harlay
44.23.01.50/
44.23.19.90
All credit cards
Parking

A long-established hotel on the south bank of the river within easy walking distance of the town centre. Burned during the war, it was rebuilt in the same style as the palace, a style very typical of many buildings in Compiègne. Bedrooms are charming: white lacy bedspreads and attractive curtains, good solid wardrobes, and all with bath, T.V., telephone and mini-bar (260f). Another bar downstairs.

The entrance hall is furnished with cosy, plush sofas, potted plants, and one of those incongruous, autumnal forest scenes covers the further wall. We were much taken with M. and Mme Boco, who speak good English. Madame has crocheted white cotton bread-baskets which go well with her crisp table linen at breakfast (25f). Private parking at the back and, although the one-way traffic in the road outside is busy during the daytime, we were assured that the hotel was quiet at night.

Hôtel de France
(HR)M
and its
restaurant
**Rôtisserie du
Chat qui
Tourne**
44.40.02.74
AE, V

Another favourite hotel in Compiègne. This small, 16th-century house, near the Hôtel de Ville, miraculously survived the war intact. The paved entrance hall has considerable charm; statues and plants make for a pleasing atmosphere of days-gone-by. On one side is the restaurant and, on the other, the hotel itself. Twenty-one bedrooms (86–210f) have pretty chintz bedspreads; the more expensive, en suite with bath. There are beams, creaking stair-treads, tall windows, and all beautifully decorated.

Mme Robert has owned the hotel for 20 years; her son Antoine (who speaks excellent English) has worked with her for the last five years. He showed us, with great pride, their elegantly furnished dining-room which they have extended this year into an adjoining house. White-painted panelling on the walls, chintz curtains, cane-backed chairs set around white-clothed tables, and a deer's head looking serenely down. In the 17th century, this was 'The Inn of the Cat that turns the Spit', named after a travelling man who gave a performance that featured a cat roasting a chicken. 69f weekday menu includes: l'oeuf mollet Florentine, poulet sauté chasseur, pommes noisettes, fromage blanc or tarte maison.

Le Picotin
(R)M
*22 pl. de l'Hôtel
de Ville*
44.40.04.06
*Closed Tues.
p.m.*
EC, V

The reputation of this restaurant in the centre of Compiègne had somewhat deteriorated a few years ago. However, under the new ownership of M. and Mme Valle (starting on their second year), we hope for better things. Certainly, the two dining-rooms looked attractive enough; and the desserts on a trolley by the door (everything, including the ice-cream, is made on the premises) quite delicious.

Menus at 56f and 89f offer a wide choice; and the à la carte is most reasonably priced as well: terrine de poissons (30f); oeuf en gelée au porte (18f); ficelle Picarde (30f); magret de canard au poivre vert (74f). Three parking areas nearby, so parking should present little problem.

**Les Jardins
d'Eugénie**
(R)M
*23 pl. de l'Hôtel
de Ville*
44.40.00.88
*At present V.
DC & AE to
follow*

M. Cahors opened this restaurant and salon de thé on 15 December 1986. With the help of a famous French interior decorator, he transformed the original café and *brasserie* into an amusing eating-place, 1930s style. 'Stained-glass' (in fact, it's coloured plastic) panels decorate the walls, the feature repeated in the windows and on the ceiling light-fitting. There are lots of artificial flowers; brass rails run along the polished wood screen at the back; seating is on a red plush banquettes at tables covered with white cloths; big windows and glass doors front to the Grande Place.

No set menus here: you eat 'à la Parisienne' (à la carte). A three-course meal would come to around 120f, a half bottle of wine 31f or a glass of good Bordeaux 13f. Lots of enthusiasm among staff; a good, jokey patron.

Hôtel du Nord
(HR)M
1 pl. de la Gare
44.86.00.66

A hotel with a good name that fronts on to the river and backs on to the station. The 20 bedrooms (225–240f) are good sized, well decorated and most of them are spacious. Hard to know whether to choose those at the front or the back. Those overlooking the street are, without doubt, troubled by some traffic noise. At the back, you have to contend with the popular station buffet. Although we were staying in the Hôtel de Flandre, further down the same street, we could hear gusts of laughter, cheers and general merrymaking bursting from the little restaurant well into the night.

Hard to find fault with the dining-room. René Laudigeois's accolades are many, among them that he runs one of the 'meilleures affaires de Picardie'. Prices in the slightly upper price range: 145f for the set menu. A la carte includes la sauté de langoustines au beurre estragon (113f); les medaillons de homard sur pousses d'épinards (110f); le pigeonneau braisé au jus de truffes (120f).

Map 6B

COUCY-LE-CHÂTEAU-AUFFRIQUE (Aisne) 243 km SE of Calais

02380

14 km SE of Chauny by the D 1. On the edge of the Forest of St-Gobain (see p.133).

A small town dominated by impressive ruins of its walls and a a13th-century castle. Its history is an exciting one. The Sires of Coucy married into the royal families of France, England and Austria, rode to the Crusades, felt themselves at times to be grander than the King himself. 'King, I'm not, neither Prince, Duke nor Count . . . I am the Sire of Coucy' was the proud boast of Enguerrand III, the 'Builder', who raised this magnificent castle in 1225. It remained, almost intact, down the centuries until 17 March 1917. The week before, Crown-Prince Rupprecht of Bavaria had met Ludendorff, the German commander, and advised him to leave the castle alone because 'it formed a valuable part of the cultural history of France'. Nevertheless, Ludendorff, a professional soldier and unmoved by such aesthetic considerations, planted 28 tons of explosives in the keep. Except for one house, the entire town of Coucy was blown apart: a single act of vandalism that destroyed seven hundred years of history.

Since 1917, much of ancient Coucy has been reconstructed: the solid entrance gates to the town and some of the buildings in the castle. Visits to the castle are 10 a.m. – 12 p.m. and 2–5 p.m. (closed Tuesdays) in the season. There are some excellent paperbacks on Coucy for sale in the tabac on the Place, Coucy Ville-Haute.

Hôtel Belle-Vue
(H)S(R)M
*Porte de Laon,
Ville-Haute*
23.52.70.12
*Closed Tues.
AE,V*

The hotel stands on a corner, just within one of the city's gates. The restaurant is billed as 'gastronomique', and it lived up to its excellent reputation: one of the best meals we have eaten in France was enjoyed at this unpretentious Logis. Menus at 75f and 115f (weekdays), 95f and 160f (Sundays). For 75f we dined on feuilleté de champignons à l'estragon, Sobiquet 'Clovis' (hard to describe, the dish included beans and was quite delicious), followed by strawberries and cream.

Rooms were simple but perfectly comfortable and quiet (although we *did* hear a mouse or two running around behind the skirting): 70f for a double; and 100f for the two of us and our small daughter, with washbasin and bidet behind a screen. Loo and bathroom in the corridor. Parking in the courtyard at the back. M. and Mme Dubois were very friendly and helpful and lent us books to read on Coucy. We intend to return, having become confirmed Coucy-philes.

| Map 1A | **COULOGNE** (Pas-de-Calais) 3 km SE of Calais |

Between the Guines road, D 127, and the N 43. A useful route back into Calais.

La Terrasse
(R)S
21.36.65.72
1 quai
d'Amérique

A bar/restaurant overlooking the canal, locally appreciated but generally not discovered by tourists. With patronne cooking, menus cost 50f, 63f and 88f. I can't say the ambience is particularly friendly but the location is useful for a first or last meal, and the value good.

| Map 7A | **CRÉPY-EN-VALOIS** (Oise) 282 km SE of Calais; 24 km S of Compiègne |

60800
(M) *Wed.*

To the north of the Automne Valley, on the southern edge of the Forest of Compiègne, there is a Way of great antiquity, which existed long before Roman times. This track (traced today by the GR 12) passes by the hamlet of Champlieu and crosses a high plateau which has been known, since time immemorial, as the 'Camp de César', although it was not until the 19th century that any intelligent excavations were made on the raised mounds that stood there.

In the 1850s, Napoleon III, a keen archaeologist, came to Champlieu from his palace at Compiègne with Viollet-le-Duc (then engaged on the restoration of the great château at Pierrefonds). They uncovered a Roman amphitheatre, the foundations of thermal baths and the remains of a temple. These remains seem almost magical today, set as they are in great sweeps of farmland, away from any habitation. To get to Champlieu, take the D 32 out of Compiègne, then right for a short distance along the D 116, before forking right again; the camp lies just before the village.

From the village of Orrouy on the D 123, just south of Champlieu, the D 116, a lovely, country road, continues south to the small fortified town of Crépy-en-Valois. It passes by Glagnes, where, below the wooded slopes to the right of the village, there is a fine example of 'le style Rothschild': a massive 19th-century château embellished with *poivrières*. Drive up the hill on the other side of the road for the best view.

Crépy-en-Valois today is a bustling little town. In the Middle Ages, it was the ancient capital of Valois, the district which gave its name to a dynasty of kings. To appreciate the strength of its fortifications, you should drive through the town and down the r. des Fosses and pass beneath the outer ramparts of the castle: seen from there, those almost vertical slopes look well nigh impenetrable.

The oldest quarter, that which contains the ruined abbey of St-Arnould, the church of St-Dénis and the ruins of the château, has great charm. Elsewhere, are some 17th-century houses and the ruins of the church of St Thomas, dedicated to Thomas à Becket. In 1165 Thomas à Becket fled to France and stayed at Crépy with the Comte de Valois, who was engaged at the time in building this large church. After Thomas's murder, the count make a pilgrimage to Becket's tomb and returned to dedicate his church to the new martyr.

Le Relais du Valois
(H)S(R)M
Pl. du Paon
44.59.11.21

A splendid little Logis, once a coaching stop, that stands on the corner of the street. Young M. Jérome Gatellier is so full of smiles and enthusiasm that it is a joy to pull up at his door. He even carried my case in from the car and up to my room – and I can count *that* experience (during a two weeks' stay in France) on the fingers of one hand.

Before Monsieur arrived here in the autumn of 1986, the hotel was named 'Les Trois Pigeons', and was, he described rather emotionally, 'like the night', whereas now, done up with spanking new wallpaper and fresh paint, it makes a most attractive stop. The 15 rooms (90–177f) are spacious and comfortable. Only complaint is that I was kept awake at night by the considerable amount of traffic that rolled through the town.

Menus at 80f and 110f. Well-cooked, traditional recipes.

Hostellerie de Geresme
(HR)M
Av. de l'Europe
44.39.63.04
Closed Sun.
p..m.; Mon.
V

A big house standing above a public park with a small lake in the middle distance. Trees, greenery, tranquillity without; and a most agreeable atmosphere of 'other days' within. The Hostellerie was originally a 17th-century priory, then a private house (or rather, château) before becoming a hotel nine years ago. M. Tony Antuners has owned it for the last six months and has furnished and decorated it in impeccable taste. Wood panelling in the reception rooms and draped, velour curtains; a wide staircase curving round from the stone-paved entrance hall to the upper floor.

Bedrooms are large and well equipped with elegant old furniture and seemed remarkably good value: 160–180f. 100f menu in the elegant dining-room was varied and a good example of classical French cooking: terrine de poissons, rillette de saumon frais, mousse d'homard . . . Friendly patron, and plenty of room to park.

More reports please for this possible arrow.

Map 7C   **DIZY** (Marne) 308 km SE of Calais

51200
Épernay

3 km N of Épernay by the N 51.

Auberge du Relais
(R)S
26.55.25.11
Closed Mon.
p.m.; Tues.;
1/2–5/2, 15/8–
31/8

Turn into the little wine village of Dizy, about whose name so many jokes have been made, to find this little auberge, recommended locally as offering good reliable value on menus that start at 47f.

Map 3D/4A   **DOUAI** (Nord) 123 km SE of Calais; 2l6 km NE of Arras; 36 km SW of Lille

595000
(M) *Daily*

Autoroute A1 8 km.

Douai is a cheerful, vibrant town that recovered quickly from the havoc wrought by two world wars. Walks down the narrow streets that run off the Grande Place (there's a disorientating one-way traffic system) bring their own rewards.

Rising above the Hôtel de Ville is a fine 14th-century belfry, which Victor Hugo, passing through the town in 1837, immortalised with his prose 'Imagine a gothic tower, covered with a roof of grey slate; on each side a weather-vane; at each corner, a turret . . . and out of all this amusing, mad and lively ensemble there sounds a carillon.' It is a rousing, jangling carillon that rings out on the hour and the quarters. Climb the long, steep staircase up among the bells to the summit of the tower and look down upon the panorama of the city. Part of the church of Notre Dame (badly damaged during the last war) dates from the 12th century. There is the Collégiale St-Pierre with a 16th-century tower, and the tangled rooftops of many 18th-century houses. Visit the Ancienne Chartreuse, an interesting ensemble of buildings dating from the 16th–18th centuries which houses the Musée des Beaux Arts and its marvellous collection of 15th–17th-century Flemish masters. Or sit in the Grande Place outside one of the cafés and watch the world go by . . . There always seem to be plenty of people going about their business in Douai.

Hôtel de Paris
(H)M
63 pl. d'Armes
27.88.95.63
Closed Sun.
lunch
AE, EC, V

Betrand LeClerq, who runs the Hôtel de Paris, is the Vice-President of the Syndicat des Hôteliers de Douai and has all the tourist information on his city at his fingertips, and its promotion at his heart. A tall, old hotel that stands on the Grande Place in 'une étape au calme', as Monsieur's visiting-card puts it. An entrance hall with a bar at the further end; local businessmen holding serious discussions over their coffee when we visited it; 'staff' (which included Monsieur's young son) very polite and helpful.

A solid, stripped wood staircase leads to the upper floors: a little creaking, and the stair-carpet worn here and there. Bedrooms (160–220f) are fresh and clean, with modern decoration, spacious old wardrobes and tiled bathrooms. By virtue of its age and style, the Hôtel de Paris has been designated a 'listed building'. It seems a very nice example of an old, classic French hotel equipped with all the modern conveniences.

'*Rooms are clean and tidy, old fashioned, staff are very friendly, just like the St-Louis in St-Omer – not trying to be anything but just good value, and they seemed to like the Brits. Double room with shower cost us 190f, twin room with shower 240f, breakfast 20f.'* – Louise Scott.

Le Grand Cerf
(HR)M
46 r. St-Jacques
27.88.79.60
AE, EC, V

This small hotel and restaurant in one of the shopping streets that run off the Grande Place has recently been totally redecorated and refurnished. The result is that the wall-coverings are predominantly that practical shade of brown, so favoured by French hôteliers when bringing their establishments forward into the 1980s. Beds in the neat rooms (130f–225f) are covered with attractive, flowered covers; the bathrooms all that one could wish for.

Downstairs, the dining-room has pretty pink cloths on the tables. Unpretentious menus (70–150f) offer rognons maison; filets de sole; coquilles St-Jacques. A long-established hotel which seems a good bet for an overnight stop. Bedrooms in the front could be noisy.

La Terrasse
(H)M
36 terr. Saint-Pierre
27.88.70.04
EC,V

A well-furnished hotel in a quiet square with only public (metered) parking. Pretty, light, chintzy bedrooms with white bedcovers (195–335f). All recently decorated and sparklingly clean. We woke in the morning to the sound of a multitude of doves cooing from the flying buttresses of the big church outside.

The 80f menu offers three choices for the first and second courses. The best and most stylish hotel that we visited in Douai.

A l'Homme Sauvage
(HR)M–S
106 r. Valenciennes
27.88.85.03
Closed Sun. p.m.
V

A small hotel (15 rooms) on the right-hand side of the big street that runs from the pl. d'Armes towards the Porte de Valenciennes and so on to Arras. It was a close, humid day and stout Mme Barbier (a lady endowed with a considerable personality) was sitting, exhausted, behind the desk in the entrance/dining-room.

Bedrooms (96–110f), she told us, were all occupied (as a shot in the dark, I would classify them as *simple*; if you visit them, please let us know!) so we never got to see the upper floors. The two dining-rooms (all recently done-up) with fresh white tablecloths, and the unusual (for these northern climes) terrace-garden, looked charming. The speciality on all the menus (65f, 105f and the carte) is fish: turbot, salmon, St-Jacques aux petits légumes . . .

For a short stay, you can park on the wide pavement outside the restaurant. Overnight, leave your car in the pl. Général de Gaulle.

Au Turbotin
(R)M
1–3 r. de la Massue
27.87.04.16
Closed Mon.; Sun. p.m.; Aug.
AE, EC

Don't be in a hurry if you plan to eat in this charming small restaurant: no-one ever is. Citizens of Douai expect to linger over the delectable food. When we went there, chic, elderly ladies were lunching à deux: there was much thoughtful discussion over the items on the reasonably priced menus (90f and 140f). Specialities are, above all, fish. With poor captive lobsters twitching their whiskers in a glass tank at my elbow, I couldn't quite bring myself to taste the delicious-sounding 'terrine de homard frais et sa vinaigrette de tomates fraîches' on the 140f menu. On the 90f menu I ate an enormous cocktail of grey shrimps, crab and avocado; guinea fowl with wild mushrooms; and an assortment of local cheese ('Délices de la ferme affinés de Maître Brébant'), the latter accompanied by a glass of red Bordeaux supérieur.

Service was slow, but then the dishes were cooked to order. Mme Philippe Mène made a charming and attentive hostess, while her husband prepared those delicious concoctions in the kitchen. Crisp white tablecloths, the two dining-rooms furnished with taste: we thoroughly enjoyed our lengthy drawn-out lunch. Parking in the marché de poissons.

'We were in jeans and I expect if they hadn't needed the money they might have turned us away (elegant interior); as the evening

wore on and they realised that we weren't British yobs they began to
warm to us but the general atmosphere was over-fussy.

'However the 150f menu was very good: starters: red mullet in
aniseed with braised fennel, oysters, foie gras and cured ham (boar);
main course: roast lamb, pepper steak, John Dory in watercress
sauce, all nicely cooked. The interesting cheeseboard included one
in beer which almost killed you when you took the lid off.

'If you like shellfish, this is the place to have a platter. Two of our
party had one, for 140f each, consisting of two crabs, 16 crayfish, 12
oysters, sea urchins, mussels, clams, sea snails, scallops, shrimps.
They were still going when we finished our second course. They
agreed it was the best platter they had ever had, with such variety
and quantity.

'Good food, moderate wine at an inflated price, welcome lacking
unless you are dressed for the occasion, fussy service.' – Louise
Scott.

Map 4C	**DOURLERS** (Nord) 186 km SE of Calais

59440
Avesnes-sur-
Helpe

6.5 km N of Avesnes on the N 2 towards Maubeuge.

**Auberge du
Châtelet**
(R)M
27.61.06.70
Closed Wed.;
15/8–15/9
AE, DC, EC, V

As you come from Avesnes, this noteworthy restaurant stands on the
left-hand side of the N 2. In spite of the considerable traffic rolling by
outside, the atmosphere is calm and quiet. Outside is a pretty garden
and a small, paved space set with white chairs and tables. Within is
an open, airy dining-room with red-clothed tables, a ceramic floor
and walls decorated a little au style rustique, but not overpoweringly
so.

Pierre Carlier speaks excellent English. He proposes before the
meal une coupe maison: 1 cm mango juice, 1 cm lemon juice, ½ cm
crème de cassis, 3–4 cm whisky, iced (25f) and delicious!

Menus (95–300f) have as their specialities: andouillette de Troye
grillée, tarte aux Maroilles, and chevreuil (in season). Children's
menu (including lemonade) 75f.

Please note: this restaurant is such a popular Sunday eating-place
that reservation for that day is essential.

Map 6A	**ÉLINCOURT-STE-MARGUERITE** (Oise) 230 km SE of Calais; 24 km N of Compiègne

---

60157

Take the N 32 out of Compiègne, then follow the D 142, which runs
through lovely wooded countryside to the large village of Élincourt-
Ste-Marguerite.

➤ **Château de
Bellinglise**
(HR)L

FE4 first visited the Château de Bellinglise in 1984 and fell in love
with it. Since then, it has changed hands, and today, quite frankly, we
are mad about it.

44.76.04.76
All credit cards
Parking

This vast 16th-century château stands in a 230-hectare park with a lake below and a beech wood to one side. It originally belonged to the Comte de St-Olive, who left during the war when the Germans used it as a military hospital, and never returned. The Château remained derelict until 1960 when it first became a hotel of endearing, but somewhat eccentric, splendour. Between November 1986 and April 1987, it was extensively renovated by an American company and is today one of the best and most luxurious hotels that we visited in the North of France.

There are 47 lovely bedrooms in the château itself (600f and 650f), others across the courtyard in the annexe converted out of the old stables (400f and 450f). Most of the bedrooms are large and all are beautifully furnished and decorated by an American interior designer, using marvellous chintzes and fabrics.

During renovation, the bannisters of a 16th-century staircase were uncovered in a wall of one of the corridors, and these are now exposed – just one of the original touches that give the place so much character.

Patrick Durant, the highly artistic young chef, arrived in June 1987. He had worked in Paris and at the Regent Hotel in Kensington, and is now striving hard to impose his personality and strong convictions on his menus.

Weekday menu at 175f, and à la carte at weekends. A few examples: 'la terrine de lapéreau confit à l'ail doux 75f; la saumon frais mariné à l'aneth avec ses toasts et son sorbet tomate 85f; le rouelles de veau à l'infusion de sauge, petits légumes tournés 85f; la farandole du Château de Bellinglise (petit tarte Tatin, opéra chocolat, opéra fruits frais, tulipe de sorbets) 55f.

Parking on the gravel outside impressive wrought-iron gates, and hall-porters ready to carry your bags up to your room. A golf course is planned, and also a swimming pool. A lovely place to spend a quiet, country weekend.

Arrowed for supreme luxury.

Map 7C | **ÉPERNAY** (Marne) 308 km SE of Calais; 26 km S of Reims

---

51200
(M) *Wed..*
Thur., Sat

Strictly speaking the southern limit of this book should stop at Reims, but I cheated a bit to include Épernay, since it would be unthinkable to write about the Champagne territory and omit it. Victor Hugo wrote 'Épernay c'est la ville de Champagne. Rien de plus, rien de moins', and President de Gaulle called it 'La capitale de la Champagne', to the disgust of the Rémois.

There is no doubt that it is here that one feels in the very heart of the champagne industry, which is not surprising when one considers that 80% of the locals are engaged in various aspects of the trade, and that as many bottles are produced in this small provincial town as in the mighty Reims.

Its most striking feature is the av. de Champagne, an impressive, if bizarre, avenue leading from the pl. de la République, lined with a series of idiosyncratic buildings that have nothing in common except their dedication to champagne.

Moët et Chandon, the best-known and biggest of the principal champagne houses, stakes its claim early. Theirs is the vast yellow pile on the right, courtyard surrounded by iron railings, statue of Dom Pérignon presiding. Almost opposite is the fantasy Petit Trianon – two identical sugar-icing pavilions, built in the last century and owned by the Moët et Chandon family, and used for entertaining their fortunate guests in considerable style. The garden, with sunken pool, forms a perfect setting for a delectable little orangery, and the whole group of exquisite miniatures has the charming effect of a rich child's set of toy houses.

Fantasy reaches its peak a little further up on the same side, with the monumental mock-Renaissance château, now a library and museum, built in 1863 by the son of the founder of Perrier-Jouët. The Mercier family have their château too – the château de Pékin, all spikes and turrets. Dotted in between these eccentricities are some delightful town houses, notably that owned by the Perrier-Jouët family, and a few Victorian villas, so the avenue is nothing if not varied.

Beneath it all runs the mile after mile of the chalk caves in which the town's life-blood is so lovingly stored. A visit to one of the champagne cellars to witness the mind-boggling extent of the millions of bottles, millions of pounds, lodging there, is a must.

Most of the *négociants* are happy to arrange a tour of their subterranean territory. Moët et Chandon, whose galeries extend for 28 km, offer a guided tour in several languages, and a free *dégustation*. Apply at their reception desk to find out when the next English tour is likely to leave.

I cannot claim that Épernay is a beautiful town, even with the benefit of the two rivers that join up there, the Marne and the Cubry. In spite of its antiquity – a community has existed there since AD 460 – and associations with many leading French personalities, its strategic position at the end of a valley leading directly to Paris has doomed it to a history of involvement in war and regular destruction. Today there are few historical monuments left to delight the eye. The pedestrianised area around the r. St-Thibault is the best for shopping. There are one or two good bars there, like le St-Thibault, where you can sit outside on the pavement and eat a snack lunch. On Thursday there's a colourful flower market in the nearby pl. Hugues.

➤ **Les Berceaux**
(HR)M
13 r. des Berceaux
26.55.28.84
AE, DC, EC

I would place this top of the list in the medium price bracket for the English traveller, for several reasons: it is situated in an old street in the centre of the town but away from the main traffic; the chef-patron, Luc Maillard, worked in London, married an English girl, and now insists that all his friendly staff speak English; the rooms are comfortable and good value, in this highly-priced area, at 210-280f; there is not only a very smart restaurant, but a wine bar too – a rarity in France.

In the wine bar you can have a glass from a wide range of wines, especially those from the region, for 9f, and perhaps a light lunch from a range of *amuse-gueules* for 34f, or a salad, or just one dish for around 40f. On Thursday, Friday and Saturday evenings there is live piano music to brighten up this not-very-exciting little town.

In the restaurant the menus are at 120f, 160f and 260f. The middle one offers, for example, a terrine of rascasse, escalope of monkfish, venison stuffed with pistachios, salad, cheese and dessert.

Altogether a comprehensive and highly organised service for the traveller in a tourist town, earning an arrow.

Hôtel Champagne
(H)M
30 r. Eugène Mercier
26.55.30.22
AE, CE, DC
Parking

I suggest this purely as a functional little hotel in the town centre. It is certainly no beauty, but everything works. 235f a double with bath.

Hôtel de la Cloche
(H)S
3–5 pl. Mendès-France
26.55.24.05

Across the leafy square opposite the station. The rooms have recently been redecorated and are good value at 135f–170f. Go for one at the side if you can (the front ones are noisy, those at the back have an unattractive outlook). It has the advantage of a pleasant restaurant (see below) and feels very French.

s Berceaux, Epernay

Restaurant l'Hermite (R)S
3 pl. Mendès-France
26.55.24.05.
Closed Mon.

Attached to the hotel, a pretty little bistro with art-deco decor. The Gault-Millau regional magazine recently featured it in its round-up of the best bistros in the area, and I would agree its 52f menu is very good news, with some interesting ideas alongside the traditional dishes.

L'Oeuil de Boeuf (R)S
40 r. de Sézanne
Closed Sun. p.m.

An attractive little restaurant, with rustic lattice on green walls, just far enough away from the main tourist attractions to be geared to the locals. In fact it is alongside the market halls, which, like the station, is so often the place to look for good eating in France.

At lunchtime it is full of local office workers, so get there early.

The menus, as the name suggests, are mostly meat-based. The 51.50f version kicks off with a good salad, or 'l'idée du jour', then a choice of two different steak dishes, or magret of duck with green peppercorns, or 'suggestion du jour', which is sometimes fish. Then a good cheese, like an unpasteurised Brie aux noix. The desserts are extra. You can also take just one dish, like the salade paysanne, which included expensive Roquefort, walnuts, potatoes, etc. for 23f. Nearly an arrow.

La Grillade (R)M
16 r. de Reims
26.53.14.74

Recommended by more than one local for prime meat cooked over a charcoal fire. It has other advantages too – a pleasant garden and shady terrace, which in the heart of a busy town can be a blessing, and an excellent wine list. Allow 70f.

Au Bon Accueil (R)M
13 av. J. J. Rousseau
Closed Sat. p.m.; Sun.

It is rare for a prosperous French businessman even to be aware of the exitsence of a Relais Routier café, let alone to have eaten there, but I had an unusually perceptive local gastro-guide in Épernay, who told me that he sometimes took his family to Mère Préjent's establishment for a bargain blow-out. I would certainly never have tracked it down or given it a second glance without his prompting, but I'm now indebted to him because for those on strict budgets it's the best value in town.

You find it, on approaching Épernay from Reims, by turning left along the river bank before crossing the river, then left again into the r. Hémart. It's the seedy looking cafe on the corner. Three courses of good solid nosh for 40f and wine for next to nothing.

Buffet de la Gare (R)S
26.55.26.36
Closed Tues.

If you do not wish to get embroiled in central Épernay, a stop-off here, where several main routes converge, could make sense. You could do a lot worse than enjoy this further example of the breed unknown in England – the upmarket station restaurant. Menus start at 40f.

La Terrasse (R)S
7 quai Marne
26.55.26.05
Closed Sun. p.m.; Mon.

Another suggestion for those *en route* who do not wish to penetrate into the town centre. La Terrasse is a cheerful clean little restaurant overlooking the Marne (but do not expect romantic riverside views – this is all heavily industrialised). Menus from 47f are way above average for that price and earn a red 'R' in Michelin for value.

It may seem odd that in a town as prosperous as Épernay there are no luxury hotels or restaurants. The explanation, I suppose, is that the wealthy businessmen prefer to entertain in their own homes or drive a little outside the town, where there is no shortage of expensive eateries. See Champillon, Vinay, Montchenot, and Berry-au-Bac, all with Michelin stars.

For those staying in the town, a further southwards diversion from Épernay, beyond my stretched limit, could include the recommended and more modestly priced Le Cheval Blanc and Hôtel de la Place at Montmort on the N 51; the Relais de Cherville at Cherville on the Chalons road; and, particularly, Le Mesnil at Le Mesnil-sur-Oger on the D 9.

I was the highly privileged guest of Moët et Chandon in their exquisite Château de Saran, where the food is as sumptuous and tasteful as the surroundings. From the château the vistas in all directions are dedicated to the vine. On my previous visit, in the autumn, the vendange had just started and the slopes, bathed in late golden sunshine, were animated with hundreds of pickers recruited to deal with the harvest. This last time, in an unusually chilly June, there was no direct evidence of human intervention; as far as the eye could see the armies of vines marched in straight lines over the valleys, as they have done since Roman times. But always in this region the landscape is washed with a unique luminosity, which perhaps has something to do with a reflection from the chalky soil – a subtle blurring of outlines, an impressionist view rather than a sharp pen-and-ink sketch, which emphasises its mellow richness.

The most spectacular views, recognisable from many a poster, are those from the Montagne de Reims towards Épernay. Stop the car on the hill (hardly a mountain) that hairpins down from Champillon, to take it all in. Some idea of the vastness of the enterprise, of the spirit of such an area given over to one idea, of the dedication of its landlords and workers to the same end, can be glimpsed here. To look at such a concentration of man's expertise, finance, industry, technology and constant care and to know that any one of the inherent dangers that threaten it – the frosts, the storms, the infections, the parasites – could nullify a year's work is cause for sobering thought.

Take a drive around some of the nearby wine villages surrounding Épernay to see where and how the growers live. The villages are not generally attractive, being built in grey stone, with windows facing away from the road, and few visible gardens. Many a modest house will offer a *dégustation* of the owner's wine. It may be fun to try some of these and indeed to back one's taste and judgment by buying, but don't forget that the small producer, however perfectly sited may be his little plot of vines, cannot have access to and choice between many other grapes, from which the skilful cuvée, or blending, of the best champagne derives.

The best drive of all is to the intensely picturesque village of **Hautvillers**, perched high, facing south down the Montagne de Reims to the valley of the Marne far below. It's undoubtedly the prettiest wine village, with well-tended old stone houses displaying their names in hand-forged iron signs ranged along the narrow streets. But the main reason for visiting this shrine is to pay respects to the man who was responsible for the local prosperity – the much revered Dom Pérignon.

In order to take a tour round the abbey where he worshipped and the new museum dedicated to his memory, you must apply to Moët et Chandon in Épernay, and if you are lucky you will be guided round this fascinating reconstruction of the life of the Dom by one of his greatest admirers and the man who caused the museum to take its present form (he hasn't stopped yet – ideas and projects bubble over) – Commander John Collard.

His aim, he says, is to allow the visitor to get inside the skin of his hero, and to understand what it must have been like for a monk in the 17th century to have combined his religious duties with those of guardian of the vineyards and cellarer – a position second in importance only to the Abbot. Stand on the terrace, now being planted with vines of the same varieties that Dom Pérignon would have used, and look down over the valley to the river far below in order to understand that to visit some of the vineyards under his control on foot, the Dom would have had to allocate days, not the few hours it would take today.

For a fascinating account of his life and times, and the effect his discoveries had on the whole region and the Champenois, I strongly recommend Patrick Forbes's highly readable book, *Champagne, the Wine, the Country and the People.* I started to read it as background research and found I couldn't put it down. It would certainly add a

new dimension to any travelling in this area.

The Dom's greatest discovery – how to put and keep the fizz in the bottle – is far from being the only aspect of his life that is illuminated in the museum at Hautvillers. There are models of the monks and copies of their belongings, furniture and furnishings, and clever lighting to emphasise salient points, to tie up with the recorded commentary. It's all for free, but I would recommend this excursion even at a considerable cost.

What is more, refreshment of the body as well as the spirit is not far away:

Le Bar Champêtre
(R)S
Closed Mon.; Tues.; 15/8–30/8

A charming little café/restaurant in the village, run by the equally charming M. Thiery Landegrin. You can eat inside his simple little dining-room or in the shady garden, where he cooks over a charcoal fire in summer.

There are menus at 49f, 70f and 90f, but this is also a good place to take just one dish, like a substantial omelette champêtre, for 38f, or a salade Thiery, both highly recommended by Commander Collard.

Map 5C

EPPE SAUVAGE (Nord) 211 km SE of Calais

59132

26 km E of Avesnes on the D 133 and D 453. 11 km E of Liessies on the D 963.

The village is a quiet and peaceful place, hardly troubled by any traffic noise, and surrounded by fields and trees – an ambience that has earned it the sobriquet 'The little Switzerland of the North'.

La Goyère
(R)M
R. de Verdun
27.61.80.11
Closed Tues. p.m.; Wed.; 1/2–15/2
EC, V

One year ago Pierre Gobron turned this little 18th-century village house into a restaurant, and already he haas earned himself a considerable reputation.

This tubby and very proud man has much going for him: a charming wife (Pierrette), room for 65 people in his dining-room, furnished *au style rustique*, and solid bookings eight days ahead for every Sunday lunch and dinner. Specialities are fish and shellfish, gleaned from the boats at Boulogne. Menus are astonishingly reasonable: 55f (except Sunday), 68f, 98f and 148f. All the food is fresh daily. Well worth booking ahead for that leisurely, good-value Sunday lunch.

Map 7A

ERMENONVILLE (Oise) 263 km SE of Calais

60440

13 km SE of Senlis by N 330.

Hôtel le Prieuré
(H)M–L
Chevet de l'Église
44.54.00.44
EC, V
Parking

Everyone's dream house, I should imagine. It stands on the outskirts of the village, well sheltered from the world without by a high stone wall, an impeccably tended formal garden and the ancient façade of a 12th-century church. Le Prieuré once housed the Sisters who ministered to the church. For the past 25 years it has been the family home of M. and Mme Treillou. Sadly, ill-health forced Monsieur to take an early retirement from his job as engineer and, as a devoted

Anglophile, he conceived the idea of running his home on a bed-and-breakfast basis, *au style anglais*. 'It was hard at first on the children', Monsieur told us, 'to see strangers occupying their rooms'. But the result is a charming blend of privacy, a hint of amateurism and the sort of treatment that one might expect as a private guest. As Monsieur deals in antiques as a sideline, there are one or two nice pieces of furniture in every room. Ten rooms from 350–400f. Breakfast (30f) includes a variety of cereals, freshly squeezed orange juice – as well as the usual coffee and croissants.

Private parking on the gravel drive in the garden. One major advantage: Charles de Gaulle airport is within twenty minutes' drive across green fields. It never ceases to astound me the way the countryside presses right up to the outskirts of Paris!

Auberge de la Croix d'Or
(HR)S–M
44.54.00.04
Closed Mon.;
15/12–1?3
EC, V
Parking

An ancient Relais de Poste that stands on the village street, once a stretch of the carriage route between Soissons and Paris. Although M. Vezier has traced the history of the inn back to the mid 18th century, he knows it goes back even further. In his *Mémoires*, Alexandre Dumas writes of it as 'l'Auberge de la Croix'.

At the time of writing, there is still much heavy traffic beating down the street between those old houses (soon, we were told, a by-pass is to be opened). There is space for a few cars on the pavement across the way and more in a courtyard at the back.

Eleven simple, pretty bedrooms upstairs. Go for the rooms that overlook the garden at the back. 80f menu was adequate, but the content, we felt, had been sacrificed to suit popular tourist taste. In other words, we have eaten far better meals for the same price elsewhere. A pity; the restaurant is full of charm and, when the new dining-room and various building projects in the garden are completed, the ambience should be even more attractive.

Map 1A   **ESCALLES** (Pas-de-Calais) 13.5 km W of Calais

02179
Wissant

The coast road from Calais to Boulogne is surprisingly underpraised. I would infinitely prefer to take ten minutes longer and follow this route rather than the N 1, arriving in Boulogne along the promenade and not via the congested suburbs. Those who think of the Pas-de-Calais as being uniformly flat and boring must surely have a pleasant surprise to discover the spectacular coastline which dips into great valleys, and sweeps up again to imposing cliffs, with views of perfidious Albion across the narrowest stretch of Channel. At Cap Blanc Nez, the road zig-zags dramatically down into the hamlet of Escalles, inland from a stony beach in a cleft of the white rocks.

➤ **L'Escale**
(HR)S
21.85.25.09
Closed 22/9–26/
2, except fêtes
and Sun. lunch.
Parking

An old and trusted faithful that has won nothing but praise from highly satisfied readers. For a family outing it's hard to beat the unassuming little Escale.

In their pretty light pine dining-room the gentle Bourdons continue to dish up their bargain plâteaux de fruits de mer – 65f with crab, 88f with lobster, both with oysters, or their 49f menus – coquille de poissons gratinée, truite meunière, predictable afters. Other smarter menus creep up to 91f and the wine is a bargain. Readers' comments say it all:

'Clean and comfortable rooms with wash-basin and bidet cost a mere 77f. We had a good and quiet night's sleep. The food on the 72f menu was good and the service quick and friendly. We later spent some time in the pleasant bar. The patron is to be congratulated on the ambience of this establishment and we will certainly hope to return.' – Joan and Alan Wadsworth.

We stayed in the annexe, which we found most comfortable and clean and actually had the luxury of constant hot water and plugs that worked – difficult to find in French hotels. The proprietor allowed us to feed my 15-month-old son early (and made an omelette for him each night), which enabled us to enjoy our meal in peace later on. – Mrs Pat Madox.

Rooms are 85f for a simple double, 140f with bathroom, or 185 for three people.

Arrowed unhestitatingly for reliable and sustained high standards in the 'S' category.

Restaurant du Cap
(R)S
21.36.01.10

Across the road from l'Escale, a large family restaurant, popular for its fish, and well patronised by French Sunday lunchers. Menus from 55f.

Map 6B   **ETOUVELLES** (Aisne) 252 km SE of Calais

Au Bon Accueil. Etouvelles

0200 Laon	3 km S of Laon, signposted off the N 2.

Au Bon Accueil
(R)M
23.20.62.09
Closed Wed.;
Feb. for 15
days;
Christmas.

The hostellerie was an 1848 Relais de Poste and the decoration of the dining-room is well in keeping with its history. Dark furniture; a deer's head on the wall; various rustic knick-knacks hanging from the beams; an old dresser cluttered with antique plates and pots.

The three-course lunch menu at 75f includes wine; others (98f, 110f, 140f) propose good, classical, French recipes with variations *à la maison*: terrine cordon bleu (rabbit); l'agneau des prés, haricots panachés (Laon is famous for its beans); foie gras garnished with chicken livers. Friendly (but slightly fussy) Mme Varlet seemed to be torn in about three different directions at once as guests arrived, all with beaming smiles, to be shown to their tables. Clearly, it seemed a popular eating-place.

Map 5C   **ÉTREAUPONT** (Aisne) 260 km SE of Calais

02140   8 km N of Vervins; 22km S of Avesnes on the N 2.

**L'Auberge du
Val de l'Oise**
(R)M
23.97.91.10
Closed Sun.
p.m.; Mon.
lunch
All credit cards

An intriguing little restaurant in this Thiérache village on the N 2. The house itself is charming: an 1880 Relais de Poste with two dining-rooms and enticing menus (52–145f). 145f menu includes a cocktail, half a bottle of Bordeaux and coffee.

Dominique Trokay is a member of les Toques Blanches and brings immense enthusiasm and joie de vivre to everything he does. A few yards down the road, at No 8, he was in the process of putting the finishing touches to 'his hotel': it should be open by the end of 1987. This lovely 18th-century château (quite obviously the pride of M. Trokay's life) was once owned by an author–judge. Starting from scratch, he has renovated the interior in impeccable taste: the lovely lines of the building and the low, curving staircase are a joy. Seventeen bedrooms (180–260f) are furnished in reproduction Louis Philippe style. We approved of the fresh colours of the wallpaper and the carpets. Should make a most agreeable stop by any account.

Not content with all this admirable entrepreneurship, Monsieur and a group of his friends have produced a pamphlet, centred on Étreaupont, of places to visit in the region. He proposed to introduce circuits that take in those lovely fortified villages; cider and Maroilles cheese-tasting. I wish him all the luck.

Map 7B   **FÈRE-EN-TARDENOIS** (Aisne) 316 km SE of Calais; 31 km NE of Château-Thierry

---

02130   Coming from Paris on the A 4 take the Château-Thierry exit, then direction Soissons. Coming from Reims, take the Dormans exit, then on the N 380 take the D 801 to the right, direction Villers-Agron.

An old town on the banks of the river Ourcq, which has been an important road-junction since time immemorial. During the First War it was served by the only railway which supplied the Germans during their occupation of the Château-Thierry enclave, and suffered greatly as a result. The 16th-century church has been much restored. Note the beautiful north portal in tiers-pont. There is a lovely covered market that dates from the 16th century; the framework is supported by large cylindrical pillars and covered with a tiled roof rebuilt after 1918.

Auberge du Connetable
(H)S(R)M
Rte du Château
23.82.24.25
Closed Mon.;
10/1–28/2
AE, DC

The name of the auberge refers to Anne de Montmorency, 'The Great Connetable', who was the faithful servant (male, inspite of the name) of six kings from Louis XII to Charles IX. His prowess on the battlefield and his immense wealth and power are legendary: by the marriages of his eleven children, he became allied to Henri II and to most of the noble families. When he was killed in battle, five sword thrusts, two strokes of a club and an aquebus thrust were needed to kill him, and when dying he broke his assailant's jaw with the pommel of his sword.

The Auberge is in the middle of the forest of Nesles. The ancient, ivy-covered front of the house was once an inn; the spacious dining-room at the rear was added at a later date. From the windows, there is a fine view over the pretty garden to the forest trees. Menus (72f, 115f, 150f (weekends) and à la carte): saumon confit à l'anette, terrine de foie gras aux langoustines . . . On the 72f menu were terrine de foies de volailles au poivre vert, les côtes d'agneau au romain, Brie de Meaux.

The four bedrooms (130–160f) were hardly up to the standard of the restaurant, being small and scruffy and in dire need of redecoration. Still, Mme Pilati is a very friendly person – I should imagine that she does a roaring trade, Fère-en-Tardenois is very much a tourist honey-pot and within 110 km of Paris.

Hostellerie du Château
(HR)L
28.82.21.13/
23.82.22.13
Closed 2/1–1/3
AE, DC, EC, V
Parking

A marvellous upmarket hotel in part of the 13th-century castle built by Robert de Dreux, a grandson of Louis VI, and at one time owned by Anne de Montmorency. It rests in 14 acres of parkland, surrounded by further castle ruins: a truly luxurious place in which to stay.

La famille Bot have run the hotel for 30 years, apparently with great success for there were many guests sitting in the elegant armchairs in the ante-rooms, and plenty of cars drawn up on the gravel outside. Bedrooms are lovely (500–660f) and there are apartments as well (830–1200f), all beautifully furnished. Menus in the large dining-rooms are 250f, 380f and à la carte. The decoration throughout is in excellent taste: good furniture, marble fireplaces and soft colours under tall ceilings.

Map 7B   **FISMES** (Marne) 226 km SE of Calais

51170
Ⓜ *Sat.*

5 km S of the N 31, half-way between Soissons and Reims and 12 km N of the A 4. A small town, with a long history, that today exists in an oasis of calm yet remains almost within shouting distance of the frenetic traffic on the route nationale.

In the Middle Ages Fismes was on the frontier of the county of Champagne. In the 13th century, the third Comte de Champagne, Thibaud, granted it a charter, thus starting the little town on its road to prosperity – one that remained fairly constant until the 20th century. Medieval princes stayed in Fismes on their way to Reims to be crowned Kings of France; the last king to visit the town was Charles X in 1825.

Throughout the centuries the old town survived the Wars of Religion, riots, and the Napoleonic Wars, but, alas, during the two world wars it was effectively destroyed. However, the 14th-century town hall and much of the old quarter have been rebuilt, and the town makes a worthwhile stop, with one excellent little restaurant and a favourite good-value 'motel'.

Le Comte Thibaud
(R)M
5 r. d'Ardre
26.78.05.30
Closed. Tues.;
Sun. p.m.
AE, EC, V

M. Blanquet changed the name of his restaurant from Le Pinot to Le Comte Thibaud in 1986 and gave his excellent little establishment a face-lift as well. It is in the centre of the town near the old Hôtel de Ville. There are pink patterned cloths on tables set well apart, glass doors that open on to a courtyard at the rear where there is plenty of space to park.

99.50f menu offers some enticing dishes but, during a lunchtime visit, we felt we couldn't cope with a full meal and ordered à la carte chosing from the entrées. 'Terrine de légumes et coulis au pistou' was imaginatively and decoratively presented with avocados and green salad (32f). 'Cassolette d'escargots' was served in a copper dish with handles (52f). Both these portions were large enough to be a meal in themselves.

Fimotel
(H)S
32 faubourg
d'Épernay
26.78.07.55
Closed Feb;
sometimes on
Sun. p.m. 'to
tidy up'.

The 'reception' of the 'motel' is an inauspicious little house in a street that runs on towards Épernay. The rather shabby exterior, in dire need of a spot of paint here and there, shouldn't put you off venturing inside. Mme Barras' sitting-room and kitchen are just within the door.

Behind the house, set around a garden planted with vegetables and fruit trees, are 13 rooms with shower, loo and wash-basin (119f). M. and Mme Barras had run a bar in a neighbouring village for much of their life, then retired here to spend their days in peace. *Then*, they saw on the television the President of the Republic, who 'called upon the nation to provide more cheap accommodation for travellers along the routes nationales'. Whereupon they hit on the idea of turning their orchard into a motel – and I'm so glad that they did!

Rooms are essentially simple but well-built, using good material, and washing facilities are up to date: there was even another sink in the sitting side of the room. Friendly old Monsieur carried out our breakfast in the morning – good coffee and fresh rolls (14.50f).

Map 2C   **FLÊTRE** (Pas-de-Calais) 71 km SE of Calais

59190

Exit Meteren from the A 25.

A large village on the D 33 9 km NW of Hazebrouck. In the Middle Ages it was the seat of the Van Houtte family, seigneurs of Flêtre. The scant remains of their old red-brick castle, said to be one of the most interesting examples of mediaeval architecture in the north of France, stands among trees on long grass beyond the church. The tower received a bomb in 1918; the present owners live in a large 1872 country house alongside the ruins. If the entrance gates are open, drive in (the owners are said to be very welcoming), but there is not a lot to see.

La Vieille Poutre
(R)M–L
Caëstre
28.40.19.52
Closed Sun.
p.m.; Mon.;
Aug.
V

Although the address is given as Caëstre, this restaurant stands on the D 933, 200 metres down the road from the village of Flêtre and its château. La Vieille Poutre was converted from a farm and stables; the name means 'the old beam', and rafters run the length of the dining-room, which is well furnished, with stained wooden chairs and tables. The mantelpiece is engraved with the initials of the people who once lived here and the date when the house was built (1836).

M. Drif has long had his own appreciative clientele who come here for the traditional Flemish cuisine. The quality is good, the helpings are substantial, but the prices high. Menus are 180f and 225f, with some reasonably priced dishes à la carte, such as une terrine de lapin ou de canard sur la confiture d'oignons grenadine (45f) or les filets de sole George Sand (75f). However, not the place for a quick snack. In fact, this would be quite definitely discouraged (in a most friendly fashion). Monsieur looked quite shocked when I asked for a small portion of ris de veau (a speciality of the house) on the list of entrées, as a main couse. Abashed, I settled for the proper *plat*: ris de veau en feuille de choix, sauce poule (90f). Service a little slow, but the cool tranquil dining-room and M. Drif's friendly personality make it into a relaxing, leisured hour.

Map 3D **FLINES-LES-RACHES** (Nord) 133 km SE of Calais

59148
(M) Thur.

On the D 938. From the A 23 take Exit 2 for Douai (11 km SW of Flines-les-Raches); the village is 6½ km from the autoroute.

L'Auberge du Bois Vert
(R)S
Bvd des Alliés
27.91.91.39
Closed Mon.;
Tues., Wed. and
Sun. p.m.;
Aug.; 2 weeks
in Sept.

A little country restaurant, once an old farm, set on the outskirts of a village that is renowned for an ancient church and a 10th-century church tower. Somewhere behind the birch wood that flanks L'Auberge are sand quarries – an industry much in evidence in this flat, well-drained land.

Mme Marie-José Caudrelier is the enthusiastic patronne. Her specialities are fish, sole in particular, and from September on into the winter months she has mussels, clams and other shellfish on her menus (50f, 70f and 120f). Very keen to show off her 'bar', thought to be in the style of an English pub. Well, there *were* several beer taps in evidence and a large, polished wooden bar counter. Also very pleased with the densely flowered wallpaper ('le style Anglais, n'est-ce-pas?') and the gleaming copper pans over the old fireplace in the dining-room. Cream coloured cloths over dark green cloths on the tables: a particularly friendly atmosphere – and all that enthusiasm!

Map 6D   FLIZE (Ardennes) 270 km SE of Calais

08160 — 8 km S of Charleville-Mézières, on the D 864.

La Cendrière
(HR)S
1 r. de Mézières
24.54.05.83
Closed Fri.;
otherwise
'usually open'
EC, V

A simple Logis in a 19th-century village house by a roundabout. Very friendly young Mme Rousseaux showed us upstairs. Nine simple bedrooms (120–170f), stair carpet a little worn, but everywhere nice and clean.

Downstairs is a small dining-room, the tables covered with brown cloths. Possibly, we felt, this could warrant a higher grade than the sleeping side of the house. The menus (45f, 75f and 120f) proposed some delicious dishes: gratin de langoustines au whisky, medaillons de veau St-George (mushrooms, calvados and crème fraîche).

Map 3D/4A   FRESNES-LES-MONTAUBAN (Pas -de-Calais) 135 km SE of Calais

62 — 12 km SW of Douai. ½ km from the A 1.

La Frenaise
(R)S
21.50.17.19
Closed Sun.
p.m.; Mon.
AE, V

An attractive, small restaurant in an old converted farm on a corner of the N 50 and a narrow village road. Friendly M. Froger specialises in steak au poivre, andouillettes, brochette de porc a la crème and a wide choice of desserts. Cheerful check tablecloths, spotlessly clean dining-room with a charcoal grill in an open fireplace below and enormous mantelpiece at the further end.

Menus at 46f, 64f and 100f. 46f menu includes museau vinaigrette; andouillette grillée, sauce moutarde; and steak au choux, pommes frites. A favourite, good-value little eating-place.

Map 7C   GERMAINE (Marne) 260 km SE of Calais; 15 km NE of Épernay; 22 km SE of Reims

When I was last in Épernay there were massive reconstructions on the N 51 heading north to Reims. (The French go about their road repairs in a different way from the British system of a stretch at a time – they dig up a whole road at once, so ignore their diversion signs at your peril.) The way therefore led through the Forest of Reims along the D 9 and, for anyone not in a hurry, may I recommend it as being a far more agreeable (and not much longer) route than the juggernauted route nationale. A further green and delightful diversion recommended for shady picnics is to turn off on to the D 271 towards the village of Germaine. Beyond that the D 71E leads to the hamlet of Les Haies.

Relais de la
Diligence
(HR)S
Les Haies
26.52.23.69
Closed Wed.
o.o.s.; 23/12–1/3

I was not best pleased to realise it was a Wednesday when I investigated this little Logis, recommended by a local friend; I could not therefore inspect the rooms, but certainly the situation, between Reims and Épernay, just a few kilometres from the main road, in deep peaceful countryside, is ideal.

It's a modern building and looked spic from the outside, so I should be surprised if the rooms were not at least adequate. At 90–150f, they're worth a risk. The menus start at 55f, and here again, in such an agreeable setting, this might be a good lunch stop.

Les Ferme des Boeufs
Les Haies
Open weekends only from 15/4–25/10

Carry on past the Diligence until the lane becomes a track and to the left, clearly marked, is the 'ferme auberge' It's a working farm, where Isabelle and Bernard Verdonk cook hearty rustic meals in the summer. During the week they do not always open and at weekends they are sometimes full. It's all very rustic, very peaceful, very pleasant, and seemingly a thousand miles from the champagne sophistication.

For 70f you get four substantial courses, with a special 36f children's menu, and la cuvée du patron is 25f.

Map 4D **GIVET** (Ardennes) 240 km SE of Calais

08600
(M) *Thur.*
Fri.

This lovely old town lies on the banks of the river Meuse, the river that was once the demarcation line between the Kingdom of France and the Spanish Empire. Today the road to Givet from the west passes in and out of the frontier with Belgium.

Givet is dominated by the ruins of the castle of Charlemont, which was built in 1555, as a result of the rivalry between Charles V and François I, and finished by Vauban. It remains as a unique example of 16th–17th-century military architecture under the Spanish domination. Napoleon slept here (in the hostelry that is now **La Maison Baudoin**) before the battle of Waterloo, while his men and horses were ferried across to the 11th-century Tour Grégoire on the *rive droite*.

Guided visits to the castle are every day during July and August. From the site of the Tour Grégoire (now joined by a bridge to the left bank) there is a lonely view of the Meuse where it flows on into Belgium.

Maison Baudoin
(R)M
2 pl. du 148 R.I.
24.42.00.70
DC, EC, V

M. Trotin, chef de cuisine, proudly showed us around this ancient auberge and Relais de Poste where, he told us, Napoleon had slept on the eve of Waterloo. It is near the bridge that replaced the old ferry-crossing; you walk down steps into the cool entrance hall and bar. Beyond that is a small courtyard where Monsieur has discovered traces of the original 16th-century building, and which is set with tables and chairs for apéritifs.

The dining-room is attractive, the menus (65–180f) propose fruits de mer, and game (in season) from the great forests that cloak the hills of the Ardennes. On the 65f menu: salade Niçoise, brochette Ardennaise (smoked meat), cheese and dessert.

A favourite restaurant with lots of atmosphere.

Map 4C **GOEGNIES-CHAUSÉE** (Nord) 165 km SE of Calais

59600
(M) *Tues.*

Take one of the straight Roman roads (D 932) from Bavay in the direction of Mons and Belgium. The village is signposted to the left, just before the frontier.

A la Porte de France
(R)M
Grande Place
27.67.90.31
Closed Mon.
V

When we visited this jolly restaurant, it was market day on the Grande Place and, as the main road runs directly down the frontier, the stalls of country produce were neatly divided: those across the road being Belgian and those on our side French. A la Porte de France has a bistro/café atmosphere, with a bar at the entrance (well patronised that Tuesday morning) and a roomy, if somewhat dark, dining-room beyond.

Menus at 50f and 80f, with some delicious dishes on both. 50f menu offers coquille de poisson gratinée for starters, followed by steack au poivre à la crème, and finishes with tarte maison. The 80f menu proposes, more ambitiously, pavé de charolais sauce diable; and there are escargots à la crème oseille (42f); and foie gras maison et son verre de Sauternes (50f) on the carte. A good-value restaurant, and do try and time your visit for that Tuesday-morning market.

Map 3C

GOSNAY (Pas-de-Calais) 86 km SE of Calais

62199

From the A 26 take the Béthune exit in the direction of Bruay and St Pol. After 2 km turn right in Hesdigneul and follow the road signposted to Gosnay.

La Chartreuse du Val St-Esprit
(HR)L
1 r. de Fouquières
21.62.80.00
Closed Sun. p.m.
AE, V

When you arrive at a T junction, the imposing entrance of this splendid 14th-century monastery stands, almost opposite, across the road. Legend has it that, following a particularly cruel set of misdeeds inflicted on the community, the area was bothered by evil spirits, and the well-meaning Countess of Artois built a monastery here, in the Gosnay Valley, to counteract their influence. In 1441, Isabelle of Portugal died in the monastery and her heart is still said to lie buried in the churchyard in the village. More recently, the building was used as a home for young offenders – a fact that is very hard to believe today.

Jean Constant bought this magnificent building five years ago and set about restoring it to its former glory: the grand opening took place in 1986. Black and white tiles pave the entrance hall, and the ante-room leads into a large and elegant dining-room. There are high ceilings; tall doors and windows; and walls covered in fabric, toning from tomato, to pale yellow, to golden-pink in the dining-room.

The 23 bedrooms (260–390f) are as elegantly furnished and decorated as one might suppose them to be. Breakfast (either in bed or downstairs) is 35 f. Menus cost from 85–195f. Specialities from the 145 menu include huitres chaudes au vinaigre de Xérès, and blanc de volaille à la crème d'ail. After only one year, the hotel has earned itself an enviable reputation: it should cause concern to other similarly-priced hôteliers in the district.

Map 1A

GUINES (Pas-de-Calais) 10 km S of Calais

62340
Ⓜ *Fri.*

A pleasant alternative to following the signs from the port to get out of Calais is to drive into the town centre, down the bvd Jacquard, get into the centre lane and take the Guines road behind the theatre.

After a bit of grim greyness, the D 127 soon runs alongside the canal, most agreeably. You can then loop back, via Brêmes, to join the N 43 at Ardres and dodge the worst of the heavy traffic.

This road passes near the site of the Field of Cloth of Gold, where in 1520 François I and Henry VIII met in ostentatious splendour, to forge an abortive alliance. The gold brocade tents of the French vied with the crystal palace of the English in this scene of unimaginable royal one-upmanship.

The sleepy little town of Guines, which Henry made his headquarters, nowadays goes about its business as a main distribution centre for cereals, with apparently little concern for the whims of the thousands of British tourists who pass by so near and yet so far, which is probably why it manages to keep such a typically French inn as:

Le Lion d'Or
(HR)S
Pl. Foch
21.35.20.51
Closed 1/10–
Easter
AE, V

Unassuming, unspoiled, in the market square. Patrick Deplanque is an amiable host, who likes his English guests; many of them have become regulars, using his hotel as a cheap stop-off for first or last nights in France.

The rooms are modest but perfectly adequate at 100–150f and good meals in the cheerful dining-room, well patronised by locals, start at 45f.

Camping la
Bien Assise
D 231
21.35.20.77

I made an exception in mentioning a 'camping' in *FE4* because I thought La Bien Assise, based on a faded 18th-century château, was such a special place. The response has been uniformly enthusiastic, further improvements have been made, and so I am happy to repeat the recommendation.

This is the home of the charming M. and Mme André Boutoille, who have converted the old stables and pig-houses into an attractive country restaurant, open to campers and non-residents, where Madame cooks simple meals for 65f inclusive. The whitewashed stone stalls, manger, and farm implements give an atmosphere of calm rusticity, and the owners are so pleasant and helpful that I am sure a night spent under canvas or combi here would be a most agreeable one.

'It is an excellent quiet site for the ports of Calais and Boulogne, with a good swimming pool. We ate in the village at Le Lion d'Or, which provided excellent value. 43f menu included an interesting crudités, daurade, frites, and good cheese. Smoothly served, plenty of customers.' – Christine Sleigh.

Map 5B	**GUISE** (Aisne) 186 km SE of Calais; 27 km NE of St-Quentin

02120
Ⓜ *Sat.*

On the D 960 37 km SE of Cambrai.

A small and cheerful town in the Oise Valley, Guise gave its name to the great dukes whose family was related to the kings of France. Visit the ruined 11th-century château above the town. It was completed by François de Guise in the 16th century and largely destroyed during the First World War. Since 1952, the young volunteers of the Club du Vieux Manoir have been engaged on its restoration. Guided tours: 9 a.m.–12 p.m., 2–7 p.m.

Hôtel de Guise
(HR)M
103 pl. Lesur
23.61.17.58
Closed Fri. and
Sun. p.m.
EC, V

Nothing much to say about the Hôtel de Guise or its owners. Grimm, they were by name, and grim by nature. Far too busy, they said, to spare us the time of day. So – the hotel is in a side-street and seemed nice, clean and respectable. One of the few blanks we drew – so please let us know your own experiences.

Hôtel Champagne-Picardie (H)L
41 r. André Godin
23.60.43.44
EC, V

Lucky (in retrospect) that we had that bad experience at the Hotel de Guise; we might never have sought out this splendid alternative.

Three years ago, M. and Mme Lefebvre bought this handsome 19th-century building (then a private house) and converted it into an elegant hotel. From the hall, a well proportioned staircase winds gently upwards to floors where there are 14 spotlessly clean and beautifully decorated bedrooms (95–175f). Two reception rooms downstairs with original mouldings on the ceilings, a heavy, marble fireplace, white panelling and formal wallpaper.

Breakfast 19f, enclosed parking and a large, pretty garden planted out with flowers, trees and shrubs. It all seemed lovely: *just* the sort of place where we would like to stay.

La Petite Auberge
(R)S–M
384 r. Sadi-Carnot
23.61.07.53
Closed Wed.; 1/ 8–15/8

Small restaurant with a good name in a quiet street near the Hôtel Champagne-Picardie. General atmosphere, a little scruffy: heads of wild board and deer – all a little moth-eaten – look down from walls covered in browning and patched wallpaper; someone has split water on the menu, causing the ink to run; round-and-about little Mme Lacourt dashes hither and thither, hair a little on end. Surprising then, to find a sophisticated menu with some really delicious classical dishes: grenadin de veau au vinaigre de cassis (45f); cassolette Stroganoff (55f). We ate navarin d'agneau on the 59f menu, and thoroughly enjoyed it. All goes to show that you can't always go by appearance.

Map 6A | **HAM** (Somme) 194 km SE of Calais

80400
Ⓜ *Sat.*

23 km S of Péronne by the D 197. The ancient town of Ham was almost completely destroyed by the Germans in the First World War. There is little of interest left except perhaps the sprawling old abbey-church in the main street and, on the banks of the Canal du Nord, the shell of the 13th-century castle where Napoleon III was held prisoner.

Hôtel de France
(R)M
5 pl. de l'Hôtel de Ville
23.81.00.22
Closed Sun. p.m.; Mon.; Feb.; 3 weeks in Aug. AE, DC Parking

The Hôtel de France is no longer a hotel – a vine-covered building in the shadow of the town hall, where M. Dumont and his son now concentrate on the restaurant, hold on to what I should imagine is a precarious Michelin star. The food is classic, a little dull, but reliable in this area where meal stops are not easy to get excited about.

Menus at 71f and 140f (weekdays only), 165f on Sundays, feature terrine of duck, fresh turbot, duck with wild mushrooms.

Domaine des Îles (R)M
Parc Fleuri
23.82.10.85
Parking

6 km N of Ham, signposted off the D 937 and D 930.

A large and abundantly wooded recreation park, with plenty of gentle amusement for everyone. French fathers, with their fishing-rods, make for the numerous étangs. Accompanying ten-year-old reported favourably on the playground, pedalos, rowing-boats, pony rides and bicyles.

There are two menus for children in the surprisingly elegant restaurant in the grounds and adults' menus ranging from the simple 'fishermens'meal' at 58f to a splendid feast at 210f, wine included.

Map 5D

HAYBES (Ardennes) 270 km SE of Calais; 35 km N of Charleville-Mézières; 9 km NE of Revin

---

08170
Fumay

Le St-Hubert (H)S(R)M
41.11.38
EC, V

A simple Logis in the street opposite the church. Most of the house is very old, although the upper floor was built on at a later date. From the bedrooms (90–100f, all very clean and tidy) there is a fine view over the roof tops and vegetable patches to the Meuse and the dense forest on the further bank.

A charming dining-room with deer heads of assorted shapes and sizes on the walls. Game on the menu in the hunting season (20 October–5 January): terrine de sanglier, chevreuil and gibiers. Menus 50–140f.

Jeanne d'Arc (H)S(R)M
32 Grande rue
24.41.11.44
Closed New year
EC

A simple Logis across the street from the St-Hubert. Fourteen bedrooms (80–100f) were clean and neat. Tiled floor in the dining-room, and pretty pink tablecloths laid ready for delicious-sounding meals: feuilleté de turbot à l'oseille (45f), escargots de Bourgogne pur beurre (45f), truite aux amandes (45f). Menus: 40f, 55f, 95f and 135f.

Map 2C

HAZEBROUCK (Pas-de-Calais) 62 km SE of Calais; 22 km E of St-Omer

---

59190
Ⓜ *Tues.*

A bustling town traversed by the N 42, the canal de Nieppe and the railway line. It was in order to aim a blow at this important railway centre that the Germans launched one of the most costly – in terms of human life – offensives of the First World War. In 1940, the spire of the old church of St-Eloi, one of the marvels of the North, was destroyed by bombing. In 1955 the carillon in the 16th-century tower was presented to the town by a Dutch descendant of the old Seigneurs of Hazebrouck. Most of the vital life of this mainly agricultural town goes on around the Grande Place, dominated by a vast, early-19th-century Hôtel de ville. Here are shops, restaurants and a large parking space: chairs and tables spill out on to the pavements, and there is a sort of jolly, holiday atmosphere engendered by the crowds of country-people who come into town for a day's shopping.

**Hôtel
Gambrinus**
(H)S
2 r. Nationale
28.41.98.79
Closed 2–4.30
p.m.; one week
in French
Christmas
school-holidays
around 20 Dec.
– 4 Jan.
EC, V
Parking

Tall, old hotel on a corner of a quiet street, with plenty of space for cars on the paved parking in front. Seventeen bedrooms, reached by a creaking, but elegant staircase, cost from 85f for a small double room with a washbasin and bidet on the top floor, to 135f for a big double room with bathroom on the first floor. Decoration is rather faded and predominately brown, but everywhere is spotlessly clean. An agreeable air of 'other days' prevails at the moment; but, as the plumbing is all in the process of being modernised, perhaps the decoration will follow suit.

A small, friendly bar at the entrance, where locals congregate. The market takes place, some weeks, in the street outside; on others, it is held in the Grande Place, five minutes' walk away.

La Taverne
(R)M
61 Grande
Place
28.41.63.09
Closed Mon.
EC, V
Parking

A lovely, small restaurant on the Grande Place. It was built in 1932 in Flemish style and hasn't changed since those days. A long dining-room, the walls lined with tables, runs back into the house. M. Pierrot's success as a restaurateur lies mainly in his ability to cater for the locals.

He specialises in Flemish dishes at remarkably reasonable prices. Sunday menu costs 100f and there are no set menus during the week: la salade magret d'oie ferme aux lardons 35f; la saumon frais mariné au citron et poivre vert 46f. And 'Ah, nos flamiches', as the menu puts it: la tourte au Roquefort 26f, la fromage au Maroilles 26f, la coquille St-Jacques gratinée 36f, crêpes 15f–25f, fresh strawberries in season, foie gras, cold chicken and rabbit in jelly . . . A really good find, we felt, and plenty of room to park on the Place.

Map 2B

HOULLE (Pas-de-Calais) 38 km SE of Calais

N of the N 43; 5 km NW of St-Omer.

Dennis Osborn, who runs a series of well-researched off-the-beaten track outings to France, has been kind enough to pass on the following recommendation to me. He uses Mme Poupart's auberge for lunch for his party and has never had a disappointment yet. It sounded exactly right for FE – small, unspoiled, family-run, good value – so I made a detour to investigate. Foolishly I left Mr Osborn's directions behind and although I found first Moulle, then Houlle, asked various passers by, I ran out of time before I could locate Mme Poupart. So hear ye:

**Restaurant
Poupart**
(R)S
21.93.05.26
Closed Sat. and
Bank Hols.; 1/
11–28/2
Eve. by
reservation
only

'Not easy to find – but worth the trouble. Taking the N 43 turn left at the top of the undulations on to the D 220, just past a garage and Auberge Franco Russe. Houlle surrounds the gaunt chimney ahead but don't be put off. Follow the road through Houlle; on the outskirts leave the road just past Au Rallye d'Artois, following the Le Camping signs. The camp site on your right, go ahead and turn left for the restaurant – a red-roofed low white building, but without a name displayed.

'The menu one day last April was: toast with Roquefort, pears and three peppers; thick slices of ham with Madeira and mushroom sauce; guinea fowl, salad and pommes frites; choice of cheeses with excellent bread; apple tart; coffee and a biscuit. All this and two bottles of Vin du Patron cost, for four persons, 420f. It is not necessary to book, but if you can order ahead, ask for frisée au foie de volailles: crisp endive and raspberries hiding warm chicken livers in a cream sauce.' – Joan and Dennis Osborn.

I shall persevere.

Map 5C	**LANDOUZY-LA-VILLE** (Aisne) 264 km SE of Calais

02140
Vervins

10.5 km NW of Vervins by the D 963 and D 29.

Domaine du Tilleul
(HR)L
23.98.48.00
All credit cards

Converted stable block set in the grounds of an 1831 château that was once the hunting-lodge of M. Le Phinée de Monaco. Large, light bedrooms (280f–340f) overlook all that lovely parkland; no sound except for birdsong and the murmured conversation of guests sitting at tables set on the grass outside. On the ground floor is a small brasserie where you can eat breakfast (30f), or grills, later in the day. Menus in the large dining-room opening off the brasserie are 140f and 190f. The drawing-room in the castle is there, should you wish to have a cocktail or just to relax in elegant surroundings. When we looked in, the debris of empty champagne glasses was much in evidence.

There is golf and tennis in the park. A very friendly lady presides over the reception. Verdict: a quiet spot in lovely surrounds. Upmarket ambience probably justifies the prices.

Map 6B	**LAON** (Aisne) 117 km SE of Calais; 47 km NE of Reims

02000
Ⓜ Tues.,
Wed.

A diversion from the ring road is a must, in order to see at close quarters Laon's unique cathedral, one of the most beautiful in France. Its towers – seven of them – can be discerned from far away across the plain, crowning a considerable hill, up which you must wind to arrive at the cobbled parvis outside the west front.

Built in the 12th century, within the short span of fifty years, the cathedral, vast though it is, has a wonderful sense of unity. Its builders allowed light to separate its slender pillars so that there is nothing ponderous about their immensity. Carved stone beasties lean out from the sides as though hesitating whether to jump, and the dribbling gargoyles are among the most hideous ever. Try and see it at least twice, with different lights illuminating the façade.

Inside is equally magnificent. The vast nave, illuminated by 13th-century glass, soars ever upwards in four distinct stages. Most impressive is the grill enclosing the choir, dating from the 17th century.

The view from the ramparts outside is a bit of a let-down – all railway sidings and factories.

The ancient town, once the capital of France, is divided into several distinct sections. The shopping area along the narrow r. St-Jacques, known as Le Bourg, is appallingly traffic-ridden, and trying to balance on the one-person pavements can be nerve-wracking. It's a relief to arrive at the tranquil pedestrianised La Cité area approaching the cathedral, with plenty of room for pavement cafés.

I had problems with the hotels and restaurants in Laon and failed to find an arrow, as I felt the town deserved. They'd done their best to spoil **Les Chevaliers**, where I stayed (see below), and in the restaurants I spent my time dodging the dread pop. Regular readers will know that this Fenn allergy is apt to cloud all judgments and be prepared to make allowances accordingly. I suspect it may be the table-for-one that makes me more than usually susceptible to the ghetto-blast, but I do find it quite impossible to concentrate on either food- or note-taking when aurally bombarded, and deem the attack all the more offensive in an old town like Laon.

Les Chevaliers
(HR)M
3 r. Serurier
23.23.43.78
Closed 10/8–18/
8, 1/3–7/3
AE, DC, EC, V

Strip lighting and carpet-up-the-walls decor worried me considerably, but the original character of the beams and walls in this old stone house wins – just. My bedroom and bathroom were O.K.ish, for 203f, but that dreadful carpet stuff gets grubby and stays grubby, and the traffic noise was not good news. However, I met a couple who had been allocated a room at the back and they liked the laid-back atmosphere, with teenagers lolling on bean-bag seating in the entrance lobby, and the little dining-room where you can eat a modest meal, so perhaps this might suit some. Parking diabolical and you hump your own bags.

La Bannière de France
(HR)M
11 r. F. Roosevelt
23.23.21.44
Closed 20/12–20/1
AE, DC, EC, V

Probably the best of a poor bunch. And the only choice if you like to eat in your hotel. Every time I have tried to inspect it, it has been full, so I haven't been able yet to see a room. They appear to be good value at 119–292f and the food is said to be reliable – apparently a little dull on the menus, but of good quality and quantity. The management might well have been spoiled by too-easy custom.

'Even more evidence of G.B. plates. We had a family room, with two double beds and shower, for 245f and my mother had a single for 85f. I feel that in view of the fact it has had so much exposure it doesn't find it necessary to spend any of the profits on replacing the wailpaper. However the food was very good. The cheapest meal is 85f and worth it: Avocados with prawns, pâté, crudités, then brochette of beef or chicken; excellent pâtisserie. Other menus looked good too.' – Lesley Bayliss.

Hôtel Angleterre
(HR)M
10 bvd Lyon
23.23.04.62
Rest. closed Sun. o.o.s.; Sat. lunch; 23/12–30/12.

Not so interestingly situated as those hotels in the Haute Ville, but highly recommended thus:
'Reasonably priced, family-run hotel with good-value food and spotlessly clean. Unpretentious outside, welcome surprise inside. Very good value. Service very efficient.' – David and Wendy Simmons.

Rooms are 120–300f. Menus from 65f.

Le Châtelain
(R)M
35 r. Châtelain
23.79.69.69
Closed Mon.
AE, DC, EC, V

Charming old stone restaurant in the pedestrianised area near the cathedral. You eat downstairs in the erstwhile cellars, in an atmosphere of times gone by, and alas of times present in the form of the boum-boum. I tried to enjoy my 79f menu but the odds were overwhelming and I fled. The deaf and immune would doubtless appreciate.

Les Chenizelles
(R)M
1 r. Bourg
23.23.02.34
Closed Sun.
p.m.
AE, EC, V

On the main street not far from the town hall. Calls itself a 'bistro gourmand'. Risking being labelled a bolshie Brit, and in utter desperation I asked them to turn down the volume a bit, which they cheerfully did.

I tried three starters as a kind of *menu dégustation*, which perhaps wasn't playing fair. My tartare de loup was a travesty. If you're going to go for raw marinated fish it must be fresh above all else. This was lumps of bass (what a waste) suspiciously chilly, in a sea of nauseous aerated cream; feuilleté de poireaux was excellent for the leeks, leaden for the pastry. I couldn't even bring myself to try the cassoulet d'escargots – the blob of aerosol cream dissuaded me from delving further. Snails with *cream*?

But I must stress that this is probably unfair judgment. Stick to the menu – terrine de lièvre, sauté de porc au curry, tarte aux poires, and for 59f you can hardly grumble, especially if you like heavy metal.

Map 6A

LASSIGNY (Oise) 238 km SE of Calais; 24 km N of Compiègne

60310

On the junction of the D 938 and the D 142. From the A 1 take exit 11 and follow signs to Lassigny and Noyon. A small town, destroyed during the First World War.

**Hôtel de la
Croix d'Or**
(R)S
*2 pl. du
Souvenir*
44.43.60.01
Closed Wed.;
15/8–15/9 AE,
DC, EC, V

A simple restaurant on the Place, near to the church and in front of the War Memorial. M. Milone says that his establishment is already well known to the English who lodge at La Tête Noire next door and come to him for their meals. Menus are certainly good value (46.50f, 86.50f and 140f). On the 46.50f menu that day were cochonailles (plate of cold meat), steak au poivre or andouillette, cheese or dessert. Atmosphere was cosy and friendly – both Monsieur and his mother found plenty of time to chat.

**Hôtel de la Tête
Noire**
(HR)S
*1 r. de la Tour-
Roland*
44.43.60.09
Closed Mon.;
15/7–15/8

An essentially simple hotel on the corner of the Place. Rooms (78–118f) are clean and cheerfully furnished. 42f menu in the large, tidy dining-room beyond the café-bar entrance.

Map 5C   LIESSIES (Nord) 202 km SE of Calais

59   24 km N of Hirson on the D 963.

Château de la Motte
(HR)M
27.61.81.94
Closed 24/12–30/1
EC, V

A most impressive 18th-century château set in a park. But the 12 bedrooms (99.50–185f) are, frankly, a let-down: shabby to a degree that is almost eccentric. Those in the best state of preservation are drably furnished with contrasting wallpaper, bath and bidet behind a screen and no loo.

Fat and friendly Madame appeared, apparently from nowhere, in answer to the bell. The château, she told us, had belonged to her parents. Menu in the empty and echoing dining-room looked intriguing: la flamiche aux Maroilles, le coquelet à la bière, le poulet au Riesling . . . A few tables on the terrace at the back overlooking that lovely parkland.

Certainly an hotel with atmosphere, set in peaceful surroundings – just don't expect too much!

Map 5B   LIGNY-EN-CAMBRÉSIS (Nord) 63 km SE of Calais

59191   14 km SE of Cambrai on the D 15.

➤ **Le Château de Ligny**
(HR)L
27.85.25.84
Rest. closed Mon. lunch
Hotel closed 12/1–20/2
AE, V

A small and exquisite château, parts of it dating back to the 12th century, set in 12 hectares of parkland. In style it is pure Flemish Renaissance, with an arched gateway leading into a courtyard, and a moat, drained and covered with mown grass, running all around. When the German army occupied the castle in 1917, they found a stone platform bricked up in the cellar walls on which the 15th-century archers had stood to defend the moat. To one side is the stable block, and beyond that are the walls of the old village houses and the tall spire of the church. It is a lovely and peaceful spot: a lawn, well shaded by trees and a magnificient old magnolia shedding its petals in the courtyard.

M. Boulard worked here as chef for three years and in 1986 took over the hotel itself. The six bedrooms are – quite frankly – splendid. Not cheap by French prices (430–550f, ranging from a double bedroom to an apartment), but ridiculously so by ours. Menus *are* expensive by any count: 250f menu in the evening which proposes, among other delicacies, raclette de Maroilles au jambon de canard; le gâteau d'homard au basilic . . . A la carte, you could get away with 200f, and there are lunchtime menus for 90f.

Arrowed as the sole representative of a luxury hotel in this area.

Map 4B   LOCQUIGNOL (Nord) 160 km SE of Calais; 23 km SE of Valenciennes

59530   A small village set in the heart of the great Forest of Mormal, the largest forest in the north of France. Consisting mainly of oak trees, and the home of countless roe deer and a dwindling number of the much hunted wild boar, this vast area is crossed by numerous signposted rides (many of which are closed to motor-traffic after dark) and walking trails. Locquignol grew up in a forest clearing, its existence due mainly to the clog-makers and wood-carvers who once lived here. Coming along the D 33 from Le Quesnoy, turn right in the middle of the village in the direction of Maroilles, following the sign for **L'Hostellerie de La Touraille**, which is set in a forest glade at the junction of four of these ancient rides.

Hostellerie de la Touraille (HR)M *Rte de Maroilles* 27.34.21.21 DC, V

Well, I like a little eccentricity from time to time. La famille Buffart (mother, father, two sons and a daughter) own this highly original converted barn that, over the last two hundred years, has served as a place of shelter for travellers along the road. Once two sisters lived here and ran it as a wayside inn, renowned far and wide for their gastronomy and for the mead they served.

Lost of frills everywhere (not the least in Madame's flamboyant style of dress); fussy white lace tablecloths in the little salon at the entrance and in the dining-room; a live parrot squawking in a cage: it could well be the set for some romantic film.

Upstairs, the bedrooms are hardly less striking. Decorated in a highly individual style: dragged paint (each bedroom is painted in a different colour), big white down cushions and, of course, frilly white bedcovers. The effect is delightful – if a little overpowering.

Bedrooms cost from 170–380f; the latter, a good-sized apartment with an extra bed.

Menus: 140f and à la carte. Specialities include: émincée de saumon au gros sel; six huîtres chaudes aux blancs de poireaux; pâtisserie des deux soeurs. Outside is a garden and, beyond that, the forest rides and all those lovely trees.

Map 7B

LONGPONT (Aisne) 289 km SE of Calais; 23 km SW of Soissons

02600

Signposted off the N 2 and surrounded by the great Forêt de Retz. This forest, incidentally, was the scene of a remarkable encounter between French and German troops in the First World War when a cavalry charge, led by Lieutenant de Gironde, destroyed a squadron of German aeroplanes near the farm of Vauberon.

The impressive ruins of the 12th-century Cistercian monastery of Longpont are in a valley that had been a swamp before the monks settled there and drained the area. The village takes it name from the 'long bridge' which crossed the marshes carrying the Roman road from Meaux to Soissons. The original monks' dormitory was so luxurious that the Abbot was put on bread and water as penance and ordered to rebuild it: the ruins we see today are the survivals of an 18th-century fire, the Revolution and the First World War. The interior may be visited at weekends and holidays from 10 a.m.–12 p.m. and from 2.30–7 p.m.

From the green expanse where the ruins stand, a cobbled village street runs between houses (all post 1918) and ends in a 13th-century gate-house. This small, turreted building was once part of the *châtelet* constructed for the protection of the monastery and housed a small garrison.

Hôtel de l'Abbaye de Longpont
(HR)M
23.96.02.44
EC, V

The hotel is at the end of the village street, just before the gate-house. The whole scene looks like a tiny mediaeval village built for a film set; in fact, the original was totally destroyed during the offensive commanded by General Mangin in 1918. Today it seems a peaceful, relaxing spot; although in high season, it could well be crowded with tourists. There are plenty of unambitious rural pursuits in the neighbourhood: walks down forest rides, and patron M. Verdun supplies bicycles for hire.

Bedrooms (140–260f) are well furnished, attractively decorated and spacious. The dining-room looks welcoming with brown and white ceramic tiles on the floor, heavy long wooden tables alongside the walls and a big, old fireplace at the further end. But, oh M. Verdun, you *have* prostituted your culinary art to the tourist! Menus (75–180f) seemed attractively unsophisticated when read: 'assiette de crudités; sardines grillées; fromage blanc'. The dish of my choice, 'langue de boeuf, sauce tomate', was exactly that and no more: slices of boiled tongue covered with thick tomato purée, and my companion's meal equally unexciting. *Not* the sort of food we come to France to eat!

Map 2C | **LONGUE CROIX** (Nord) 60 km SE of Calais, 22 km E of St-Omer

---

59190
Hazebrouck

Take the N 42 Hazebrouck road from St-Omer and turn north on to the D 238 to find the crossroads in the middle of the flat Flanders plain.

➤ **Auberge de la Longue Croix**
(R)M
28.40.03.30
Closed Sun. p.m.; Mon. p.m.; Tue.; 22/ 6–30/6; Dec. Dinner by reservation only

'We were surprised', said the local restaurateurs when Stephane Maerten won the most recent Michelin rosette in the limited Northern ranks. 'He's closed half the time and then he only does dinner by reservation.' But bully for Michelin to overcome technical considerations and recognise talent. M. Maerten's intention is emphatically not to allow his new station to change his modest ways. He and his wife run the tiny auberge in the middle of nowhere between them. Fifteen covers are all they can or want to handle.

His hand-scrawled dinner carte is commendably short, majoring on fish, with perhaps four dishes in each section. At lunch there is a 120f menu.

He explained that the scallops entrée would be served in their shells, simmered in their own juices ('etuvée' sounds much more interesting than 'stewed'), or there was salmon marinaded in lime and olive oil, flecked with chives, or home-made duck foie gras.

Commendably there are local dishes – a carbonnade of monkfish, with the fish poached in locally brewed beer, with a dash of *genièvre*; accompanying veg. are dug down the road, all interestingly presented without any hint of the chi-chi.

Madame Maertens recites the desserts, which included that wonderful but unlikely dish that everyone should try once – strawberries with pepper. They, like the chocolate charlotte, the genièvre and fruit feuilletés, were perfect.

It's just as well that the beamed and tiled auberge is such a comfortable place to pass the time, since everything is cooked to order, and this is no place to eat in a hurry. Rather reserve it for a special evening. The wine list is impressive and well chosen, but it is possible to pay only 42f for a modest Sylvaner, so, with coffee, you could get away with a total bill of less than 200f. Good value and arrowed accordingly as being of particular interest.

Map 2B **LUMBRES** (Pas de Calais) 42 km S of Calais

62380
(**M**) *Mon.,*
Wed.

Moulin de
Mombreux
(R)L
Rte de
Bayenghem
21.39.62.44

A well-known gastronomic hideaway. Jean-Marc Gaudry has been cooking in this idyllically situated mill on the river Bléquin for over twenty years now, and his Michelin rosette is well established.

The fact that the surrounds – the busy N 42, the mean little town of Lumbres and the dusty paper-mills – are so dreary accentuates the pleasure of bumping down the lane, well signposted from the route

Moulin de Mombreux.

Closed Sun.
p.m.; Mon.; 15/
12–1/2
AE, DC, EC

nationale, to come across the well-tended courtyard, with expensive loungers overlooking the little river, around the erstwhile millhouse. You eat on the first floor, up a corkscrew staircase.

The 155f no-choice menu can sometimes seem a little uninspired, but if its components suit your tastes you should stick with it because the bill à la carte can get out of hand, especially with the expensive wine list. However, it must always be remembered that although the Moulin's prices are high for this region, the equivalent standard would cost much more at home.

The *menu dégustation* I took last time, at 200f, offered five mini-courses of splendid quality – a hot ducks liver pâté on a bed of diverse saladery, a chunk of freshly poached lobster flecked with herbs, and a fillet of lamb served in a superb sauce flavoured with truffles. The cheeses came from Olivier of course, and the dessert was a refreshing gratin of oranges. Some of the more simple-sounding dishes – like a roast chicken from Licques up the road – should not be scorned.

I was disappointed to find that building had not even begun on the new rooms, due to be ready by autumn of '87, but I understand that planning permission has at last been given and they should be ready for the high season of '88. Their luxury will be more in keeping with the high standards of the restaurant, and so will their three-star prices. At present the six existing rooms though cheap (155f a double) are a let-down, with paper-thin walls and built for doll-sized customers.

Persistent complaints about the lack of accueil and grumpiness of the waiters mean that this is sometimes not a happy place to eat, and so the arrow must go.

Map 4C | **MAUBEUGE** (Nord) 171 km SE of Calais; 34 km E of Valenciennes

---

59600
(M) Wed.,
Sat., Sun.

A noisy, traffic-thronged industrial city originally established around a 7th-century convent. Little today, except some good restaurants and hotels, to recommend it to the tourist. It stands on the ancient route from Paris to Brussels and in its long history the cruel events of war have been too often repeated: seized by Louis XI in the 15th century, burned less than a hundred years later, besieged in 1793, occupied by the Prussians in 1814 . . . On 17 May 1940, the city was so effectively destroyed that only 10 per cent of its houses survived. After the war it was rebuilt to the design of the architect André Lucat, and is considered a model of modern city architecture and has also won many prizes in the contests for *villes fleuries*. In spite of all that dreadful destruction, vestiges of the city's ancient fortifications, designed by Vauban, still remain: La Porte de Mons, the only surviving of the city's four entrance gates; a portcullis restored by the Vauban association; and, a little outside the city, the remains of the north-facing ramparts.

Hôtel de la
Poste
(H)S
15 r. Henri-
Durre
27.64.65.34

A small hotel (14 bedrooms) in a side street that runs parallel with the r. de France. Mme Daunoit has owned the hotel for the last 12 years and, during that time, has had many British visitors. She is a very friendly lady who, if you arrive and find the hotel full, will telephone around to find your other accommodation. She is quite genuinely concerned that we should not recommend L'Hotel de Provence, a door or so further down the same street. It was noisy (with a night-club adjoining it) and, she told us, had a poor reputation.

Rooms are simple and spotlessly clean and cost from 90f–120f. Breakfast is 15f. Lots of little restaurants, pizza places and fast-food dining in the r. de France. Plenty of space to park your car in the quiet street outside the hotel.

Le Grand Hôtel
(HR)M
1 pte de Paris
27.64.63.16˙
All credits cards
Garage

A sparkling clean hotel on a corner at the furthest end of the r. de France on Paris road. The best hotel and restaurant in Maubeuge, with a light, cheerful atmosphere and a very friendly owner. We thought the bedrooms (170f–260f) a little tatty, but approved of the vast dining-room, where menus range from 65f to a gastronomic 230f. Mouth-watering dishes, à la carte, include foie gras de canard du chef au sauternes et sa brioche (80f); carré de veau doré au four et au thym (65f); charlotte de la mer et ses coulis de légumes frais (58f). Parking is outside the hotel; or in four garages (25f).

M. Marszolik (who speaks good English) is, apparently, the benevolent Mr Big of Maubeuge. As well as the Grand Hôtel, his empire includes the Concorde, the Bar du Zoo and the Forestière (in the Forest of Mormal – see Locquignol).

Joseph
(R)M
7 av. Jean
Mabuse
27.64.68.14
Closed Sun.
p.m.
AE, DC, EC

Young M. and Mme Petit took over Joseph two years ago and the restaurant has already earned them a reputation for gastronomy. A large, light dining-room, well furnished and hung with pictures of sailing boats, seems quite remote from the traffic in the busy three-lane road outside. The oldest part of the building is to the right of the entrance: here, small, round tables are set for apéritifs or coffee beneath lacy lampshades like old women's bonnets.

Menus (64f, 85f, 115f and 170f) are simple, but impressive in their content. A sample 64f menu (they change all the time) offered: salade de ris de veau composée, longe de porc au citron, cheese or île flottante. Mme Petit speaks perfect English: indeed, I judge that she must almost be bilingual. Parking is no real problem – provided you have time to hunt around a bit and don't mind a short walk. It's right in the central shopping area, so plenty of interest in the immediate surroundings.

Map 2C

MOLINGHEM (Pas-de-Calais) 66 km SE of Calais; 5 km SE of Aire-sur-la-Lys

---

62330
Isbergues

The villages of Isbergues (where the sister of Charlemagne was born), Molinghem and Berguette make up one commune: all date from after the First World War and are unremarkable – except, perhaps, for the well-thought-of little restaurant Le Buffet.

Le Buffet
(R)M
21.25.82.40
Closed Sat.
lunch; Sun.
p.m. (other
eves by
reservation
only); last 2
weeks in July
and first 2
weeks in Aug.
EC, V

From Aire-sur-la-Lys, follow the D 188 through Isbergues, cross the major D 186 into Molinghem, turn left by the Place and follow signs to the station – easier than it sounds.

Le Buffet (once the station restaurant) is in a quiet cul-de-sac opposite the little station of Berguette: plenty of room to park in front.

Young M. and Mme Wident have worked hard on their little restaurant. The result is a cheerful, modern place that still retains a café/buffet atmosphere: ceramic floor, entrance bar and small, light dining-room. Monsieur's credentials are impressive: he trained at **le Buffet de la Gare** in Arras and gained further experience at **l'Ambassadeur**, Le Touquet, and at the **Moulin de Mombreux**, Lumbres.

Menus: 52f, 85f, 118.50f and 150f. Speciality of the house is tourte aux cinq fromages. 52f menu includes la salade aux noix et au bleu; le medaillon de porc aux baies de genièvre.

Reports particularly welcome – an arrow in the offing?

Map 2C   **MONT DES CATS** (Nord) 70 km SE of Calais

A 25, exit 13 direction Poperinge, D 948, D 18.

As you leave the flat plain of the Lys, a line of distant hills appears on the horizon to mark the French/Belgian frontier. They are Mont Cassel (178m), Mont des Cats (158m), Mont Noir (130m) and the Monts de Boeschepe (137m): ancient boundary markers that were protected by their rocky cores from the erosion that affected the surrounding countryside.

At the summit of the Mont des Cats, the distinctive outline of the Trappist monastery, surrounded by a wood planted by the monks, dominates the entire range of hills. These worthy men, while respecting a vow of silence, pass their days in prayer, study, working in the fields and making cheese – the fromage du Mont des Cats is on sale, although the monastery itself is not open to visitors. Here, also, is a First World War memorial to Canadian soldiers killed in the Battle of the Monts in 1918.

There are numerous marked footpaths to follow on the hills. Maps available from the Tourist Office in Bailleul.

La Sapinière
(R)M
28.42.50.89/
28.41.96.04
Closed Thur.;
p.m. except Fri.
and Sat.
AE, V

I have to admit that I visited La Sapinière in early spring when this modern building, set in a pine-wood near the summit of the Mont, looked a trifle bleak and 'caff-like' – but then out-of-season visits are no great advertisement. Once inside, having met the friendly and helpful manager, it was easier to see what a lively destination this remote clearing could become, later on, when the trees on the hill were clothed in leaves, the ample dining-space echoing to the cheerful clatter of knives and forks, and children playing on the swings, and so on, outside.

Apparently a favourite destination for grannies from Lille, who come here on coach tours to breathe some country air. Philippe Dehonger, who presides over his kitchen, caters for large groups as well as individual tourists. About once a month, he organises special evenings with a particular theme: Flemish menus, rural feasts; or (incongruously) carnival evenings with a Brazilian buffet.

Day-to-day menus present such country-style dishes as tourte au fromage des moines du Mont des Cats (25f); gigôt d'agneau à la fleur de thym (65f) and les petits salades gourmandes au chêvre chaud. A particularly good point – the restaurant can, subject to availability, point you in the right direction for somewhere to stay the night. I'm just a little intimidated at the thought (during the daytime) of all those rollicking grannies!

Map 2C	**MONT NOIR** (Nord) 78 km SE of Calais

59299
Boeschepe

On the D 10, between exits 13 and 12 of the A 25.

Hôtel du Mont Noir
(HR)M
28.42.51.33
Closed Fri.;
Feb.; Aug.
AE, DC, V

Take the D 23 and the D 223 6 km north of Bailleul. This old hotel, a Logis de France, stands beside the road on the windy summit of a hill planted with chestnut trees. From the belvedere that lies beyond it, you can look far away to Ypres, over to the other Monts and down on to the flat plains of Flanders and into Belgium, the frontier-post and the slow-moving cars below.

M. Sévin acts as a friendly and relaxed host in the small bar beyond the entrance, in between times preparing his substantial local cuisine. Madame presides over the dining-room with a certain gruff kindness: she didn't turn a hair when we came down at 10.30 for breakfast one morning, having forgotten to change our watches (and only discovered our mistake the following afternoon).

A stuffed fox and a pheasant guard the staircase that leads from the dining-room up to the bedrooms. Rooms with twin beds and bath are furnished with attractive chintz bedcovers and flowery wallpaper (120–150f). Menus range from 65–150f. On the 65f menu were ficelles Picardes (crêpes filled with ham), and jambon braisé à la bière de 3 monts et au cidre.

Map 7C	**MONTCHENOT** (Marne) 293 km SE of Calais

51

11 km SE of Reims by the N 51.

Auberge du Grand Cerf
(R)M–L
Closed Tues.
p.m.; Wed.; 15/
8–1/9; 20/12–3/
1
AE, CB

A favourite retreat from the city for the Rémois in summer and popular with every local I asked, from Épernay northwards. Particularly useful for an en route stop if you don't wish to get embroiled in Reims' traffic, since you could hardly fail to be soothed and refreshed by the welcoming atmosphere. It's a sophisticated restaurant, however, and probably not the place to tumble into all travel-stained and hung about with hungry kids.

One of the owners, Alain Guichaova, comes from Brittany, and his latest innovation is a menu entirely composed of seafood – a salad of lobster claws with a julienne of mango, buckwheat pancakes stuffed with the coral of the lobster and anointed with a sauce from the same

lordly crustacean. There is a good-value 180f weekdays-only menu,
otherwise they are 220f or 300f. Astonishing collection of
Champagnes. Michelin star.

| Map 5D | **MONTHERMÉ** (Ardennes) 290 km SE of Calais |

08800

18 km N of Charleville-Mézières by the D 1.
  A small and ancient town, surrounded by mountains, that is
situated on the confluence of the rivers Meuse and Semoy. A tourist
honeypot in summer for excursions into the two river valleys, a
centre for *ski du fond* in winter.

Hôtel-
Restaurant de
La Paix
(H)S(R)M
24.53.01.55
Closed Sat.
o.o.s.; and
'sometime in
December'
AE, EC, V

A 1952 Logis by the bridge that crosses the Meuse, in the centre of
this little town. Outside is very much '50s style, but the interior could
have come from an earlier age. Ten good, simple bedrooms up a
solid staircase (85–110f), all very clean and shortly to be redecorated.
  Menus (50–130f) looked appetising. Hotel well patronised by
tourists when we visited it.

Franco-Belge
(R)M
24.53.01.20
Closed Fri.;
Sun. p.m.; 10/
1–25/1
V

Hôtel Franco-Belge is in the main street that passes by the little Place
where, incidentally, the Syndicat d'Initiative is situated.
  We arrived at this Logis during l'*heure du service* and therefore
everyone was naturally too occupied to show us the bedrooms
(95–130f). But what a good excuse it was to relax and enjoy a
leisurely lunch. Two dining-rooms, one by the bar, with pink
tablecloths, the other (more tranquil) with white cloths over brown,
and very popular they were – by 12.30 both were crowded. Our meal
was delicious: on the 70f menu we ate cassolette d'escargots de
Bourgogne à la creme, salade frisée au magret de canard fumé,
cheese and dessert. Other delicacies included caille cocotte à
l'Ardennaise, medaillons de veau forestière . . . Menus: 70–150f.

| Map 2C | **LA MOTTE-AU-BOIS** (Pas-de-Calais) 61 km SE of Calais |

59190

5 km S of Hazebrouck on the D 946.

Auberge de la
Forêt
(HR)M
28.48.08.78
Closed Sun.
p.m.; Mon.;
mid Dec.–mid
Jan.
AE, V

This chalet-like Logis stands on a corner of the village, in the heart of
the forest of Nieppe. In a park across the road is a grand château,
now occupied by the French Air Force.
  Blonde Mme Bécu runs the two dining-rooms (one very large, the
other small and intimate) with her husband and two helpers. Menus
run from 100f up to a seven-course feast at 250f. The 100f menu
included rillettes, papillote de cabillaud (cod), petit salé aux lentilles,
cheese, tarte or ice-cream.

Auberge de la Foret   La Motte-au-Bois

There are 15 bedrooms, some with twin beds, which cost from 90f (without bath) up to 210f. When we last visited the hotel, three years ago, we were much taken by the light and attractive decor. Since then, the bedrooms have been 'modernised' and lost something in the process. A featureless brown predominates; and the powder room (which was formerly decorated with style and imagination) now has a strictly functional character.

Map 4B   **NAVES** (Nord) 150 km SE of Calais; 7 km NE of Cambrai

---

59400

L'Auberge du Champart
(R)M
Chaussée Brunhaut
27.37.84.65
Closed Sun. p.m.; Mon.
V

Take the Valenciennes road out of Cambrai, fork left for Naves, driving across flat farmland and red earth to this quiet village on the D 114.

The Auberge is an imaginative conversion from an old barn into something like a tiny château, designed on strictly Heath-Robinson lines. Entrance door leads to a circular staircase that winds round the tower to the upper floor.

The dining-room is of conventional barn-type structure: exposed beams and rafters. Upstairs (reached by another winding staircase) is a gallery with more chairs and tables. 100f menu includes six escargots, assortiment de terrines et ses salades, suprême de volaille grillée au coulis de tomate. Menus at 78f, 110f and 160f.

Map 5B	**NEUVILLE-ST-AMAND** (Aisne) 202 km SE of Calais

02100 St-Quentin	3 km SE of St-Quentin by the D 12.
Le Château (R)L 23.68.41.82 *Closed Sun.* *p.m.; Wed.* *p.m.; Mon.* *All credit cards*	A lovely restaurant in a large country house well signposted down a private road. 　The dining-room is splendid: large and airy, furnished with orange tablecloths and tall, tapestry-covered chairs, and overlooking 3 hectares of tranquil parkland. Grandfather of the brothers Meiresonne was Belgian: Claude is the chef, and the charming Jean-François is in charge of the restaurant. Menus start at 130f and run, on Sundays, up to 260f. Classical cuisine includes (on the 130f) cocktail de poulpes aux herbes fraîche. The speciality of the house is probably fish, with locally killed meat coming a close second. Lots of room to park. Guests are treated with warmth and good manners.

Map 2B	**NORDAUSQUES** (Pas-de-Calais) 25 km SE of Calais

	Just N of the autoroute, 2 km from the Nordausques exit.
Auberge de la Hem (R)S *Rte de St-Omer* *21.82.94.41*	A little roadside inn, recommended to me by Mme Béhaghel at la Ferme de Wolphus (see p. 165), who says her clients always return well satisfied after a meal in Michel Gressier's rustic, check-clothed dining-room. Menus from 56f.

Map 5B	**LE NOUVION-EN-THIÉRACHE** (Aisne) 259 km SE of Calais

02170 (M) *Wed.*	47 km SW of Valenciennes on the D 934 and N 43; 46 km SW of Cambrai.
Hôtel Petion (H)S(R)M *Tel. No.??* *Closed Thurs.;* *15/1–15/2* *EC, V* *Parking*	A very good-value hotel with a long history. The original was burned down during the First World War and rebuilt in 1920: miraculously the stained-glass windows that date from that era have survived. I asked for the most simple room (most expensive 180f) and for 80f got a large, clean bedroom, furnished with several chairs and a wardrobe, and a spacious 'bathroom', with wash-basin and bidet, opening off it. 　The Hôtel Petion is one of those excellent family hotels that, one imagines, has a struggle to survive, now that the autoroute has left the town high and dry and the hotels on the more international N 2 have poached much of their custom. 　The dining-room, that night, was well patronised by French and Belgian families and, as M. Albert Eldarai is a renowned chef (1st prize in the Section d'Art gastronomique for the Belgian frontier), the meal was predictably good. From the 75f menu, I ate avocat au crabe; jambon sous le cindre, crême de mousserons, salad; and there was a great variety of delicious desserts to choose from. 　Out of the 11 bedrooms, only 2, in fact, overlook the road. As it was the weekend there was little traffic passing through the town, so that

night a good sleep presented little problem. A modern extension at the back is probably a safer bet; it overlooks a little garden where, incidentally, there is room to park your car.

Map 6A

NOYON (Oise) 239 km SE of Calais; 20 km SE of Roye; 24 km NE of Compiègne

60400
Ⓜ *Wed.,*
Sat.

A thriving industrial town with an ancient history. Here, in 768, Charlemagne was crowned king of Neustrie, and in 987 the coronation of Hugues Capet as king of France took place. The 16th century saw the birth of Calvin (1509) and of the great sculptor Sarazin (1592). Visit the Musée Jean-Calvin (9 a.m.–12 p.m., 2–5 p.m., closed Mondays), which is in a house reconstructed (1927) on the foundations of the great reformer's birthplace. In the first room is the 'Chaire de Desert', the travelling chair from which Calvin preached his sermons in the countryside. On the second floor are some 16th-century bibles; most of their covers were destroyed when they were buried to avoid discovery.

The fine cathedral and the semicircle of houses on the Grande Place were largely rebuilt after the First World War. There's a good deal of traffic in Noyon, which is merely an adequate overnight stop with a few worthwhile restaurants.

Hôtel Saint-Éloi
(HR)M
Bvd Carnot
44.4.01.49
EC, V

Thirty bedrooms (260f) in this 18th-century, old-fashioned sort of house by a roundabout. The sleeping side of the hotel is in an annexe; the rooms are all very fresh, with pretty wallpaper, although dark stained wood furniture and bedheads combine to give them a slightly gloomy atmosphere. They were all occupied when we visited the hotel in August. Hotels are thin on the ground in Noyon.

The main part of the hotel has an architecturally eccentric and, let's face it, crumbling exterior. Wrought-iron gates and fences enclose a little garden; a night here should be relatively quiet.

Menus are 60f, 785f, 120f and 180f. On the 60f menu were terrine de lapin maison, côte de porc, gratin dauphinois, cheese or dessert.

L'Auberge
(R)M
R. Jeanne-
d'Arc, Pont-
l'Evêque
44.44.05.17
Closed Sun.
p.m.; Mon.;
Feb.

From Noyon take the Compiègne road for 2 km out of the town. Pont-l'Evêque is signposted to your left.

L'Auberge is on the corner of a village street: an ancient inn that was reconstructed after the First World War. There are beams, a paved floor and pink tablecloths. On the wall behind the big, wooden bar-counter are gleaming copper pans, a boar's head and a set of antlers. Cheerful patrons and reasonably priced, always changing menus. On the 90f menu that day there were salade de ris de veau, steak of gigôt aux herbes, plâteau de fromage ou Crottin roti (+25f).

Les Alliés
(R)M
5 bvd Mony
44.44.01.89
Closed Tues.
p.m.; Wed.
EC, V

On the corner of a boulevard that runs east towards Chauny and west towards Amiens, not far from the cathedral. A cosy restaurant, not particularly smart, with reasonably priced menus and a nice, friendly patronne, Mme Guelbone.

A terrace dining-room at the front overlooking the street, another at the back and yet another upstairs. Menus: 44f and 70f. On the 44f menu were: pâté en croute, choux farcis, camembert or crème caramel. 70f menu offered coquille de morue à la parisienne, darne de colin blanc à la Dieppoise (mussels and shrimps in a white sauce), cheese or dessert. Both menus change frequently.

Auberge de Crisolles
(R)M
44.09.02.32
Closed Wed.;
Tues. p.m.
EC, V

This little restaurant is set back from the road, on the D 932, direction Ham. Menus cost 65f (lunch only), 85f, 120f and 160f. On the day we ate there, it was sadly empty of clients – a pity, as there were some really interesting dishes from which to choose: coquelet de poivre vert, terrine de canard maison, sorbet aux fraises, foie gras d'oie frais fait maison . . . and all the menus include a half carafe of wine, and coffee to follow. We ate the *table d'hôte* menu (65f), which consisted of charcuterie as an entrée, viande garnie, followed by dessert.

The owner is charming and runs his restaurant with flair and good manners. If only, he sighed, there were more tourists around this year (1987). Perhaps his dream will come true – so go soon, before the crowds arrive. We can thoroughly recommend this restaurant.

Map 5A

PÉRONNE (Somme) 170 km SE of Calais; 35 km SW of Cambrai; 29 km NE of Roye

---

80200
 Sat.

11 km from the A 1.

A favourite stop. Péronne is an old, fortified town built on the confluence of the Cologne and the Somme and still affected by the commercial traffic of the Canal du Nord that runs to the north across the outskirts. The town was almost totally destroyed during the First World War and only fragments of the 16th–17th-century walls and city gate, Porte de Bretagne, remain. A 13th-century château has been partly restored and is open to the public in July and August.

Hostellerie des Remparts
(H)S(R)M
21 r. Beaubois
22.84.01.22
Rest. closed 3/
8–13/8
AE, DC, EC, V

The Hostellerie des Remparts has changed little, if at all, since *FE4* was here in 1984. Mme Drichemont still sits comfortably behind the high desk in the entrance hall of this charming 19th-century Logis de France. Good-sized, old-fashioned bedrooms cost from 160–185f, the best looking out on to the green bank below the ramparts, although those facing on the street are almost as quiet. Menus: 60f, 80f, 90f, 140f and 170f. On the 60f menu we ate hors d'oeuvres, moules and strawberry tart. Service is swift and efficient. Judging by the amount of people arriving to dine until late in the evening, the restaurant enjoys a considerable reputation locally.

'This lived up to the expectations from your recommendation. Comfortable rooms, excellent cuisine and friendly helpful and professional service. A delight to eat in the restaurant.' – Robert Duncan.

Auberge la Quenouille
(R)M
Ave. des
Australiens
22.84.00.62

1 km outside Péronne, set back from the road, off the N 17, direction Arras.

We liked both Bernard Thiery and his restaurant very much. Monsieur started his business 11 years ago; the house itself was built in 1925. He hails from La Rochelle and trained in Lille, Paris and Bordeaux, so there is a wealth of gastronomic experience in his art.

Closed Sun.;
Mon.; and at
the end of Jan.
AE, DC, EC, V

Menu costs 95f during the week and 145f at the weekend. 95f menu offers 9 escargots, côtes d'agneau, cheese and dessert.

Monsieur's recommended choices à la carte are: filet du sole farcis 'Auberge'; aiguillettes de canard sauce poivrade, pommes sarladaise; chèvre chaud, chiffonade de salade. Lots of energy and pride go into the running of this well-established restaurant. Guests are invited to inspect the kitchen – which looked gleaming and smelled delicious.

Le Saint-Claude
(HR)M
42 pl. Louis
Daudre
22.84.46.00
Closed Sun.
p.m. o.o.s
AE, DC, EC, V

In the main street and not a lot of traffic passing by. Although the hotel would be a second choice to Hostellerie des Remparts, it has a great deal of character, is comfortable and well thought of, and the restaurant enjoys a considerable gastronomic reputation.

The house dates from 1663 and traces of its origins, although it was badly damaged during the First World War, remain. It had been a hotel before 1914. Twelve years ago the place was extensively renovated. The modern entrance leads into a surprisingly elegant interior. Bedrooms (120–260f) are large and well furnished, reached by a winding, slightly tilted and creaking staircase.

Menus are 80f and 120f. On the 80f *menu gastronomique* that day were julienne de langue au vinaigre de cidre, onglet poêlé à l'échalote, fromage blanc à la crème, mousse au chocolat (it changes every day). Specialities of the house include terrine de canard; ficelle picarde; matelot d'anguille; assiette du terroir (poissons fumés de la région).

Map 7A   **PIERREFONDS** (Oise) 272 km SE of Calais

60350
(M) *Fri.*

14 km E of Compiègne by the D 973.

A small and attractive town set around a lake and dominated by its spectacular castle. For nearly three and a half centuries, the massive ruins of Louis d'Orléans' fortress had overhung the town. At the time of the Revolution, Napoleon III, a keen archaeologist, bought the romantic remains for under 3,000f and commissioned Viollet-le-Duc to turn the castle into an Imperial residence at a cost of a further 5 million francs, much of it coming off the civil list.

By 1857, the Gothic revival was in full swing. The work of Viollet-le-Duc (who restored among other buildings the great cathedral in Chartres) has been criticised – like that of his English contemporary Gilbert Scott – as being 'too perfect'. Whereas Pierrefonds is not in the true style of the feudal age, it is an exciting and competent example of how the 19th century considered that age should be. Viollet-le-Duc was a considerable scholar and, as he said himself, 'there are only too many ruins in France . . .'

Visits to the castle (in season) 10 a.m.–12 p.m. and 2–6 p.m. Closed all year on Tuesdays. (Out of season) open 10 a.m.–12 p.m. and 2–4.30 p.m.; and on all public holidays.

Hôtel des
Étrangers
(HR)S–M

A good hotel with charming bedrooms (90–140f), all very clean and well decorated; those at the front have views over the lake and up to the castle. You sleep here on condition that you eat in the hotel

10 r. de Beaudon, Cuisse La Motte 44.42.80.18 Closed. Sun. p.m.; Mon.; 1/ 1–20/2 V

dining-room. No problem: it is a large, comfortable room decorated *à la chasse* with small stuffed wild animals, an owl standing on a perch and the heads of wild dear looking gently down.

Menus at 48f, 60f and 80f. 48f menu features potage de légumes, langue de boeuf sauce piquant, brie ou fromage blanc ou dessert. M. Boulin, a great traveller during his holidays, has decorated the bar with trophies brought home from Africa and Asia: they seem a little incongruous with that Gothic pile outside. Monsieur is a cheerful, friendly man who speaks a little English.

Map 6D   **POURU-ST-REMY** (Ardennes) 300 km SE of Calais

08140
Douzy

8 km SE of Sedan on the N 43.

Hôtel de France (HR)S *24.26.30.02 Closed Wed.; 1/ 10–1/2 EC, V*

Small hotel on the N 43. Charming patron who first treated us to cups of excellent coffee in the café-entrance before furnishing us with the nitty-gritty. The house has been a hotel for the last fifty years and it is essentially a good, simple auberge with clean, spacious bedrooms and a low-priced restaurant. Monsieur was about to embark on extensive redecoration of the interior and plans to build a terrace outside for a few chairs and tables. Five rooms cost from 79f; and a special package which includes wine, dinner, bed and breakfat costs 120f each. Menu 41f (46f and 78f on Sundays).

Map 4B   **LE QUESNOY** (Nord) 152 km SE of Calais

59530
(M) *Fri.*

17 km SE of Valenciennes on the D 934.

A beautiful example of a fortified town, surrounded by greenery and water. In the Grande Place (which becomes totally emptied of cars around lunchtime) is the 18th-century Hôtel de Ville, with a fine bell-tower and a rousing carillon of 48 bells. Housed in it is the Tourist Office and, on the first floor, in the salle des fêtes, a remarkable Maori tribal sculpture that was sent to the town by the people of New Zealand.

In November 1918, in the final offensive of the Great War, the New Zealanders were immobilised below the town and under heavy bombardment from the Germans, who were entrenched in the Grande Place. On 4 November, two lieutenants of the New Zealand Rifle Brigade set a ladder against the walls, scaled the ramparts and led the liberation of the city. A memorial set on the spot reads 'In honour of the men of New Zealand through whose valour the town of Le Quesnoy was restored to France'. Within these lovely bastions is a green park where rooks caw and nest in the trees, and there are splendid views over jumbled back-yards and roof-tops. The fortifications were designed by Vauban in the 17th century and are remarkably well preserved: ask at the Tourist Office for a pack of leaflets that will guide you around the walls. Between the Grande Place and the park are the scant remains (the entrance gate, the cellars and some vestiges of the walls) of the mediaeval château of Marguerite de Bourgogne.

Hostellerie du Parc
(HR)M
7 r. Victor Hugo
27.49.02.42
Rest. closed Mon.
AE, EC

A fine small hotel and restaurant housed in an 18th-century building that was, until 1956, a private house. There are only six bedrooms (105–200f), so telephone ahead to see if one is available. We were very much taken with their attractive sprigged wallpaper, pristine white bedcovers, tall sunny windows and large, ceramic-tiled bathrooms. An old-fashioned, and somewhat leisured atmosphere throughout, like that of a private house.

The dining-room, with white-clothed tables set with flowers is charming. Menus cost from 63f up to 200f (the last includes apéritif and wine) and specialise in Flemish cooking. So renowned is the restaurant that people come from as far afield as Valenciennes and Maubeuge to dine here. Closed parking in a courtyard at the back. Friendly M. Pierchon took a lot of trouble showing us around. He has been here two years, and, incidentally, he speaks excellent English.

Arrowed for delightful setting, regional cooking.

Les Vanneaux
(R)L
Louvignies-
Quesnoy
27.49.15.40
Closed Mon.

In a road of suburban villas on the outskirts of the village: the D 934, direction Englefontaine, 2 km N of Quesnoy.

'La tradition culinaire d'hier dans un cadre d'aujourd'hui' proclaims the visiting card of M. and Mme Cappon, owners of Les Vanneaux for the last 18 years. Monsieur is now 64 and has been cooking since he was 15. The restaurant is very much in a *cadre d'aujourd'hui*.

No set menus: prices à la carte are in the slightly upper-price bracket and probably worth it – the restaurant's gourmet catchment area extends to the discerning city-dwellers of Valenciennes, 15 km away. Speciality of the house is foie gras de canard frais de Landes (88f). There are long windows running round two sides of the light and pretty dining-room, green curtains patterned with roses, pink tablecloths set with vases of flowers and a fine view of green and garden. A painting of vanneaux, described by Mme Cappon as 'oiseaux de chasse', were identified as 'lapwings'. But don't worry – they may shoot the poor things in France, but, at this restaurant anyway, you are unlikely to eat them.

Map 4B

QUIEVRECHAIN (Nord) 147 km SE of Calais; 12 km NE of Valenciennes

---

 Thur., Sat.

A large and unremarkable village whose only advantage to tourism is that it lies 3 km from the A 2. Coming from Belgium take the Onnaing exit; from Paris, leave at Crépin.

Hôtel le Petit Restaurant
(H)S
180 r. Jean Jaurès
27.45.46.06
V

This small hotel (11 bedrooms), owned by M. Dubois, is (strangely) not to be confused with the adjoining restaurant of the same name. Some co-ordination is apparent, however: parking for instance 'can be arranged with the restaurant'.

General impression was of a simple but rather shabby hotel with plain bedrooms. Pale yellow bedcover, stained and spotted, made an unfortunate initial impression; although a quick, sneaky look under them revealed clean bedlinen. Prices were comfortingly reasonable: 90f with bath; 70f with wash-basin. Possibly worth a night's stay, if only to dine in the acclaimed **Au Petit Restaurant** next door.

Au Petit Restaurant (R)M
182 r. Jean Jaurès
27.45.43.10
Closed Mon.;
Aug.
EC, V

M. Legrand opened this restaurant 21 years ago, turning it from an inauspicious turn-of-the-century private house into a charming and popular eating-place. Dark flowered wallpaper, pink and white tablecloths, flower-patterned plates. A large boar's head looks grimly down onto the few tables and chairs set aside for that preliminary apéritif.

Menus are 55.80f and 95f. The former includes saucisson de montagne, côte de porc garnie, cheese or dessert. Homard du vivier grillé beurre Nantais (lobsters bought off the boats in Roscoff) costs 35f for 100g (two people). Monsieur showed up his gleaming kitchen with great pride, where apricot and apple tarts were lying enticingly on stainless-steel shelves. Although there is room for up to 120 people in the three dining-rooms, at the weekend it is best to telephone ahead for a reservation; no problem during the week.

Map 4B

RAISMES (Nord) 140 km SE of Calais; 5 km NW of Valenciennes; 5 km S of St-Amand

59590
 Thur.

Exit Raismes from the A 23.

La Grignotière (R)M
6 r. Jean Jaurès
27.36.91.99
Closed Sun.
p.m. Mon.;
Aug.
AE, DC, V

M. Renoult, patron and chef, runs this cheerful restaurant that fronts on to the main road. Parking in the Place, nearby. La Grignotière means, loosely translated, 'He who nibbles nut'. The squirrel, Monsieur's mascot, is much in evidence: stuffed on the wall and printed on the admirable menus in the dining-room.

They cost from 90f, up to a gastronomic 140f. The 110f Sunday menu includes a half bottle of wine, beer or mineral water. Fish is the speciality. The dining-room is furnished with tapestry-covered, high-backed chairs round white-clothed tables; copper pans gleam dully on the walls, and the windows overlook the garden. A favourite restaurant for business lunches of *hommes d'affaires* from Valenciennes and St-Amand-les-Eaux.

Map 1B

RÊCQUES-SUR-HEM (Pas-de-Calais) 20 km SE of Calais

62820

A turning off the N 43, just by the Nordausques exit from the A 26; it's a tricky turn; best go on to the Cheval Noir to double back. The Château is well marked from all roads.

Le Château de Cocove (HR)M
21.82.68.29
AE, DC, EC, V
Parking

It must be a red-letter day for Calais to discover that at last a smart, new, and interesting hotel has opened up on its doorstep. Previously I have been stumped when asked where to head for a comfortable and spoiling weekend not far from the port. Now M. Calonne has provided the answer.

He and his wife came across the dilapidated 17th-century château by chance, during a walk some two years ago, fell in love with its elegant grey stone façade, and saw its potential as an hotel. Recruiting his brother, an architect, who lived on the premises while restoration was going on, they set about restoring the crumbling masonry, adapting the high-ceilinged salons to the requirements of a modern hotel, and rescuing the grounds from the encroaching jungle.

Now they have 22 light and airy bedrooms, a delightful dining-room and bar, and many many plans for future embellishments and improvements. The 'parc' in front of the house is being transformed into a 9-hole golf course, the 'potager' is already yielding the first vegetables and herbs for the restaurant, and sheep have been recruited to attack the undergrowth that chokes the orchard.

There is still a long way to go; the rooms are comfortable and well-equipped with mod. cons. like colour T.V.s and telephones, but there are few character-bestowing extras. M. Calonne intends to collect good pieces of furniture gradually, as and when he can find and afford them, and add them to the basic furnishings. Some of the more expensive rooms already boast a polished chest or pine cupboard that make all the difference between a homogenised plastic hotel and one with the owners' personality stamped upon it.

I regret that the ceilings have had to be lowered and the cornices lost, so that the heating might be effective, and that the fireplaces have been sealed up for the same reason, but can see why. This is not a luxury hotel, with prices to match; it is two-star* (see over), there are no pictures on the walls, the carpeting is basic, the bathrooms are uniformly white, with lino on their floors; the bedroom furnishings are all the same, but the fabrics are light and cheerful and the effect generally pleasing. They cost from 260–450f, all with bathrooms.

The dining-room has been the greatest success. The stone has been knocked out of the arches in one of the wings, to let in lots of light through the windows, the stone floor has been scrubbed to a pale yellow-grey, and the white cane chairs are a delightful change from the sombre tapestry of most aspiring French restaurants. It is already popular with locals, and I was the only non-French eating there. Here, as everywhere else in this establishment, the staff smiled. I suspect I shall soon be receiving letters on this very aspect. A friendly management and helpful staff are number-one priority at whatever level of readers' experiences. M. Calonne weaves his way amongst the tables, and I watched the diners' faces light up as he chatted to them all in turn. He speaks enough English to make us all feel at home. Gentle Mme Calonne takes the orders and gives advice, and the knowledgeable young sommelier, though impressively dressed in the black apron of his calling, is not above helping to take the dirty dishes to the kitchen. The young waitresses are well trained too – Calonne daughters doing duty when I was there.

The cooking is like the hotel – not quite there yet, but already so good that the outcome is in little doubt. The young chef is confident enough to try his hand at new ideas as well as old favourites and M. Calonne encourages him to use the best ingredients. Ultimately all the fresh veg. will come from the kitchen garden, so here is one restaurant that will never be on my black list for lousy légumes.

Most of the French seemed to go for the 90f menu, which gave them three good courses; I'd been saving up all day for the treat, so I tackled the 160f *gastronomique*. The mousse of sea trout and smoked salmon with red pepper sauce was O.K.ish – mousse a bit chewy, sauce not reduced enough – but the second-course fresh salmon was among the best I've ever tasted; if the quantity of fennel sauce had been reduced by four that too would have been sublime. Lamb noisettes with thyme were perfect – tender pink, flavour-full – and the rough purées of spinach, turnip and carrot were fine.

The sommelier knew all about the cheeses, picked by Philippe Olivier as the best in season, including some local choices, and there were lovely seasonal desserts – mint charlotte, peach tart, fruit gratins – all so good I had to ask advice from the sweet young waitress. She advised the chocolate marquise, and was not wrong. No house wine but a good choice of wine by the glass – unusual again. Cheapest otherwise is 55f.

M. Calonne was, or rather is, a wine merchant, and I have no doubt that the château's cellars influenced him in making the decision to buy. He has set up a display of fine wines down there, and finds that English visitors are only too pleased to buy their allowance here, under his expert guidance. This is not the place to buy gut-rot; there is some reliable Bordeaux, red and white on offer at 16f, but the Brits

apparently usually choose something classier, and go home boasting about their private French wine merchant.

I think that, even allowing for teething problems, the Château de Cocove and the Calonne family are quite exceptional. Their hotel is a beautiful building, set in peaceful grounds; their restaurant is attractive and serves food streets ahead of most hotel cooking; the position, just off the autoroute and the N 43, so near to Calais and St-Omer, make it ideal for an overnight stopover; the rooms, already comfortable and well equipped will be getting better all the time, and their price is reasonable for this quality; most of all, the Calonnes are trying hard. I am sure that my Hotel of the Year will be everyone's favourite very soon. Go while you can still get a booking.

> **To celebrate their nomination as Hotel of the Year, M. Calonne is making the following Special Offer to French Entrée readers.**
> **For two people: a double room for two nights (out of high season), four meals, two of which can be taken from the** *gastronomique* **menu, breakfasts – 1200f.**

* STOP PRESS: Since Pat Fenn's visit, Le Château de Cocove has been re-classified as a three-star establishment.

e Château de Cocove   Recques-sur-Hem.

Map 7C   **REIMS** (Marne) 282 km SE of Calais

Ⓜ *Mon.–Sat.*
*(various
locations)*

There's been a settlement here for over two thousand years. Some
say the city derives its name from a powerful Gallic tribe, the Remes,
who lived here at the time when Julius Caesar was busy conquering
Gaul (58-49BC); others favour the theory that it was named thus after
Remus, who is depicted on the Porte Mars, with his brother Romulus,
taking milk from the wolf.

It became the capital of a Roman province, the 2nd Belgian Empire.
Evidence of this impressive pedigree is still to be found – the remains
of the Porte Mars, the biggest triumphal arch in the Roman world,
and the Place du Forum, with its sunken gallery, are two, but the best
known of all are the caves in which much of the champagne is stored.

In 496 St-Remi, the Gallic apostle, converted and baptised Clovis
the Franc here, instituting the tradition that the kings of France
should be crowned in Reims. Joan of Arc forced here way through
the English territories to present Charles VII for his coronation in
1429.

Reims had need of a cathedral worthy of its status, and Notre
Dame is undoubtedly one of the great cathedrals of the world, a
superb example of Gothic architecture. Marking this site of the
baptism of Clovis, it was begun in 1211 and completed two centuries
later, in a remarkable unity of style.

The façade is particularly impressive, a setting for the great rose
window above the deep-set portals, surmounted by the Gallery of
Kings and the two towers. Decorating the doorways are fine
specimens of mediaeval statuary, sculpted in the 13th century,
including the instantly recognisable flirtatious 'Ange au sourire'. The
damage effected to these treasures by the Germans in the First
World War shocked the whole world, but they have been wisely
restored.

In dramatic contrast to this extravaganza is the dignified simplicity
of the interior, illuminated by that wonderfully rich 15th-century
glass and the tapestries of the same date that hang on the walls.

Just as impressive and in total contrast is the magnificent Basilica
of St-Remi, an ancient Benedictine abbey, constructed in the 11th
and 12th centuries on the site where St-Remi was buried. Here it is
the interior that I find most moving, the vast space of the abbey
exuding calm and peacefulness. Walk down the seemingly infinite
arcades and listen to your footsteps echo. Peer upwards past the
Romanesque columns, sculpted with bizarre animals, to the soaring
nave. The Gothic choir has four harmonious levels, on which the
12th-century glass shines down; surrounding it is a lovely and ornate
Renaissance screen, contrasting with the simplicity elsewhere. On
one wall is a thought-provoking tablet of all the kings, queens,
archbishops and nobility interred nearby.

The quartier of St-Remi, in one of the oldest parts of the city, is not
an easy one to find, and probably too far from the centre for all but
the sensibly-shod, car-allergic to walk. Odd though it seems to set off
in the opposite direction, the quickest and easiest way to drive there
is to get on to the autoroute, in the direction of Épernay, and turn off
at the exit marked St-Remi.

Reims.

Near the cathedral is the former archbishops' residence, the Palais du Tau, where once the kings of France feasted before their coronations; it is now a museum containing fragments of the monumental sculptures once installed outside the cathedral, as well as coronation souvenirs. The 13th-century chapel of the archbishops links the palace to the cathedral.

In June 1987 there began in Reims the most sophisticated 'Festival of Light' in the world, featuring the cathedral, its architecture and history of coronations and pageantry. At 10.30 every night laser beams point to each relevant detail of three separate programmes. 'A Cathedral of Light' is free; 'Cathedral of Coronations' costs 40f and 'Apocalypse' is 30f. For summer visitors to the city, I strongly recommend the booking of a seat (from the kiosk near the cathedral) at the first opportunity, in order not to miss this unique exploitation of modern science and historic splendour.

Everyone visiting Reims for the first time will want to see at least one champagne cellar. Down beneath the city, deep in endless labyrinths of chalky caverns, is another world. Visits to some, like Ruinart, the oldest cellars of all, are by private appointment only; some, like Piper Heidseick, let a train take the strain; some, like Mumm, give free *dégustations*. All will give one of the best freebies I know – an hour's enlightenment of a world phenonemon.

Most of the essentials for making champagne found assembled uniquely in Champagne, I will leave to the expert John Doxat to explain (see p.187). I would just point out that the chalk in the soil is twice blessed; not only does it generate the special conditions for the viticulture that give champagne its individuality, but it furnishes the Champenois with perfect cellarage, easy to hew out, needing no air conditioning. The temperature remains constant throughout the year, an absolute requirement for storing the wine. Beneath Reims are 120 miles of such cellars.

The most remarkable – and a visit to these should be contrived if at all possible – are the chalk pits, or crayères, quarried to a depth of 60ft by Roman slaves, in pyramid shape, so that the minimum amount of chalk should be exposed to the crumbling effect of the air and frost. At the end of the 18th century Claud Ruinart acquired 250 chalk pits, which had not been reopened since Roman times. He cleverly converted them to ideal cellars by excavating further down to 100 ft and linking the pits by a series of galleries. Subsequently glass tiles were substituted for the stone slabs that had previously closed the pit entrances, so that now the light filters through and is emphasised by the white chalk, creating an unforgettable cathedral-like effect that never fails to dazzle the bemused visitor.

Some one hundred years ago the indefatigable Madame Pommery (see **Boyer**) persuaded the Ruinart descendants to sell her 120 of these cellars, and proceeded to let her imagination run riot. Between the seemingly infinite galleries she added arches in different styles – Roman, Norman and Gothic – and named them after the world's leading champagne consumer cities – London, Rome, New York, etc. She then commissioned an artist to carve bacchanalian scenes out of the chalk in elaborate bas-relief; her final fling was to construct a splendid staircase of 116 steps down into her sugar icing domain.

Best pay a visit to the efficient Tourist Office in the r. Jadart to check on times and to get general advice on which cellars are receiving visitors.

Altogether Reims is a city hard to label. Wartime devastation has taken its toll, but glorious squares like the pl. Royale remain and lend considerable character, and the restoration of the cathedral and abbey have been discreet and convincing. The northern climate lacks gaiety, but there is an abundance of open-air tables for conviviality. It's a large city and yet its interesting section can be comfortably covered on foot (with the possible exception of St-Remi). Away from this area, the streets tend to be grey and depressing, but the park by the station is an unusually extensive stretch of cool greenness and flowerbeds (good for picnics). It is a tourist centre, yet its hotels are undistinguished (but its restaurants are many and varied).

For the tourist the heart of the city is the pl. Drouet d'Erlon. From the fountain to the bvd Foch can be found a series of hotels, restaurants and many lively cafés, like the Lorraine and the Gaulois. I find it particularly agreeable because it is the kind of hotchpotch you only seem to find in France, with superb *boulangeries*, *chocolatiers*, wine merchants, *charcuteries*, hotels, a fresh pasta shop, all mixed up with *tabacs*, bars, opticians, *pharmacies* and a wonderful walk-round beauty shop where you can get gallic make-up advice, or at the very least a free spray of any perfume that suits your mood that day.
Elsewhere in the town, the main shopping street is the r. du Vesle, with all the cheaper shops, chain stores and even a Marks and Spencer for the homesick.
Leading off is the cours J.-B. Langlet, with probably the city's most elegant shops and a super old-fashioned chocolate shop, **La Petite Friande**, where they've been making superb chocs for 150 years. Champagne and champenois specialities on sale too. Next door is **Aux Ducs de Gascogne**, for a special take-home present of foie gras.
Parking is diabolical. The av. Foch has hundreds of parking spaces under its avenues of chestnut trees, but because they are free they are usually taken up all day with office workers. Better try further up by the markets or cruise around until you find a meter.
Two specialised shops/caves/cafés I can recommend are:

Le Marché aux Vins
3 pl. Jean Bourgeois
26.40.12.12

An excellent place to buy duty-frees. Between the halles and the pl. du Forum, with private parking. Here is a clever little *musée du vin*, not to be missed by anyone thirsting for spoon-fed vinous knowledge, and well-laid-out displays, usually with some special promotion. It is a reliable place to buy your champagne, at very fair prices.

La Boutique de Périgord
av. Drouet d'Erlon

Here is a delightful little shop which sells all the specialities of the Perigord region – like foie gras, *confits*, preserves of all kinds. Behind the counter are six tables at which you can sample before you buy. There are various kinds of foie gras, costing 50f for two slices; a glass of Sauterne goes well with them. Otherwise there is a 49.90f menu, on which I ate a salade Périgoudine, with slices of smoked duck-breasts and walnuts and a substantial casserole of goose *confit* and melting haricot beans. A pichet of Périgord wine costs 16f.

➤ **Hôtel Crystal**
(HR)M
86 pl. Drouet d'Erlon
26.88.44.44.
AE, DC, V

I have no doubt that this is where I would choose to stay in Reims. The trouble is a lot of other customers agree with me; it is small, so often full. It is a friendly little hotel, with the inestimable virtue, in a city, of an interior garden, where you can eat in fine weather and which separates and insulates the hotel from the city noise. I know nothing about the food, but the restaurant looked pleasant enough and there is no obligation to eat in anyway.

To reach the bedrooms, you ascend in a bird-cage of a lift, very French. The rooms are all different, all pleasant, and cost 250f with bath, 145f without.

Arrowed for its position and its character.

Grand Hôtel du Nord (H)M
75 pl. Drouet d'Erlon
26.47.39.03
Closed 24/12–4/1
AE, DC, EC, V

An old-fashioned hotel, modernised to a good standard of comfort. Good value at 143–238f.

Continental
(HR)M
93 pl. Drouet d'Erlon
26.40.39.36
Closed 18/12–4/1
EC, V

I chose to stay here, and rather wished I hadn't when I saw my dreary, dark and shabby room, which, at 260f, I thought expensive. However, the owners and staff are all particularly friendly, it is conveniently situated near station and shops and has a very good restaurant. It is a huge rambling building, on several levels, and its 60 rooms differ somewhat, but none of them is exactly luxurious. The cheapest single is 180f.

L'Univers
(HR)M
41 bvd Foch
26.88.68.08
Rest. closed Sun. p.m.
AE, DC, EC, V

An even better restaurant here, well worth considering even for those staying elsewhere.

It overlooks the very busy bvd Foch, so lower rooms might be noisy, but certainly the top floors are high enough to be protected, and they look out to the park.

Again an old hotel, but the rooms are good-sized and comfortably refurbished. Good value at 200f for a double with bath and 130f without.

Paix
(HR)M
9 r. Buriette
26.40.04.08
AE, DC, EC, V

Just off the pl. Drouet d'Erlon, an agressively modern hotel, whose receptionist has agressively modern manners. The rooms are bleak and functional, but well equipped, and there is a swimming pool and restaurant, so would probably suit the overnight businessman who wanted to work off his expense account lunch and go straight to bed (248–305f).

Hôtel Welcome
(H)S
29–31 r.
Buriette
26.47.39.39
Closed 20/12–5/1
AE, EC, V

The only hotel in the 'S' category I found to recommend. This one is central and cheap. The 70 rooms, if undistinguished, are perfectly adequate and well equipped, at 160f.

Boyer (Les
Crayères)
(HR)L
64 bvd Henry
Vasnier
26.82.80.80
Closed Mon.;
Tues. lunch; 22/
12–12/1
CB, AE, DC, EC

Too often a long-anticipated meal at one of the great restaurants in the world can be a let-down. Expectations are too high, prestige is too puffed up, acceuil lacks conviction, intimidation numbs the appetite. Perhaps the chef has become complacent and/or greedy; perhaps the client should never have hoped for perfection. If this has been the picture of past disillusionment, may I urge a visit to Boyer to redress the balance. Here is the nearest to gastronomic perfection I am likely to find on this earth.

I suppose first impressions always set the tone of the evening and there could hardly be a finer setting for a distinguished meal than Les Crayères, the 19th-century château to which the lucky Boyers have recently moved, ten minutes from the heart of the city, yet seemingly in deepest countryside. This happy arrangement was conceived by Louise Pommery, who ran the great champagne house of Pommery & Gréno for 30 years after her founder husband died in 1858. Before her own death in 1890 she bought the land opposite the Pommery château headquarters and set about establishing a landscape fit for the beautiful château she hoped her descendants would build there. They fulfilled her wishes about the turn of the century and the present Les Crayères is the result.

It's an upliftingly attractive as well as impressive building, perfectly in proportion, very formal, very French, built to take full advantage of Mme Pommery's 7 bosky hectares, sloping down towards the dome of St-Remi. On each side of its garden façade are glass rotundas built out on to the terrace. One houses the bar, the other the most prized table in one of the stunning dining-rooms.

There is little doubt that Gérard Boyer's talents as a chef and the location of his restaurant are outstanding. The bonus is that the ambience and accueil are just as attractive. Gérard and his wife Elyane, unlike many gastro-megastars, are rarely absent from kitchen and dining-rooms. Everyone I spoke to who had eaten often chez Boyer confirmed that their welcome and concern are both genuine and constant. This seems to be reflected in the attitude of the entire staff, who are totally professional but manage to be nice with it. As a single female diner, if anyone were going to find out differently it would be me. Not so.

So, after a *coupe* in the rotunda (and it would be inappropriate to order anything else here) and with all auspices favourable, it's into the serious bit. If you have to ask what the prices are, you can't afford it. This meal is going to cost around £50 a head and if that hurts, best forget it. All I can say is take out a double mortgage, live on berries for a week, cancel the double-glazing – you won't regret it.

I agonised over the decisions. The carte is not long, but every item seemed indismissable. In fact what it does not make clear is that you can split your order, having a half-portion of two choices on both starters and mains, with the knowledgeable maître d', Werner Heil, advising on a suitable balance.

So I kicked off with half the terrine de poireaux I had originally ordered, followed by a *dégustation* of Breton langoustines with fresh morilles, then a whole portion of Rouennais duck breast cooked with olives and artichokes. I won't go on about how sublime they all were,

because for once words fail me. It's hard to describe simple obvious virtues, like freshness, delicacy, judgment, balance; they were all present, topped up with a shining kitchen genius which is instantly recognisable but impossible to define. Perfection in other words.

Those suspicious of what the new cooking has to offer should benefit from a pilgrimage here. Gérard Boyer has effortlessly taken on board its broader precepts, without for one minute lapsing into its

Boyer Reims.

clichés. He is still a comparatively young chef, who I'm sure will continue to learn, assimilate and discard culinary ideas new and old until he hangs up his toque.

Certainly the dessert trolly would shut up those who say they never get enough to eat nowadays. The waiter will ask if you prefer a selection based on fruit or on chocolate. If you choose the former, your plate will be decorated with tastes of gâteaux, tarts, sorbets, soufflés of whatever fruits are in season; if you plump (!) for chocolate, it will come dark and bitter in slices of terrine, charlotte, mousse, relieved by vanilla-bean ice-cream. How clever.

The arrow is for excellence in a class of its own.

The rooms echo the standard of the restaurant. It is difficult to imagine any more comfortable or beautiful. Furnished in Louis XVIII style, they are not only luxurious but tasteful with it. Breakfasts are as exquisite. One runs out of superlatives, and that goes for the prices too; 897–1321f for two people *and* 15 per cent service charge.

➤ Le Florence
(R)L
43 bvd Foch
26.47.12.70
Closed Sun.
p.m.; 20/7–11/8
AE, CB, DC, EC

Mme Maillot and her staff were celebrating when I visited them, having just won the Gault-Millau Clé d'Or award for culinary excellence. Justly awarded, I consider, since Le Florence has all the requirements on my list for an arrow. It is extremely elegant, in a typically French *hôtel particulier* facing the bvd Foch, yet light and airy, thanks to its tall windows, pale walls and a little rear garden, where lunch on a fine day, in the heart of the city, is a great pleasure. The welcome is warm and efficient, and the service irreproachable. Prices for such a standard of comfort and cooking are reasonable; there is a good 160f menu, or a 310f *Repas des Gourmets*, or 240f with half a bottle of champagne.

On the cheapest of these I ate an original and refreshing *soupe* of melon and grapefruit flavoured with ratafia, then sea trout cooked in champagne, an excellent cheese selection and passion-fruit mousse. Yves Méjean, the young and talented chef, student of the great Michel Guérard, changes his menus frequently; on them you might find a rich pot au feu of foie gras with a purée of garlic, a chunk of salmon with all its juices preserved by being cooked in a casing of salt, or a fillet of beef in local red wine. The wine list is equally distinguished.

Arrowed for excellent cooking, in central Reims.

Le Chardonnay
(R)M–L
84 av.
d'Épernay
26.06.08.06
Closed Sat.
lunch; Sun.; 22/
12-13/1, 4/8–4/9
AE, CB, DC, EC

Dominique Giraudeau, an ex Boyer chef, cooks here in what used to be Boyer's restaurant. Here is classic French cooking in a pleasant restaurant overlooking first a garden, then countryside. Very popular with the Rémois (so booking advisable), who recognise the good value of the 160f menu, with items like salmon marinated with dill, duck with cherries, rib of beef with Bouzy wine. I particularly appreciate being able to buy wine by the glass, a custom rare in France.

Le Vigneron
(R)M
pl. Paul Jamot
26.47.00.71
Closed Sat.
lunch; Sun.; 23/
12–21/1, 27/7–
19/8.

Something different. Patron Hervé Liégart has created a museum of Champagne wines in his charming little restaurant, decorated with ancient tools and implements used in the wine trade. His cellar is unique in France, in representing 150 different *marques* of champagne (brut, sans année, millesimé, blanc de blancs, rosé, cuvée de prestige, côteau champenois).

His menu too is strongly regional, featuring simple country dishes, like potée champenoise, and andouille from Troyes. Don't bother with the desserts though.

Carte only. Allow 180f and expect an agreeable and edifying evening.

Le Colbert
(R)M
64 pl. Drouet
d'Erlon
26.47.55.79
AE, CB, DC, EC

Reims is well endowed with restaurants in the 'L' and 'S' categories but is a bit thin in the middle. This probably says a lot about the composition of its year-round inhabitants, who after all make up the bread-and-butter trade. A prosperous wine merchant said: 'When we want to celebrate a special occasion we have Boyer – otherwise we entertain at home'; a hotel worker said: 'We eat in our neighbourhood bistros or a brasserie'. Le Colbert fills the gap. Usefully open at weekends, when most of the other restaurants shut their doors, unrepentantly middle-of-the-road, with reliable provincial cooking, in a reliable provincial setting, at reliable provincial prices. Menus start at 63f, bu the 84f version represents the best value.

Le Verzenay
(R)M
Cour de la Gare
S.N.C.F.
26.47.54.46

Once again, cherchez la gare for a sure-fire good meal. At Reims the station buffet is too good to keep for the travellers. It's an elegant comfortable restaurant, with an intriguing rear view of trains pulling in and out of the platforms. The chef, Christian Gross, cooks sophisticated food based on regional dishes and wines, like scallops in champagne, fillets of sole Dom Pérignon, and calves sweetbreads flavoured with ratafia, on menus from 75f. Usefully open every day.

Le Cornouaille
(R)M
217 r. du
Barbatre
26.85.57.59
Closed Sun.
p.m.; Mon.;
Aug.

Reims is a long way from the sea and its fish restaurants are few, but Marie-Angèle Le Gouider, patronne of Le Cornouaille, comes from Brittany and buys with the benefit of her familiarity with all things fishy of prime quality. Fish, as in England, is an expensive commodity all over France, so if you wish to try her specialities, like fricasée of lobster, or a tart stuffed with oysters and leeks, or a gratin of prawns, you must expect a bill of about 250f for three courses à la carte. However, there is a daily fish-of-the-day on a 60.20f menu, which would make a cheap alternative.

La Champagnière
(R)M
27 r. des
Créneaux
26.85.17.42
Closed Sun.;
Mon.; 15/7–10/8

The prettiest restaurant in Reims. In an old beamed house not far from St-Remi, in the St-Nicaise *quartier*, Martial Derraux has sited his little restaurant. He was once 'Champion de France des desserts', so here is one place where you should leave room for pud. Before that it's all pretty good too, with weekly changing menus at 53.50f at lunchtime and at 102.50f otherwise, comprising a dozen entrées, four *plats garnis*, regional cheeses and the justly famous desserts. An arrow for good value in a delightful setting.

➤ **Le St-Nicaise**
(R)S
8 pl. St-Nicaise
26.85.01.26
Closed Sun.
p.m.

If you've been visiting St-Remi or the Taittinger champagne cellars, refreshment is near at hand. Le St-Nicaise is one of those little French bistros outwardly unexciting, inwardly rewarding. You go through the bar (tables outside for fair-weather drinking), full of locals, to a little dining-room, where the friendly family Fauster dish up splendid value meals at 45f, 60f and 90f.

On the cheapest menu I ate a fine salade composée with chicken livers and croutons, a fillet of haddock with copious veg, and a selection from the cheeseboard, which was left on the table with an invitation to eat as much of the good-nick cheeses and fromage blanc as I wished. A demi pichet of house plonk cost me 7f. You can't go wrong.

Arrowed for excellent value in this category.

➤ **L'Impromptu**
(R)S
18 av. de Paris
26.08.44.73
Closed Sat.
lunch

This Parisian-style bistro is still probably the best value in Reims, but has recently been written up by Gault-Millau and is in danger of becoming fashionable. Go soon and in the charming atmosphere of the first-floor dining-room, all *fin-de-siècle* old rose, or on the large terrace in summer, you will eat for 65f a menu that includes a terrine of chicken livers, home-made black sausage, cheese and sorbet.

For 100f you get snails or Bayonne ham, duck with green peppers and an assortment of desserts, and the carte is getting more and more ambitious all the time. An arrow for a fun atmosphere, excellent food at currently affordable prices (but for how long?).

Le Boulingrin
(R)S
1 r. du Champ
de Mars
26.47.39.01
Closed Sun.

Another good bet for honest no-nonsense food at honest no-nonsense prices in a site near the central markets. Le Boulingrin is one such, a large *brasserie* alongside Reims' *halles centrales*, with a very untouristy clientele, both in its bar and in its somewhat characterless and harshly-lit restaurant. Open late at night, it would be a good choice for those who wish to eat quickly, one dish perhaps, without any fuss, but for those with more time, the 75f menu is good value. It changes every week but the choice is always between three entrées (house pâtés are good), three meat dishes (like coq au vin or stuffed pigs' trotters), with cheese or pudding. Carafe wine is 27f.

Le Jardin de Rome
(R)S
66 pl. Drouet
d'Erlon
26.88.52.33

A pretty, light, latticed little restaurant, specialising in salads and pasta dishes. Good for a simple lunch.

Map 6C | **RETHEL** (Ardennes) 231 km SE of Calais; 39 km NE of Reims

08300
Ⓜ *Thur.*

44 km SW of Charleville-Mézières on the N 51; a busy market town.

Au Sanglier des Ardennes
(HR)M

In the bar there is a photograph of this long-established hotel taken in 1902 and still identifiable, although the town was destroyed during two world wars and the hotel itself rebuilt in 1946.

1 r. Pierre-Curie *24.38.45.19* *Rest. closed* *Sun.; 24/12–3/1* *DC, EC, V*	Good, big bedrooms (105–230f), with high ceilings, are modern and well decorated and reached by way of a wide, wooden staircase. Specialities on the menus (58f and 98f) include gibier and boudin blanc, and there is a wide selection of other dishes.

Map 6A	**RETHONDES** (Oise) 260 km SE of Calais; 17 km E of Compiègne

---

60153	On the D 81 just north of the N 31 Compiègne–Soissons road. A village in the forest of Compiègne, not far from the Clairière de l'Armistice.

Auberge du **Pont** (R)M *44.85.60.24* *Closed Sun.* *and Mon. p.m.;* *Tues.; 3 weeks* *in Sept.* *V*	A good little restaurant by the bridge that crosses the Aisne. There are 45 *places* in the attractive dining-room that is well furnished with white cloths on the tables, beams and flowery curtains. Beyond are a garden and trees: a relaxing, rural scene. Menus (130f, 180f and 425f *dégustation*) are essentially *cuisine nouvelle*: 'chair de tourteaux frais en feuilles d'épinards et coulis de crustacés; escalope de foie gras chaud de canard et petits radis roses confits au vinaigre de framboises; le grand dessert (pâtisseries et sorbets maison) . . .' If the food lives up to these splendid descriptions, it should be a good-value eating place in the gastronomic bracket. Mme Blot organises the menus while her husband Alain executes them in the kitchen.

Map 5D	**ROCROI** (Ardennes) 261 km SE of Calais

08230	18 km SW of Haybes on the D 877.

Le Commerce (HR)S *pl. Aristide-* *Briand* *24.54.11.15* *Closed 5/1-10/2;* *Mon. o.o.s.* *V*	If you want a thoroughly French old-fashioned little hotel, the sort that features in old tales of travel – this is it. The hotel was built in 1764 and, like the other buildings in the centre of this little market town, it mercifully escaped the destruction of the wars. Upstairs, there are nine good, simple rooms with big beds, old furniture, flowered wallpaper and tall, double doors. Downstairs, is a café-entrance room, much favoured by locals, with banquettes, tiled floor and large, chromium-plated bar. Beyond that, a dining-room, large enough to seat 60 people, where menus cost 60f, 95f, 100f and à la carte. 100f menu looked a good bet: salade Ardennaise, sanglier (*suivant arrivage*), fromage de Rocroi (evil-smelling, but delicious), dessert au choix. Very friendly and helpful owners.

Map 6A	**ROYE** (Somme) 223 km SE of Calais; 74 km S of Arras

---

80700 (M) *Fri.*	Autoroute A 25 exit 12. Small market and industrial town, with an important sugar refinery.

Hôtel Ste-Geneviève
(HR)S
9 r. d'Amiens
22.87.10.65

'This is a very old, probably 17th-century house on the main street and certainly something different. Run by an old lady, Mme Carpentier Vasset, with the real personal touch.' – Annabel Greenwood.

The Ste-Geneviève is an old favourite with the British and bully for them, because it's a charming institution, not over-publicised in other guides. It's cream-washed and half-timbered, with lots of character, not least on the part of its venerable patronne, who takes great pride in her hotel and does most of the cooking – all fresh, nothing frozen – herself.

But one reader has a valid grumble: *'This year's stay left much to be desired. After our evening meal – very good – we informed Madame we would like to leave early next morning. She was most irritable. We had only requested to leave at 7 a.m. and this in the past had never been a problem. It was only later in the day we realised that we had been overcharged'.* So perhaps it's all getting too much for Madame Carpentier Vasset.

Rooms 50f with shower and 80f with bath must be bargains. The food is simple but good, and the menu costs only 46f.

Motel des Lions
(HR)M
Rte Rosières
22.87.20.61
AE, DC, EC, V
Garage

It goes against the grain to include a motel that everyone can find for themselves, but this one would certainly make an easy overnight stop in an area short of accommodation, just off the autoroute. What is more it has a better-than-average restaurant, the Relais de Santerre. Functional rooms cost 270f and there is a *soirée étape*, which includes dinner, at 450f for two people.

The restaurant is run by the Dillon family, and uses regional ingredients on menus at 80f and 125f. Try flamiche Beauvaisienne. Fillets of haddock are lightly curried, noisettes of lamb come with a sauce contrived from avocados and there is a trolley of desserts.

La Central
(HR)S–M
36 r. d'Amiens
22.87.11.05
AE, DC, EC

'We found our room extremely noisy, but the ones at the back were quiet. All rooms had showers but otherwise were not particularly inviting. Just adequate for a night's stopover. However the restaurant Le Florentin on the ground floor was prettily decorated with proper napkins and real flowers and attractive white chairs. A pleasant room to relax in after a long day in the car. There were some excellent specialities of the region and it was full of locals.' – Annabel Greenwood.

➤ La Florentin
(R)M
36 r. d'Amiens
22.87.11.05
Closed Sun.
p.m.; Mon.; 23/
12–3/1; 30/3–6/4

Definitely one up on the '2 étoiles tourisme' with which Le Central is classified. The dining-room has been newly decorated with trompe l'oeil marble columns, but the prices remain modest. Denis Devaux cooks regional dishes on menus starting at 65f (weekdays only). Others at 85f or 110f on Sundays might include some interesting items like a 'choucroute de la mer' or a magret of duck with pears and ginger. The wines too are good value. Not nearly so well known as La Flamiche, but a valuable alternative, arrowed for good value.

'It is Italian in style inside, like a pavilion, large room, high ceiling, columns, very nicely decorated and high standard of presentation. Menus are excellent, typically: brill in lovely creamy sauce, followed

by veal kidneys à la moutarde and excellent desserts. Service efficient but very friendly, and they were busy.

'Must also take into account our circumstances – on motorbike, wet day, arrived at restaurant soaked, dispirited and bit muddy, walked in timidly (as it is a nice place), but they were very kind and did not make us feel out of place in the elegant surroundings.'

La Flamiche
(R)L–M
18 pl. de l'Hôtel de Ville
22.87.00.56
Closed Sun.; Mon.; 19/12–19/1
AE, DC, EC

'The best table in the Somme', affirm all the guides, and they may well be right. The young chef Wilfred Travet uses only the best ingredients and cooks them *à point*. He uses eel from the Somme, fish from Boulogne, wild mushrooms from the nearby woods. His salmon is barely poached, just to the point of retaining its juices without being in any way raw, then served with a light creamy sauce. One could call his cooking generous modern.

The weekday menu at 150f is the one to go for. Otherwise it's 320f or the carte. The portions are so lavish that it is perfectly feasible to share one between two and there are no eyebrows raised.

The elegant and stylish restaurant, with its beige and pink decor and collection of wooden ducks, and helpful services, make this one hard to fault, and it is arrowed accordingly.

Le Croix d'Or
(R)M
123 rte de Paris
22.87.11.57
Closed Wed.; 1/8–24/8
AE, DC, EC, V
Parking

Suggested only in the event of a Sunday evening stop, when both the Flamiche and the Florentin are closed *'Wooden panelled dining-room with stags' head on the wall, pink linen tablecloths, several dogs wandering around. Friendly management, but they shut up shop early.'* – Annabel Greenwood. Others readers have been very happy to eat here.

Map 4B

ST-AMAND-LES-EAUX (Nord) 122 km SE of Calais

59230
(M) *Wed.*

14 km NW of Valenciennes on the D 169. Exit 3, 4 or 5 on the A 23.

A busy, lively little town set on the borders of Flanders and Hainut. Long before you even reach its outskirts, you can see the majestic, baroque abbey tower rising above the old weathered roof-tops. It is all that remains of the ancient abbey rebuilt in the 17th century by Abbot Nicolas de Bois, of whom it has been said: 'He had the ideas of a king or of an emperor'. Even today, these somewhat crumbling remnants of his work seem more like the remains of a royal palace than of an ecclesiastical building. The tower dominates the Grande Place and, indeed, most of the town. Leave your car in the ample parking space in front (you can't get lost with that tall tower to orientate you): St-Amand repays exploration on foot.

The Tourist Office is situated in the tower (27.48.67.09). Among much of interest to see on the different floors above it, is the Museum of Porcelain: a display of fine bone china and pottery made in the town between 1705 and 1950. A spiral staircase of 362 steps leads up to the belfry whence there is a wonderful view of the surrounding countryside. Here is suspended the great bell, Amanda, which was forged in the 17th century and weighs 4,650 kg. The carillon of 47 bells rings out each day at midday: a tuneful cascade of sound that lasts half an hour. In the early 19th century it was played from 11 to 11.30 a.m. to tell workers in the fields that it was time for the midday meal. You may watch the *carillonneur* operating the mechanism any day except Tuesday, from 1 April–30 September. And so seriously is this form of music taken that, in its College of Music, St-Amand has created the first class in France for carillon studies.

Elsewhere in the narrow streets (particularly in the rues de Bruille, de Condé and de Wocq) there are houses that date from the 18th and 19th centuries, where you can catch the flavour of the old St-Amand. Lots of attractive shops, a certain amount of traffic and several restaurants renowned for their cuisine.

Hôtel La Tour
(H)M
19 r. Thiers
27.48.45.31
Closed. Sun.
Lunch; 15/8–1/9
EC, V

M. Napionteck (who also owns the supermarket across the way) is the patron of this cheerful hotel. There are 17 rooms: all bright and light with modern furniture and decoration. Carpets a little worn here and there; but there *is* a lift to the three floors, rather a bonus, we thought, for a small French provincial hotel.

Parking is in the street or near the church (wherever you can find a place). The Grande Place itself is but a short walk away.

Brasserie Alsacienne
(R)M
23 Grande Place
27.48.50.62
Closed Sun., Mon. and Tues. p.m.; 14/7–15/8
AE, DC, EC, V

A two-hundred-year-old restaurant on the Grande Place. Old wood panelling and a big fireplace make for an attractive, old-fashioned, rustic atmosphere. Unsuccessful in his attempt to convert the townspeople to the rarified cuisine that he had learned during his sojourn at the Belle Époque in Lille, M. Buisine has formulated a *cuisine bourgeoise* apparently well suited to the purses and tastes of the most discerning Amandinois. Menus cost 54f, 75f and 96f, and offer selections from a wide choice of dishes. A sample 54f menu includes terrine de foie de volaille, followed by poularde pochée, sauce suprême, and cheese or dessert to finish.

La Mandigotte
(R)M
68 r. Thiers
27.48.21.29
EC, V

Six years ago, Nicolas Dupont turned this corner house (once a flower shop) into a popular and much acclaimed restaurant. *Where* does he get his energy? He not only organises the kitchen, but is to be found looking after his guests in the dining-room, and is open, both for lunch and dinner, day-in and day-out.

Menus cost 68f, 82f, 120f and 168f and (except for Saturday evening and Sunday) a quarter bottle of wine, beer or mineral water is included.

From the 68f menu, we ate tomato soup, grilled lamb, and dessert, and drank mineral water 'Source de Clos de l'Abbaye', bottled in St-Amand Thermal and said to be good for rheumatism, arthritis etc. Other items on the menu included six escargots en terrine, andouillette à la Dijonnaise, foie de veau à l'ail doux, ragouts de poissons frais . . .

When M. Dupont made the conversion, he extended the dining area from the original flower shop. Beyond this he built another restaurant: **Le Perigourdin**, 4 pl. de l'Église, 27.48.62.52 (closed Mondays and Saturday mid-day).

Both restaurants have their own entrance but share the same kitchen and, I presume, M. Dupont. Mon cher Nicolas, you worry me! Please take the occasional holiday!

Le Bergerie
(R)M
403 r. de
Vaucelle
27.48.67.92
Closed Tues.
and every p.m.
except Sat.

Coming from St-Amand-les-Eaux in the direction of Lille, Le Bergerie is on the right of the road, on the outskirts of the town. Surroundings are peaceful and rural.

Running true to its name, the restaurant was once an old sheepfold. Built in 1860, the buildings (stables, barn and homestead) were grouped around a yard in the style of the old Flemish farms. Twelve years ago the very friendly M. Lorimier opened the restaurant, turning the barn into a *salle de réunion* and the stables into the simply furnished dining-room. The floor is paved with ceramic tiles and the walls are whitewashed or wood panelled, in the rural style. Menus cost 55f, 70f, 93f and 120f. The kitchen is the domain of Madame Lorimier, who, Monsieur admits, is 'the boss'. On the 60f menu she offers turbot au concombre, soufflée aux fruits de mer, ris de veau aux pommes . . .

St-Gobain – The Forest

Oak and beech shelter herds of deer: in the season, the hunt meets two or three times a week, as indeed it has since the time of Louis XV. There are signposted rides deep into forest glades. In the village of Prémontré is the vast abbey complex founded in the 12th century by St Norbert, rebuilt in the 18th century and now used as a psychiatric hospital. Follow the road through Suzy for the D 55 and the ruins of the 14th-century abbey of St-Nicolas-aux-Bois: the road follows the moat that once helped protect the abbey walls, and the jagged outline of the monks' lodging stands in private grounds behind a little château. The surroundings are magnificent: deep woods and sloping meadows filled with flowers. When we went there in late spring, the forest was echoing with birdsong and hundreds of cuckoos were literally shouting from the trees.

Just south of St-Nicolas-aux-Bois, 400 metres to the west of the D 55, is La Croix Seizine. On this spot in 1256 the violent Enguerrand IV, Sire of nearby Coucy-le-Château, hanged three young Flemish noblemen, studying at the abbey, for poaching game. For this action – high-handed even in those days – he was brought to trial and, although he escaped the death penalty, was imprisoned 'during Louis IX's pleasure': a famous 13th-century experimental case which shook the equanimity of the bad barons who were becoming unbearbly autocratic.

Map 6B   **ST-GOBAIN** (Aisne) 230 km SE of Calais

02410
(M) *Sun.*

30 km S of St-Quentin, 18½ km W of Laon by the D 7.

St-Gobain was one of those early Irish missionaries whose faith drove him far from home. He is buried in the churchyard. The town of St-Gobain is famous for the manufacture of glass (Louis XIV founded the industry in 1692), which is exported far and wide.

➤ **Hôtel Roses de Picardie**
(H)S
11 r.
Clémenceau
23.32.88.74
EC, V

How nice to meet someone who actually prefers us, the English tourists, to the French variety! The French, Mme Maroigner told us, expect breakfast in bed, make a lot of noise . . . Madame speaks good English, learned as an *au pair* in England in her youth.

Two and a half years ago, she and her husband built this small hotel out of a café. The bedrooms (110–150f) are enchanting: spotlessly clean, decorated with pretty chintz and attractive bedlinen and all decorated by Monsieur himself. We slept in the most expensive (150f), with tiled bathroom en suite and a little kitchen. It was the back of the house (those in front are probably just as quiet) and the view was over terraced vegetable gardens and fruit trees to the tall spire of the church and the old chimneys of the little glass-making factory. Nothing to disturb the peace in the morning except for birdsong and the cooing of doves. Enclosed parking above the terrace below the bedroom windows.

Arrowed for good value in the 'S' category, with friendly helpful owners, in an attractive situation.

➤ **Restaurant du Parc**
(R)M
Luce-de-Lancival
Closed Sun. p.m.; Mon.; 15/ 7–15/8
V

The old house – once a private dwelling – is in a quiet street that runs off the centre of the village. An enormous black mountain sheep-dog rushes out to meet guests. Usually followed by young and very smiley M. Eck himself. His parents ran this excellent restaurant for 26 years; since last October, he has taken over, and his mother helps him in the dining-room. Two dining-rooms: one large, the other small and intimate with a handsome Renaissance fireplace and an antique buffet. Twenty *places* to eat on the terrace in fine weather.

In season, game features on the menus (65f and 120f): the local hunt meets in St-Gobain twice a week. On the 65f menu were pâté de hure de sanglier, boeuf à la Burgondine, followed by cheese and tarte aux pommes. A delightful evening; we can thoroughly recommend it all.

Arrowed for good food, pleasant surroundings and attentive hosts.

Map 7A	**ST-JEAN-AU-BOIS** (Oise) 278 km SE of Calais; 17 km SE of Compiègne

80320

From Compiègne take the D 332, direction Crépy-en-Valois; after 8 km turn left on to the D 85, direction Pierrefonds.

La Bonne Idée
(HR)L
44.42.84.09
Closed Tues. lunch; Wed.; Jan.; Feb.
EC, V

The reputation of La Bonne Idée has travelled far and wide. It is an old house in a village in the heart of the great forest of Compiègne. In the Middle Ages, St-Jean-au-Bois was a monastic town and, just down the road from the hotel, a 17th-century church, the only surviving monument of those days, lies beyond a fortified gate. Today all is calm and quiet: a lovely place in which to stay, or just to dine on a summer's evening . . .

M. and Mme Boyer run their restaurant and hotel with sophistication and warmth. The restaurant is furnished in Louis XIII style, well in keeping with its age. Monsieur uses only, he told us, the best ingredients and buys them fresh from the Rungis market outside Paris. Menus are in the higher price range: 210f, 330f and

350f. Specialities include 'potée d'escargots forestière, l'aiguillette de canette à la fleur de moutarde et cuisse grillée avec salade aux noix'.

The 24 bedrooms (230–380f) are in an annexe a couple of steps away from the house. They are charming, simply and tastefully furnished with reproduction Louis XVI furniture here and there.

Map 2B   **ST-OMER** (Pas-de-Calais) 40 km SE of Calais

62500
(M) *Wed.,*
Sat.

The first real French town after leaving the Channel ports. Most English tourists don't bother to give it a second glance, by-passing hastily on their way south, and once the autoroute is finished no doubt there will be even fewer GBs in the town centre, but there is plenty of attraction for at least an overnight stop.

It's an interesting many-faceted little town, set at the junction of the river Aa and the Neuffossé canal, amidst a complicated network of canals and waterways – the watergangs – tourable by boat in summer. Like its big counterpart, Amiens (see *FE6*), this region is inhabited by sturdy market gardeners who glide from their particular rich dark plot, intensively cultivated to yield several crops a year, to the market depots, in time-warped flat-bottomed punts, laden down with cauliflowers, leeks, chicory. At weekends the roadside to Clairmarais is lined with stalls selling their produce; the Lillois drive over to pick up the freshest and best in the region. The bungalows here have mini-canals marking their borders and small boys sit bemused, watching their fish floats drift on the water.

Information about the Émeraude, the boat that cruises through the canals, is best attained by ringing 21.98.66.74, since the service is not regular, but basically there are three trips starting from the canal on the D 209: one around the St-Omer marais, one to Arques as far as the unique hydraulic boat-lift at Fontinettes (which in 1887 used to do the work of five locks), and one along the Aa to Houlle, with lunch at Mme Poupart's (see p.94). Given a fine day with a glitter to the pervading wateriness, it's all very peaceful and miles away from the traffic tangle.

Hard to believe now that St-Omer was once a prosperous maritime town; its rich merchants invested their profits in the substantial classical houses lining its wide streets. Those in unsuspected quiet backwaters like the r. Gambetta have recently been sympathetically restored, revealing their honey-coloured stone and intricate ironwork.

The town is a series of squares, but its centre is the cobbled Grande Place, where the dignified town hall (tourist information here) is confronted with a disreputable collection of cafés leaning drunkenly on the other side. This disparity of styles and moods is a feature of the whole town, with the ruins of the 15th-century St-Bertin, the ponderous Gothic cathedral of Notre Dame, the chapel of the Jesuits, and the elegant 18th-century Hôtel Sandelin, now a museum.

For picnicking you have a choice of the formal or informal. St-Omer is rightly proud of its public gardens, built on the ancient ramparts of the town, where the neat beds and bedding make a colourful background for a sandwich and glass of wine. For those who prefer to set up tables and have a wholehearted French-style picnic, the nearby forest of Clairmarais is deep and green and silent. St Thomas à Becket took refuge here in a Cistercian abbey, of which only the farm now remains. The lake of Harcelles is the haunt of modern fishermen just as keen to land a trout for supper as were the monks who first stocked the water.

Buying the picnic in the town is an easier proposition than it used to be when I researched for *FE4*, with several attractive new food shops recently opened and a pleasant pedestrianisation of the r. des Clouteries, which makes dilatory window-shopping much more agreeable. Here is the charming **Le Terroir**, with a good range of cheeses from the North, which the proprietor is happy to explain. **La Ferme** in the r. de Dunquerke likewise. A plethora of *chocolatiers/pâtisseries* includes **Mme Degraves'** little shop in the r. des Clouteries, where you can buy local specialities in nostalgic old-fashioned tins, like Quinquins or Babeluttes. **Cadart** in the pl. Mar. Foch has good chocs and pastries too. On the adjoining side of the Grande Place **Dassonval**, '**Feu au Bois**' is the place to dash into for a bag of croissants to take home; opposite is **La Miche d'Or**, a *boulangerie* specialising in *pain de campagne*. **Soutrain** on the corner of the rue d'Arras is the best *charcutier*. Highly recommended for wines is the **Caves St-Arnould** on the r. de Calais.

Those who like to do all their shopping under one roof will enjoy the Mammouth hypermarket on the Arques road, with fewer trolly-happy Brits than in the port; in Arques itself is the big glass factory, with a shop selling rejects at excellent prices – worth a Christmas sortie.

Best of all is the Saturday market – the most important in the area, when the marais produce is displayed in a great splash of colour in the Grande Place.

➤ **St-Louis**
(H)M(R)S
25. r. Arras
21.38.35.21
Closed 25/12–
1/1
Garage

The bar is more than ever the favourite hang-out of local students and undoubtedly gets very noisy and smoky. It depends on one's mood. On a miserable grey day it is sometimes a cheer-up to open the door and be confronted with a cheerful buzz of conversation; on others it can be irritating to be made to feel an outsider in a private club. But there is no need to sit here if the atmosphere is uncongenial – breakfast and drinks can be served in the little courtyard, there is a quite separate restaurant and reception area with armchairs and T.V.

The general reaction has been overwhelmingly favourable once again for this old-time French Entrée favourite, and the addition of the new rooms overlooking the courtyard has meant that more readers have been able to experience M. Bill's brand of hospitality. They are functional, if a little impersonal for my taste; those on the ground floor have direct access to the courtyard, via a french window, so they would be ideal for the disabled. *'The new rooms are well-appointed and roomy, with good reading lights. They cost 192f – more than the main hotel but splendid value. My wife liking the bedspread and curtains, the ever helpful M. Bill offered to have copies made for her. Try that on the English hotelier . . .'* – Dennis Osborn.

A welcome new facility is the small restaurant recently opened in the hotel. Readers have been happy to eat in after a long drive, on menus that are simple but good value. *'Very comfortable – very nice rooms and an excellent meal. The 48f menu had three good courses. At last I've eaten andouillettes – and bought some next day to bring home.'* – Elizabeth Madge. *'Breakfast cost us 19.50f – fresh baguette, croissant and brioche, orange juice and chocolate. So enjoyable that we booked again for the return trip.'* – Elaine Rubach.

Another blessing is the car-park behind the hotel, but take warning from the following: *'The Hotel St Louis and the Restaurant du Cygne were splendid, as you have written about them. The only difficulty we experienced was that while we had lunch at the Restaurant du Cygne on Sunday, we left the car in the car-park at the St Louis. We didn't realise that they locked up and when we returned we couldn't get the car out until 4 p.m., so we missed our boat.'* – G. T. Crook.

Rooms from 120–192f.

Arrowed once again for efficiency and friendliness in a useful position.

La Bretagne
(HR)M
2 pl. du Vainquai
21.38.25.78
Closed Sun. p.m.; Sat.; 12/8–27/8, 2/1–18/1
AE, DC, V
Parking

Time perhaps to reassess the Bretagne. I would not include this well-known hotel in previous FEs because I believed it didn't merit its Michelin star, nor its general praise in other guides; I did not like its atmosphere nor its accueil. Now the star has gone and the management – the same Beauvalot family as at the Georges V in Calais – seems to be trying harder. There are few other choices in the town and the St-Louis is often full, so please now reconsider this one (reports particularly welcome).

It is a chunky modern building some 10–15 minutes' walk from the town centre. It has private parking and a choice of three restaurants: 'The Best', with a vaguely art nouveau décor, they call their gastronomic restaurant (closed all day Sat. and Sun. p.m.), which, in addition to a sophisticated carte, offers a 150f buffet, including wine. Then there's the 'Petit Best', with a 59.50f menu, and the exotic Maëva grill (closed Sat. lunch and all day Mon.), with a tropical theme and a 58.50f menu. This, with three choices in three courses, e.g.: eggs Mimosa, grey mullet, fruit salad, and inclusive of ¼ bottle of wine, is not at all bad value.

One reader who was not happy with his room or the accueil readily admitted his surprise at the high quality of the meal, so it's swings and roundabouts.

The hotel rooms, at 155–280f have a great range of permutations of double or twin beds, bath or shower. The new rooms cost 280f and have one double bed, one single and English T.V., so the kids at least would be well catered for.

Le Cygne
(R)M
8 r. Caventou

I discovered this charming little restaurant soon after it opened six years ago and was able to arrow it after many confirmations that the food was exceptionally good. It is based in an elegant 18th-century

21.98.20.52
Closed Tues.;
Sat. lunch
V

house in a quiet square, with a smart ground-floor restaurant and another in the ancient cellars. The name is taken from the fountain of the swan in the courtyard, but the house speciality is duck, appearing on the carte in nine different guises.

I have always eaten well there, but rumbles of discontent are beginning to mix with the praise: *'Hardly any choice on quite a small menu, wine expensive, restaurant very cold and only five other people in.'* *'The food was disappointing. My wife chose the lamb on the four-course menu, which was very tough. We were told there was no house wine.'* But there are compliments which contradict this impression: *'An excellent four-course dinner. The decor of the two tones of brown and the white table linen, with fresh flowers, added to the first-class evening.'* David Dunham. *'Definitely the best meal we had during our stay. Four-course meal now 70f is still good value but no longer any house wine and the minimum price for a bottle is about 50f.'* – Barry Kimberly.

So it's anybody's guess how things will progress. I continue to arrow the Cygne because in my experience it is still the best restaurant in town and I think the expertise which M. Maertens, the chef/patron, acquired at the prestigious Parisian Lucas Carlton is reflected here in daily changing menu, which at 70f for four courses, is good value in such an attractive setting. I regret the passing of the house wine, but 50f nowadays is not excessive in a restaurant of this calibre – it is only the cheapness of the menu that makes it seem comparatively so. However, it's a borderline case, and further reports will decide the fate of the arrow in the next edition.

La Cremaillère
(R)S
12 bvd
Strasbourg
21.38.42.77
Closed Sun.
p.m.; Mon.; 20/
7–10/8, 21/12–
4/1
All credit cards

This restaurant, on the encircling boulevard to the north of the town, has produced fewer reports than Le Cygne but all of them favourable, and I think it is a good and reliable choice. Menus start at 52f.

'We have had many interesting meals here and it is always packed with locals. The couple who run it are quite an interesting pair, she a pneumatic blond who greets male diners with an embrace (my husband is still hopefully expectant) and a military-style husband who runs the restaurant with great élan. – Dr and Mrs Peter Brook.

'Excellent meals lunch and evening, nearly always crowded with locals and very friendly. – Chris Owen.

L'Entrecôte
(R)S
1 r. Henri
Dupuis
21.98.14.38
Closed Sun.
AE

A newish little restaurant near the cathedral, specialising, as its name implies, in meat. Nothing elaborate, but the place to head for if you fancy a straightforward steak grilled on a charcoal fire, for 42f. Menus, e.g. onion quiche, spit-roasted beef, choc. mousse, start at 59f, with an unusual 15% service charge. At 110f you get wine thrown in.

La Belle Époque
(R)S
3 pl. Paul
Painlevé
Closed Sun.
and Mon.

Just off the main square, a pretty little restaurant specialising in Flemish dishes.

'An excellent meal at La Belle Époque. The 85f menu was the best value anywhere.' – Glyn Mathias.

**Caroline's
Garden**
R)S
28 r. des Epéers
21.93.13.90
Closed Mon.

A new *salon de thé* which also serves light, salad lunches.
Recommended not only by local friends but by the poor unfortunates
who had their car locked up in the St-Louis garage all Sunday
afternoon and found this their only consolation.
   'Whilst we were waiting around we found the small and new
Caroline's Garden. They have a wide variety of teas and delicious
pastries.' – G. T. Crook.

Les Frangins
R)S
3 r. Carnot
21.38.12.47
Closed Thur.
p.m.; Fri. lunch.
All credit cards

A new one on me but another reader found this simple grill good
value for a quick and unpretentious meal. 54f menu, house wine
included.

Map 1B **ST-PIERRE-BROUCK** (Nord) 36 km SE of Calais

59630
Bourbourg

**Restaurant du
Château**
(HR)M
Rte de la
Bistade
28.27.56.05

A late recommendation arrived for this entry, which I have not had
time to check for myself. I include it because the Château does seem
to promise all the things this area so badly needs – an interesting
restaurant and the promise of some comfortable accommodation.
Further reports particularly welcome.
   I have no details of opening times and the directions 'between
Dunkerque and St-Omer' are sketchy to say the least, but it would
seem to be about 8km south of Bourbourg.
   'With Monsieur as Chef and Madame to wait at table we sat in a
pleasant dining room, with nine other diners, all French. Two of us
chose the 110f menu and had feuilleté de saumon, pintade à la
Normandie and a sorbet; scampi en croûte, tournedos forestière and
ice-cream, and the other two went for the 140f menu and had pâté
with grapes, pintade and a delicious sorbet of green apple and pear;
smoked salmon, magret de canard and a pear sorbet.
   'The presentation was original and plentiful – not nouvelle cuisine.
The smoked salmon was accompanied with red and black caviare,
egg and radicchio. Monsieur told us he grows his own potatoes and
all other vegetables are very fresh and locally grown.
   I understood Madame to say that there will be six bedrooms open
later this month (September '87) and several more planned for later.'
– Mrs V. J. Hughes-Narborough.

Map 5B **ST-QUENTIN** (Aisne) 201 km SE of Calais

12011
(M) Wed.,
Sat:

Easy to be put off St-Quentin by the industry (textiles mostly) on the
left bank and the excessively futuristic residential quarter to the
north, but it does have an attractive centre, undiscovered by many
tourists.

It's certainly a most important town in the area, thanks to its position, a long-term strategic one on the hub of several major routes; by road from the Channel to the Mediterranean and from the Netherlands to Paris; by rail to the European capitals; by water via the St-Quentin canal, which together with the Canal du Nord is the busiest canal in France, carrying mostly coal from the North to Paris.

The extension of the A 26 autoroute, skirting the town, will no doubt relieve the dreadful traffic congestion that has hitherto made the town a black spot, to be passed through as quickly and painlessly as possible.

Should an overnight stop be indicated here, these are the assets to look out for:

The town is built on a chalky hill overlooking the course of the canalised Somme. From l'Étang d'Isle, a wide expanse of water around an island, there are impressive views of the town. The lake has been well capitalised, and there are now *plages*, with changing cabins, deck-chairs and so on for a hot day's refresher, along with more violent activities like canoeing and windsurfing. Another calm cool refuge is the Champs Élysées – extensive gardens and park with wooded walks.

It's an easy town to explore, centring on its wide Grande Place, dominated by the Renaissance town hall, with a flamboyant façade of seven arcades, delicately and intricately decorated with sculpture. Its 18th-century carillon has a peal of 37 bells.

The nearby basilica is named after the town's namesake, St-Quentin, who came to evangelise the region and was martyred for his pains in the third century. It is a miracle indeed that it still stands here; having survived a prolonged siege during the Battle of St-Quentin in 1557, a serious fire a hundred years later and a bombardment in 1917, it came nearest to total destruction in October 1918 when the Germans wired up 300 mines around its pillars – you can still see the cavities – but never had time to explode them.

The massive porch on the west façade is the oldest part of the basilica, dating from the 12th century; walk round to the left, to the Square Winston Churchill, for the most photographic view, with some very dashing flying buttresses. Inside, the beautiful choir is 13th century; amazingly some of the old glass has survived in one of the chapels. Don't miss the voluptuous Renaissance organ loft on the way out.

But for me the prime reason for visiting St-Quentin would be to pay my respects to its most honoured son, the painter Quentin de la Tour. 78 of his wonderfully evocative pastel portraits of the royalty and high society of the 18th century are on show in the Musée Antoine-Lécuyer (open weekdays 10 a.m.–12 p.m., 2–5 p.m. (6 p.m. on Sats); Sun. and Hols 2–6 p.m.; closed Mon.)

Grand Hôtel and Rest. Président
(HR)L–M
6 r. Dachery

Here is another good reason for coming to St-Quentin – the be-starred, be-toqued Rest. Président. The Grand Hôtel, conscious that it cannot live up to its prestigious appendage, is about to be completely redecorated and refurbished, so it's pretty futile to go into any detail on the state of its rooms at present, except to say there

23.62.69.77
Rest. closed
Sun. p.m.;
Mon; 3'8–23/8,
3/2–16/2
AE, DC, EC, V
Parking

are 41 of them, costing between 245f and 260f. Expect to pay double that when they have been up-marketed.

The Président goes from strength to strength, with a disciple of the great Robuchon in the kitchen. It is altogether a delightful surprise to find not only a young chef of great talent and a delicate touch, but a light and carefree décor in a restaurant in the heart of a fairly sombre town in the fairly sombre North. Raymond Brouchard pays scant attention to the locally prevailing accent on substantial cold-weather food. His predilection is for the fresh and subtle – lots of fish, like scallops in a warm salad starter that incorporated fennel and a sprinkling of caviar, salmon cooked in a chicken stock, lobster flavoured with orange zest. In an unusual combination of Maître d'Hôtel and *pâtissier*, Dominique Cholon produces some fittingly suave desserts; most customers, spoiled for choice, make for the 'farandole des desserts' – a selection of mini helpings of the trolley temptations.

The menus represent remarkable value at this level of cooking. The 'petit' at 135f has no choice, but offers, for example, a compôte of rabbit with foie gras, a fricassée of liver and kidneys, and a dessert. There is more choice on the 230f version, but both compare excellently with similar standards back home.

All this is served in the charming peachy dining-room, all white ceramic floor, chintzy armchairs, exposed brick walls – nothing pompous or 'grand' about this one.

The sad thing is that as I have not been able to visit the Président this year, and neither apparently has any of my readers, I cannot award the arrow I am confident is deserved. Someone please remedy.

Nothing like making the boss do all the work. I asked publisher Jeremy Greenwood and his wife Annabel to suss out St-Quentin and Roye for me on their route to Paris. Here are their reports:

Hôtel de la Paix et Albert
(HR)M
3 pl. du 8-
Octobre
23.62.77.62
Rest. closed
Sun.
AE, EC, V
Parking

'An attractive-looking hotel with window boxes and a welcoming lounge. Very efficient staff, English speaking. Centrally placed near the station. Could be a bit noisy, so ask for a back room. Has two restaurants: Le Brésilien is a pizzeria plus a plat du jour, not too expensive, and round the corner, Le Carnotzet, specialising in Alpine food such as raclette, rösti, all reasonably priced.' – Annabel and Jeremy Greenwood.

Hôtel Diamant
(H)M
Pl. de la
Basilique
23.64.19.19

'A brand new hotel right opposite the Basilique. Rooms from 298–330f, or an apartment for 304–480f. All very attractively decorated with copies of Latour paintings. Bar food available downstairs in the breakfast room until late.' – A. & J.G.

Hôtel Mémorial
(H)M
7 r. de la
Comédie
23.09.20.09
All credit cards
Parking

'A rather unusual hotel, very quietly situated up a side street and built round a courtyard. The 16 rooms are decorated with repro furniture in old French style, with brass beds. The downstairs breakfast room is more like a château room than that of a hotel. Rooms 280–360f.' – A. & J.G.

Le Petit Chef
(R)M
31 r. Émile-Zola
23.62.28.52
Closed Sun.

'We were a little doubtful about the soup – was it entirely home-made? And they were rather mean with the bread. They spoke very little English and looked a little annoyed when we repeatedly asked the waiter to tell us what various dishes included. The specialities are trout, stuffed and served in a champagne sauce, and veal kidneys with wild mushrooms. Menus at 60f and 140f.' – A. & J.G.

Map 2B

SALPERWICK (Pas-de-Calais) 35 km SE of Calais, 5 km N of St-Omer

---

Turn E off the N 43 just before St-Omer to a lane leading to the peaceful hamlet of Salperwick.

Relais de l'Amitié
(C)
21.93.41.41 or
21.38.11.91
Open all year

This one got me into trouble in *FE1*, when, on the recommendation of a trusty friend, I included it. She had had a pleasant, peaceful, cheap stay here, in an area short of interesting accommodation, and sent me an appealing photo of an old grey stone house. I thought we were on to a winner. Letters of protest at the general shabbiness followed and I investigated for myself. At that stage it turned out that Mme Cossart was in a state of flux, with son wavering about joining her as cook, and I could well see why readers had not been pleased. I hastily omitted the place from *FE2*.

Now it seems that the Cossarts have got their act together and it's time for a reassessment.

'We stayed at the Relais de l'Amitié and I think it should be reinstated at once. Room for three, large, clean, lino on floor. Beds v. comfortable. No shades on lights and wiring looked none too healthy. Breakfast: large jug of coffee, large pot of apricot jam, more on request. Meals: three courses: fresh vegetables. No choice but all dishes delicious. On a dead end, no traffic at night. Absolute rural peace.' – John Holberton.

I had another look and reckon that, although in an area like Normandy (see *FE3*) and the Loire (see *FE8*), where the chambres d'hôte are many and excellent, this would not stand a chance, Mme Cossart's welcome and the situation make it worth a cautious entry. Prices are now 150f for two with shower and own loo, or 120f for demi pension. Rooms for four people cost 210f, and a simple meal is 50f.

Map 4C	**SARS-POTERIES** (Nord) 190 km SE of Calais; 20 km S of Maubeuge

59216
(M) *Thur.*

5 km E of the N 2 (Maubeuge–Avesnes).

Auberge Fleurie
(R)L
67 r. du Général
de Gaulle
27.61.62.48
Closed Sun.
p.m.; Mon.; 15/
1–15/2
AE, DC, EC, V

A splendid up-market restaurant which was originally a farm. Converted 33 years ago, it now enjoys a considerable gastronomic reputation under the patronage of young M. and Mme Lequy.

The three dining-rooms are quite charming: tiled floor, floral wallpaper and matching curtains, lots of fresh flowers on the tables. Blond and sophisticated Josette makes an attentive hostess.

Menus (123f, 180f and 220f) specialise in regional food: asparagus, duck, fish. The 125f menu includes dishes like: saumon cru mariné, lapin aux raisins. 'Dessert à notre suggestion' offers 'les soupes de fruits, profiterolles au chocolat'. And there is a quiet and peaceful courtyard at the back for those pre-meal drinks.

Hôtel de l'Auberge Fleurie
(H)M
65 r. du Général
de Gaulle
27.61.62.72
Closed 15/12–3/
1
Parking

The twin sisters of M. Lequy (Claudine Carrié and Thérèse Guinto) run this excellent little hotel (eleven bedrooms) in the old stables across the courtyard from the Auberge Fleurie. The original farm had belonged to their grandparents.

Bedrooms (150–200f) are beautifully furnished with antiques, most of which have been in the family for generations. Downstairs is a paved hall set with an old oak table. Mesdames are very friendly – it has all the agreeable atmosphere of a welcoming visit to a private house. Breakfast 25f. Plenty of room to park in the yard.

Map 6D	**SAULCES-MONCLIN** (Ardennes) 244 km SE of Calais

13 km NE of Rethel, just off the N 51. A small village surrounded by fields and farms.

Hostellerie des Sources
(HR)M
24.72.13.20
Closed Sun.
p.m.; Mon.
o.o.s.; Jan.
AE, DC, V

M. and Mme Raymond Alemany bought this hotel, now a Logis de France, eight years ago in a run-down state and are working hard to turn it into the sort of establishment that its charming situation deserves. It's all there: 5 hectares of well-tended, wooded parkland, trout-fishing in the Saulce (a tributary of the Aisne), which runs between the trees, a little 18th-century château (the private house of the patrons) that adjoins the hotel itself. There is a ping-pong table on the grass outside and tables and chairs on the stone-flagged terrace.

Bedrooms (103–160f) are large and well-furnished with good, big bathrooms en suite. A good night's sleep seems guaranteed – the only sounds we heard were a cat-fight below our window in the night, and birdsong in the morning. Truly, as the brochure states, 'the calm of the countryside within two strides of the town'.

Dining-room was decorated with pretty pink tablecloths and flowers; the head of a wild boar and a gun (they seem ubiquitous in the Ardennes!) on the wall. Three young girls waited on us with grace and politeness. Menus at 65f and 95f included specialities from the district: pâté en croute garni, truite braisée à la crème.

It was a favourite overnight stop from which we found it hard to drag ourselves away next morning. But, in spite of the most relaxing atmosphere, we could not help noticing that a certain gloom prevailed amongst the staff and patrons. Without doubt, much effort and hard work goes into the running of an hotel, like this, a little off the beaten track. I wish them all the best of luck.

Map 4B	**SEBOURG** (Nord) 145 km SE of Calais

59990

10 km E of Valenciennes. Turn E off the D 50.

A tranquil village in the green valley of the Aunelle. Much favoured by the citizens of Valenciennes and Lille who come here to visit their weekend cottages, or to walk in the Forêt de Mormal, the largest forest in the north of France.

The 12th–16th-century church is worth a visit. Inside are the 14th-century tombs of Henri de Hennin, seigneur of Sebourg, and his wife; and a chapel dedicated to Saint Druon of Sebourg, patron of the village. Saint Druon was a 12th-century nobleman who travelled to Rome (no mean feat in those days), returned to Sebourg to become a shepherd and a hermit, and died in 1186 with a saintly reputation. On Trinity Sunday each year, there is a pilgrimage to the church: prayers are invoked for the miraculous cure of hernias.

On a sadder note – this quiet spot was fiercely fought over during the two world wars. There is a 1914–18 English war cemetery in the village.

Au Jardin Fleuri
(HR)M
Exit Onnaing
(from Belgium)
Hotel:
27.26.53.31
Rest.:
27.26.53.44
Rest. closed
Sun. p.m.;
Hotel and Rest.
closed 168–6/9;
20/1–5/2
EC, V

A quiet, peaceful retreat. Monsieur Delmotte-Leroy is a Sebourgeois who opened a restaurant here 42 years ago. 22 years later he built the charming little hotel down at the bottom of the garden. It has twelve rooms (95–150f), all very neat and clean, well decorated and furnished *au style rustique*. A ladder staircase leads to the first floor. Our room had a loo behind a folding screen (another on the landing), washbasin, bath and duvet.

In the evening we walked up through the garden to the restaurant past a dovecote in a tree, children's swings, and by a field where chickens pecked and scratched.

The windows of the restaurant overlook the garden. Menus are 50f, 72f and 110f. Speciality of the house is Langue Lucullus (tongue with foie gras) on the 110f menu. There is a garage with room for four cars (free); otherwise plenty of parking space either by the restaurant or down by the little hotel. Breakfast is served on the ground floor of the hotel.

Map 3D	**SECLIN** (Nord) 139 km SE of Calais; 11 km S of Lille

---

59113
Ⓜ *Mon.*

Exit from the A 1 direction Seclin, then follow the signs for the centre of the town.

Auberge du Forgeron
(HR)M
17 r. Roger-
Bouvry
20.90.09.52
Closed Sun.;
Aug.
V
Parking

We had had such good reports of the Auberge du Forgeron that we left our visit there for the final night of our holiday.

Now for the bad news. Having enquired after the prices of the rooms (130–250f), we asked the receptionist for the least expensive. Upstairs we were shown two, one with a double bed, the other with twin beds, and chose the latter. All right, so we should have examined the price pinned up behind the door, but it was not until we were presented with the bill the next day that we realised we had been put (without explanation) in the most expensive bedroom. For 250f we got a small room with wash-basin, shower and lavatory behind a screen. It overlooked the main road along which heavy traffic rolled all night, making sleep very difficult.

Our list of grumbles continues . . . The dining-room probably lived up to its reputation for good regional cooking, but our dinner (menus at 70f and 152f) was spoilt by slow and poor service. Having asked for a small carafe of wine, we were told that it came only in the half bottle. Fair enough – but the wine brought was the least drinkable that we had tasted on our holiday, the bottle placed in its cooler just out of our reach and no-one quick off the mark to refill our glasses. Before we had finished a waiter told us to move the car into the private and locked parking as soon as possible. Having driven there, the gates were still locked and we had to dig out the waiter to let us in. Final insult came when we tried to settle the bill next morning and were told that credit cards were not accepted before 9 a.m.! So go forewarned: ask for a bedroom at the back and put firecrackers under all that unhelpful staff!

Map 6D

SEDAN (Ardennes) 292 km SE of Calais; 19 km SE of Charleville-Mézières

---

08200
Ⓜ Wed.,
Thur., Sat.

The town lies in a beautiful area on the right bank of the river Meuse, near to the Belgian and Luxembourg borders. Dominating the town is a fortress claimed to be the largest in Europe, the Château Fort, which houses a military museum (open daily, April to September, 10 a.m.–6 p.m.).

3 km outside Sedan at Floing is the Monument du Chêne Brisé, where signposts direct you to the Memorial des Chasseurs d'Arique and the 1870 cemetery of the Franco-Prussian War. Leaving Sedan on the Bouillon road, you come to a plateau where the 1870 battle took place: mass graves marked with black iron crosses stand as a moving testimony to the dead. At Bazeilles on the N 43 to Montmedy is the Musée de la Maison de la Dernière Cartouche (last cartridge) where the French marine unit fought a heroic battle against the Germans (open every day except Friday, 8.30 a.m.–12 p.m. and 1.30–6.00 p.m.).

Sedan is of special significance to those interested in military history. For the more general tourist, there is little to warrant a detour – except for a couple of good, overnight stops and one outstandingly good-value little restaurant.

Le St-Michel
(HR)M
3 r. St-Michel
24.29.04.61
Closed Sun.
p.m.; 15/7–18/8
EC, V

In a quiet street below the Château Fort. Seemed a clean, decent-looking establishment from the outside but, having arrived during the annual holiday, we had no chance to inspect it more closely. M. Copine was certainly friendly: in spite of being rudely interrupted in the middle of a siesta (he arrived on the doorstep shoeless, but with a beaming smile) he found the time to tell us a few details.

So – 20 bedrooms (145–170f). 150 *places* in the restaurant, menus (75f and 100f) specialise in local dishes: côte de veau Ardennaise; sauté de marcassin (young wild boar). We would be glad to hear your own experiences.

Restaurant Chariot d'Or
(R)M
20 pl. de Torcy
24.27.04.87
Parking

One of the best meals we ate anywhere during the holiday and – wait for it – the price was only 45f. This little 19th-century house (an old hotel) is on the main street that runs in from the direction of Charleville-Mézières. Young M. and Mme Jean-Claude Theys have been here four and a half years and they, and indeed the whole establishment, are charming. The interior is delightful: beams, wooden ceiling, upright, exposed timbers and red tiled floor. There were several choices on the menu: one of us ate cucumber salad in sour cream, the other, tongue in vinaigrette as starters; the *plat* was emincé de boeuf and there was charlotte aux fraises as dessert. Another menu at 85f.

Space to park in an enclosed courtyard. Altogether: thoroughly to be recommended.

Buffet de la Gare
(R)S
24.27.02.12
EC, V

A large dining-room, big enough to seat 120 peole, is beyond the café entrance. Menus: 39f, 48.50f, 57f, 70f and 110f. On the 39f menu was mousse de foie, rissolette de veau, cheese or dessert. A friendly young couple, M. and Mme Gaudicheau, running it, and a sudden rush of trains as background music to your meal.

Map 7C | **SEPT-SAULX** (Marne) 301 km SE of Calais

51

23 km SE of Reims by the N 51.

A pretty village, punctuated by the river Vesle; a good stopping place, all green and calm and strategically near to Reims.

➤ **Le Cheval Blanc**
(H)M(R)L
r. du Moulin
26.61.60.27
Closed 15/1–15/2
AE, CB, DC, EC
Parking

The 22 rooms, in a separate building across the road from the restaurant, are pretty, comfortable and good value in this area, at 285f. The only snag is that there is an obligation to eat in the restaurant. It is a very good restaurant and this should be no hardship, but if, like me, you thought you might sneak off to Boyer and save a few bob by sleeping here, forget it. Madame is adamant.

Remarkably, the same family has run the Cheval Blanc since 1610! Generation after generation has worked to transform this simple relais into a comfortable hotel and acclaimed restaurant, with Michelin star. Nowadays it's father Bernard Robert and his daughter Laurence who share the cooking.

Between them they offer interesting items like Assiette de Vesle, composed of river fish and frogs' legs, all in a butter sauce. Lots of other river-fish dishes, like fresh salmon and pike, feature strongly,

Le cheval Blanc. Sept-Saulx.

and breast of pigeon from Bresse, or calves' sweetbreads with fresh pasta. Super cellar handed down from father to son, or in this case, daughter.

The menu at 150f is a good buy. Otherwise it's 250f, or around 300f on the carte, pushing up the price of dinner, bed and breakfast into the luxury category.

Arrowed for the only example in the area of a combination of comfortable quiet hotel and excellent cooking in the M–L bracket.

Map 6C	**SIGNY-L'ABBAYE** (Ardennes) 281 km SE of Calais
08460 ► **Auberge de l'Abbaye** (HR)M	33 km SW of Charleville-Mézières An exceptionally well-run, welcoming Logis in this quiet village surrounded by farmland and the forêt de Signy. Near the hotel once

24.52.82.27
Closed Wed.
p.m.; Thur.;
Jan,; Feb.

stood a rich Cistercian abbey (destroyed in 1793), around which the old village grew up.

M. Lefèbvre's grandparents ran the hotel (the patron is now of a grandfatherly age himself) and the atmosphere is lovely: cheerful and clean with little maids bustling around under the eagle eye of friendly Madame.

Red and white tablecloths in the two dining-rooms, a low ceiling and wild boar's head over the fireplace. Menus 57f, 60f and 100f. 57f menu includes hors d'oeuvres or soup, jambon Ardennaise, cheese, dessert. Rooms: 100–210f.

'This was good. Two pleasant rooms, one 100f and the other 180f. Comfortable beds. Extremely helpful patron. We ate very well, having chosen the 100f menu. It was delicious and only marred by the fact that two puddings were brought up, the second being crème anglaise – it was just too much, after five previous courses. Everything was beautifully prepared, with a sorbet between courses and an excellent cheeseboard. Breakfast (20f) was good too, fruit juice served and lots of good coffee. Definitely worth a visit.' – Evelyn M. Walter.

It certainly is, and earns itself an arrow for good value.

Map 7C   **SILLERY** (Marne) 299 km SE of Calais

1500

11 km SE of Reims on the N 44, and, clearly marked to the right, on the D 8E.

If you look at a map, this looks like a suburb of Reims, squeezed between the autoroute and the route nationale, but in fact Sillery is a peaceful little Champenois village. At its approach is:

**Le Relais de
Sillery**
(R)M
26.49.10.11
Closed Sun.
p.m.; Mon.; 1/
2–15/2
EC, V

An attractive old creeper-covered building, where Jeanine Adin, Grande Dame de l'Association des Restaurateurs cooks in the regional tradition. No menu but dishes like foie gras with ratafia, sweetbreads with morilles and a local cheeseboard will result in a bill of around 180–220f. The wine list consists entirely of local wines.

Map 6B   **SINCENY** (Aisne) 227 km SE of Calais

02300
 Wed.

6 km SE of Chauny by the D 1 and D 1750.

**L'Auberge du
Rond d'Orléans**
(R)M
23.52.26.51
Closed Tues.

A charming restaurant set in a glade on one of the lone rides that cut through the Forest of St-Gobain. Friendly Mme Matthieu and her husband built the modern building ten years ago and have an established clientele. A large, light room with pretty pink tablecloths and big windows; an old clock ticking by the wall: a peaceful spot on a *circuit touristique*.

All the food (including terrines and bread) is made on the premises. Menus at 98f, 150f and 109f. We thoroughly enjoyed our choice: confit de canard maison (69f) and a glass of dry white wine (11f).

| Map 7B | **SOISSONS** (Aisne) 296 km SE of Calais; 56 km E of Reims |

02200
(M) *Wed.,*
Sat., Sun.

Soissons was almost entirely rebuilt after the First World War. Nevertheless, some of her ancient monuments stand to bear witness to her varied history, and to the achievement of her citizens in their restoration.

Visit the lovely cathedral St-Gervais-et-St-Protais, that dates from the 12th century, and is considered one of the most beautiful examples of Gothic architecture in France. Near the bvd Jeanne d'Arc is the old abbey of St-Jean-des-Vignes, founded in 1076, whose twin spires dominate the townscape.

By the 15th century it had become one of the richest monasteries in the north of France; gifts from benefactors paid for the construction of a large abbey church and cloisters, refectory and other fine monastic buildings. In the early part of the last century the abbey church itself was largely demolished, the stones used in the restoration of the cathedral that was then in progress. Today little but the façade remains, as well as the refectory and the bones of the cloisters. Guided visits every day (except Tues.) from 10 a.m.–12 p.m. and from 2–5 p.m. Son et lumière each year in June.

Le Picardie
(HR)M
6–8 r. Neuve St-
Martin
23.53.21.93/
23.53.34.10
Rest. closed
Sun. p.m.
AE, DC, EC, V

A 1970 hotel in a quiet street off the centre, within walking distance of the cathedral and the shopping streets. Bedrooms (185–205f, including breakfast) are on two floors: all constructed in a uniform sort of way, with rather boring decoration.

A large and comfortable dining-room with menus at 65f, 80f and 120f. Specialities are local dishes: coq à la bière and rascasse en papillotte. Pretty pink cloths on the tables; an extensive wine list; and a polite and helpful patron.

| Map 4C | **SOLRE-LE-CHÂTEAU** (Nord) 194 km SE of Calais |

59740
(M) *Tues.*

31 km N of Hirson on the D 963

La Potinière
R(S)
27.61.64.55.
Closed Mon.
V

Small, café–restaurant in a little old house in the main street. On one side, a bar, a few tables and the odd fruit machine. On the other side, a clean little dining-room with a three-course 50f *menu touristique*.

All very simple, but a pleasant stop.

Map 4B   SOMAIN (Nord) 140 km SE of Calais

59540
(M) *Thur.*

17 km E of Douai by the D 13; 20 km W of Valenciennes.

A small, straggling town stranded in the desert of coalfields. The largest coal-working station in France operates from Somain and, yet, parts of the town retain a village atmosphere: there are some 18th- and 19th-century houses, and the chapel of St Christopher is the object of a pilgrimage for parents with 'grizzling' children, who hope that the saint will cure them of their complaints.

Search out the 18th-century Priory of Beaurépaire as you leave Somain in the direction of Marchiennes; after the cemetery turn right, then immediately left along the paved road that leads to the monumental gate. A priory has existed at Somain since the 9th century; now this vast, classical building belongs to the coalfields.

Les Années
Folles
(R)M
25 r. Vaillant
Couturier
27.86.61.07
Closed p.m.s;
Sat.; Aug.
AE, EC, V

What an unusual place to find in the rather prosaic surroundings of this corner of Somain, known before the war as 'Petit Paris'. Earlier a brewery stood on the spot, serving the little bistros in the town. The Château la Dent, now the restaurant Les Années Folles, was the brewer's home; the barns and stables standing at the back housed the drays, hops and barrels. Guy Boumane bought the place as a private house four years ago and turned it into this somewhat eccentric looking restaurant. *Les années folles* were those years in the 1920s that produced such a camp style of decoration.

Next move is to plan a terrace-garden around that cobbled yard at the back and make a feature of the brewery buildings. Lots of parking in the Grande Place in front of the supermarket, a couple of minutes' walk away.

In the suitably cluttered dining-room, the tall, dry fronds of pampas grass lean from a glazed pot, greenery trails across the ceiling above dark red tablecloths. Menus are 70f and 125f; the speciality, local beef. The carte offers la coupe Années Folles, 32f (a giant crab and salad cocktail); mousse de filet d'oie Roquefort 35f.

Map 2C   STEENWERCK (Nord) 82 km SE of Calais; 6 km S of Bailleul

59181

From the A 25 take exit 9 from Nieppe driving N; exit Meteren, driving S.

Lying on the rich plain of the Lys, the village was almost completely destroyed during the First World War. In spite of this, Steenwerck is still remarkable, as it has been in centuries past, for the number of little shrines (80 in all) that stand in the hedgerows or in niches on the walls of houses. On the far side of the green grassy Grande Place is the College of Music, housed in a Gothic mansion: here one can attend recitals on a Sunday morning. Once a year, in summer, the village organises an event which enables tourists to visit M. Collier the potter, M. Debaene the basket-maker, and to inspect a farm and watch a horse being shod. Information from the Syndicat d'Initiative: 28.43.08.34.

Auberge du Brigand
(R)M
42 Grande Place
28.49.96.38
Closed Sun. p.m.; Mon.; Jan.; Feb.
AE, V

A 19th-century house set back from a green and leafy Grande Place. Quiet and peaceful surroundings – if you can disregard those young bucks on their erratic motor-bikes who buzz around as irritatingly as wasps. Friendly, red-haired M. Fauchoit has owned the restaurant for ten years: he is in charge of the impressive cellar. Mme Fauchoit, a talented and self-taught cook, specialises in fish bought off the little boats that put into the Channel ports. Rouget à notre façon (75f) and petit pâté chaud de crabe (65f) are but two of the mouth-watering delicacies from the carte. Set menus range from 115–240f. Dining-room decorated in a rustic fashion in keeping with the surroundings: rough-cast, whitewashed brick walls, lacy tablecloths and white napkins. Small bar on one side of the entrance with pretty flowered curtains. In summer, meals may be eaten outside on the terrace.

Map 1C **TETEGHEM** (Nord) 49 km NE of Calais; 6 km SE of Dunkerque

---

59229

Signposted off the D 4.

▶ **La Meunerie**
(R)L
28.26.01.80
Closed Sun. p.m.; Mon.; 21/ 12–15/1
AE, DC, V

Incongruously elegant in this hamlet near the residential/industrial sprawl of Dunkerque, this is a large, squat modern building on the site of an old mill, from which it takes its name. They have made an attractive feature of the old mill machinery, cleverly lit, in the middle of the dining-room. Everything else is new, plush, ultra-luxe (tapestry chairs, deep-pile carpet, round tables well apart), and functional (super-efficient service, from booking to bill). And book you should. It's a long way to any other starred restaurant in this area and an even longer way to one of this calibre; gastronomes are prepared to drive from Calais in one direction and from Belgium in the other to eat here.

Jean-Pierre Delbé, relying strongly on the Dunkerquois fishing fleet and local market-gardeners for his ingredients, cooks with imagination and style, but his dishes are presented unfussily – none of the superfluous garnish or ostentatious artwork so often standard in an up-market restaurant.

It is tempting to go Banco on an expensive menu here, confident that the money will be well spent. The 260f 'Rétour de Pêche' has three hard-to-resist fish courses before cheese and dessert, and the 330f 'Composition du Moulin' is seven masterly *dégustations*, but there is really no need to spend more than 160f.

For me this 'Menu de Printemps' yielded first home-made pasta laced with miniscule shrimps, their cooking juices incorporated into a light creamy sauce, flecked with chervil. Then a whole veal kidney, roasted to tender pinkness, set on a thin cushion of foie gras mousse.

The temptation to exploit to the full the extraordinary cheeseboard – local cheeses knowledgeably explained, everything in perfect condition, appealing to eye and taste, served with home-made nut and raisin bread – should be firmly resisted, in view of what is to come next.

The star turn of La Meunerie is undoubtedly the sweet trolley, wheeled in with justified beam by Mme Delbé. The agony of indecision is helped somewhat by her encouragement of multiple choices from the all-equally-commendable mousses, feuilletés and gâteaux. And then along comes a sister trolley, this time a deliciously bedewed sorbetière of Edwardian aspect, from which two or three *parfums* must be selected.

Of the same high standard as the rest of the meal are the petits fours with the coffee, and the splendid but pricey wine list.

A new building, linked to the restaurant, was almost ready when I last visited La Meunerie in July 1987; it is now functioning, with nine luxurious rooms, furnished in different styles, offering a choice of mood – Louis XV, Restoration, 19th-century Romantic, or Roaring Twenties, all with marble bathrooms, his 'n' hers wash-basins; the price of 400f for a double seems very reasonable, compared with the cost of similar accommodation in England.

Arrowed for exceptional cooking, probably the best in the North, and what I confidently expect to be the most comfortable accommodation in the area.

LA THIÉRACHE (Aisne)

A region of deep, green fields and gently rising hills, bordered by the Vermandois, Champagne, Ardennes and the Laonnois. This lovely, rural countryside is little known to tourists – either French or from abroad. It is Marches country: over the centuries, the Thiérache has been open to attack on every side. Today it is chiefly remarkable for its architecture: low, brick houses, many with thatched roofs, that are surrounded by apple orchards and tightly grouped around their lovely, little fortified churches. There are 60 of these churches, some of which date from the 12th century; you can see them all around on the rolling countryside. In most cases the body of the church is of white-painted brick with red-brick fortifications and roofs of grey slate. An excellent booklet, available at most tourist offices in the area, traces the history of the churches and lays out a tourist trail: start at Marle on the N 2 – exploration of these narrow, winding lanes results in some charming discoveries. Near La Capelle on the D 285, direction Flamengrie, is the 'Pierre d'Haudroy'. This monument marks the spot where, on the 7 November 1918 at 8.20 p.m., representatives of the German parliament presented themselves to the 1st Battalion of the 171st French Regiment to request an armistice. The stone was destroyed by the Germans in 1940 and raised again in 1946.

Map 6C	**THUGNY-TRUGNY** (Ardennes) 230 km SE of Calais
08300 Rethel	5 km SE of Rethel on the D 983.
M. Robert Camu (C)	A charming 18th-century house in a quiet, farming village. M. and Mme Camu live in another part of the village and run this spotlessly clean establishment like a little hotel.

24.38.34.48   Five large bedrooms (98–117f, the most expensive with loo etc.) are attractively furnished, with clean, fresh colours on the beds.

Downstairs, there are wooden floors with rugs, old fireplaces and antique furniture. A big garden with swings for the children. Lots of tourist information lying around, and a young lady (whose husband works on a nearby farm) is employed to look after the guests. Breakfast, but no evening meal.

Map 7C   **TOURS-SUR-MARNE** (Marne) 13 km E of Épernay

51150   Follow the Marne on the D 1 to the village of Tours, where river and canal lie side by side.

a Touraine Champenoise   _Tours - sur - Marne._

La Touraine Champenoise (HR)S R. du Pont 26.58.91.93 AE, DC, EC, V

This is the place where I would stay if I wanted a friendly, cheap, no frills, quiet stop. It's a pretty little low whitewashed inn, with only the road between it and the canal. The rooms are all different and some are much nicer than others, but all are clean and country-comfortable, bargains at 100–170f. You'd certainly pay at least double for the same standard 13 km down the road.

The food served in the rustic dining room is simple but ample and menus start at 59.50f, with wine similarly modestly priced. Mme Schosseler is a helpful and amiable patronne.

Arrowed for good value, in a peaceful setting.

Map 6A	**TRACY-LE-MONT** (Oise) 268 km SE of Calais; 14 km NE of Compiègne

60170	From Compiègne take the D 130 NE to Ollencourt, turn right on to the D 16 for 1 km.

Auberge de Quennevières (R)M *16 r. de la Elouriette* 44.75.28.57 *DC, EC, V*	Good restaurant in the Forest of Compiègne. Jean-Louis Dumatras (who speaks English) has done well with his dining-room since he converted it from an old café seven years ago. There are red tiles on the floor, wood-panelled walls and cosy fire in the big fireplace during the winter months. He serves lots of different fish dishes on his 120f menu. A good feast à la carte, including wine, costs from 200–250f. Mouth-watering items include ris de veau braisé au Champagne; grenadin au poivre vert; escalope de saumon à l'oseille.

Map 6B	**URCEL** (Aisne) 259 km SE of Calais

02000 Laon	7 km S of Laon on the N 2.

Hostellerie de France (R)M *23.21.60.08* *Closed Wed.; 3 weeks in Sept.; 3 weeks in Feb.* *EC, V* *Parking*	The best restaurant around Laon, so a local tells me. It stands on the right-hand side of the N 2 Soissons– Laon road with plenty of room to park around the back. The building was constructed in the 1920s, *au style rustique*. A large and relaxing dining-room: in the body of the room, there are stained-wood chairs set around white-clothed tables; on a slightly elevated level near the window are fresh, white cane chairs, and tablecloths with a pretty floral design. Flowers everywhere and trailing greenery gives the place some of the atmosphere of a conservatory. Outside is a garden with more tables. Menus: 60f (during the week), 100f and 160f specialise in fish. On the 100f menu is salade de pêcheur gourmand; marinade de saumon cru au citron et l'huile d'olive; cailles en brasière; cheese; fondant au chocolat. Well worth a visit!

Map 6B	**VAILLY-SUR-AISNE** (Aisne) 310 km SE of Calais

02370	14 km E of Soissons on the D 925; 24 km S of Laon. For much of the way, coming from the west, the road follows the Aisne, running through water meadows and fields. At Vailly-sur-Aisne, the D 15 branches north for the 'Chemin des Dames' – the famous ridgeway that separates the valley of the Aisne from that of the Ailette. This *chemin* took its name from the daughters of Louis XV – 'Mesdames' – who used to travel along it to the château of the Duchess of Narbonne. Since time immemorial it had been a way of military importance: all along the spine of this high land there are wide views of the valleys on either side. Near the Plâteau de Californie, Napoleon directed the Battle of Craonne and, around one hundred years later, German and Allied forces fought over the same land, with terrible

casualties resulting on either side. At one end of the road stands a gigantic cross. At the Fort de la Malmaison, in the German cemetery, small crosses set in serried ranks seem to stretch to infinity.

In spite of all those great sweeps of green fields, and copses bursting with birdsong beyond them, it is one of the most haunted stretches of road that I have ever visited.

Vailly-sur-Aisne is a sleepy little village on the D 15. Confusingly, in its main street, facing one another are two hotel/restaurants, the Cheval d'Or and the Cheval Blanc. Go for gold!

Le Cheval d'Or
(HR)S
23.54.70.56
Closed 15/12–
15/1
EC, V

Hard to find really cheap accommodation in this area, but the Cheval d'Or has spacious old-fashioned rooms for 60f (or 99f with shower). Next year there will be baths!

The menus start at 60f and there is a special exclusively fish menu. Full pension is 130f a person. Wines tend to be disproportionately dear.

Diana checked it out:

'I arrived for lunch, late in the afternoon; there was only one couple left, but as they were elderly and French and interested in their meal, this could be a recommendation in itself. However, having ordered hot pâté en croute on the cheapest menu, I found it overcooked and greasy; the quail had suffered much the same fate, which the tinned peas and onions that accompanied it did little to relieve. Still the Maroille was excellent and so was the tarte aux pommes. If you eat there at a sensible hour and have better luck, please let us know.'

Map 4B **VALENCIENNES** (Nord) 135 km SE of Calais

59306
 Wed.;
Sat.

A city with ancient foundations lying on the flat chalk plains of the Escaut and the Rhonelle. Penetrate the industrial outskirts, making always for the centre – the pl. d'Armes – and you will find the city's core surprisingly small and easy to negotiate.

Although the two great wars took their toll, there are many fine old buildings preserved from a troubled past. In the 16th century, through the marriage of Marie of Burgundy, it became part of the Hapsburg Empire. Charles V, the Holy Roman Emperor (nicknamed 'Charles of Europe' because of the political and physical power he exercised over his vast dominions) visited the city in 1524 and 1544. Two hundred years later, Valenciennes rose up in arms against Hapsburg domination: the statue which stands outside the 19th-century Hôtel de Ville in the pl. d'Armes represents the citizens defending the ramparts in 1793. It is the work of Carpeaux, one of France's most famous sculptors, born here in 1827. Another of Valenciennes' most famous sons was the painter Watteau. The Musée des Beaux-Arts, in the bvd Watteau, houses some of his work, as well as one of the finest collections of Flemish paintings from the 15th–18th centuries. Another room displays the work of Carpeaux: particularly interesting is the vast collection of designs that he made for his sculptures.

From the pl. d'Armes (a large and lively square, well served with restaurants) take a right turn into the r. Askière. No. 1 is known as the 'Spanish house', a lovely example of a 16th-century wooden dwelling that now houses the Tourist Office (27.46.22.99).

➤ **L'Alberoi**
(R)L
Pl. de la Gare
27.46.86.30
Closed Sun.
p.m.
AE, DC, EC, V

One of the great gastronomic experiences of northern France. How often have I travelled by a train which has pulled in briefly to Valenciennes station, and never realised what delights lay beyond the crowded platform! L'Alberoi is the 'Station Buffet' – what a prosaic description for this restaurant. Glimpses of the trains beyond its windows merely seem a surreal and sophisticated contrivance to complement all that elegance within.

François Benoist bought the old Station Hotel 22 years ago. In opening his splendid restaurant, he has endeavoured to retain the atmosphere of those railway-station hotels built in the mid 19th century, which catered for a more leisured age, when aristocrats hired their own particular carriages, if not their own trains, and travellers stopped to take on hampers to sustain them on their way.

Menus are from 100–130f. Service is swift and efficient; the wine waiter, distinguished by his black apron over his black suit, always on hand to anticipate an empty glass. We ate Langue de Valenciennes Lucullus (the speciality of the house), followed by sole served in a delectable cream sauce, on plates patterned with yellow geraniums. The reputation of M. Benoist's cuisine is such that chefs who have worked here put 'chez Benoist' as an honour after their names. Parking in front of the station.

Arrowed for one of the best station buffets in France.

**Hôtel Nôtre-
Dame**
(H)M
*1 pl. Abbé
Theillier de
Poncheville*
27.42.30.00
*Closed Wed.
afternoons;
Sat.*
EC, V

Exit Valenciennes Nord.

Some of the rooms date from the 18th century and those are the ones to go for: high ceilings, elegant dimensions and bathrooms en suite. The newer bedrooms face on to the road: by no means a busy throroughfare, or noisy either – unless you take into account the peels of bells from the belfry opposite, which, on weekdays, would wake the deepest sleeper at 9 in the morning. The church itself is 19th century and was built on the foundations of a much earlier one; that noisy bell, called 'The Bell of Jeanne of Flanders', dates from the 14th century and comes from the older belfry.

Bedrooms 110–175f. Breakfast in a small anteroom, 20f. The hall porter sits at his desk at the entrance, only too happy to recommend nearby restaurants. Plenty in the street just around the corner; and lots more in the pl. d'Armes, a short walk away.

**L'Hôtel de la
Coupole**
(H)M
*Pl. de la Gare,
25 r. Tholozé*
27.46.37.12
AE, V

M. Benoist, proprietor of L'Alberoi and the Café du Roy at the station, recommends this clean and cheerful hotel to his guests. Mme Matex has run it for the last two years. There are 40 light and well-decorated bedrooms, a lift, and a little breakfast room with strawberry coloured, stippled brick-walls in the old cellar.

Bedrooms: 115–180f. Breakfast 18f.

Café du Roy
(R)S
Pl. de la Gare
27.46.86.30

Within a stone's throw of L'Alberoi and also owned by the estimable M. Benoist, serving good food at remarkably low prices. Menus at 59.60f and 66f both include a quarter bottle of wine or beer with the meal and coffee to follow.

Some examples: terrine de foies de volailles; terrine de poissons, sauce Grelette; brochette d'agneau; l'onglet poêlé à l'échalote.

Le Relais de Maître Kanter
(H)M
34 pl. d'Armes
27.46.29.61
Dinner served up to midnight

We chose to eat in Le Relais de Maître Kanter quite by chance: the collage of oysters, pink lobsters, gleaming fish and other seafood looked so beautiful and the menu, in its glass case outside, so reasonable that we went no further. It was 8.45 p.m. and we found that many other people had had the same idea: so book ahead if you don't want to be kept waiting.

We lingered for twenty minutes or so over an apéritif while waiting for a table, our appetites further whetted by the sight of silver platters of oysters on ice (33f) whizzing by on waiters' shoulders; or big plates of assorted fruits de mer (136f), as decorative as paintings.

When our turn came, we found the service as prompt as the packed dining-room made possible; and, most important, the meal was as delicious as it had promised to be. Not being very hungry that evening, we ate sparingly. Excellent fish soup for one of us, half a dozen snails for the other, followed by three different sorts of ice-cream and accompanied by a carafe of vin rosé came to 100.05f for two.

Map 7A   **VAUDRAMPONT-MORIENVAL** (Oise) 266 km SE of Calais

60127   10 km S of Compiègne by the D 332 through the forest.

Auberge du Bon Accueil
(H)S(R)M
44.42.84.04
Closed Mon. p.m.; Tues.; Feb.
V

The Auberge de Bon Accueil stands beside the D 332 in the forest, five minutes drive outside Compiègne, in the direction of Soissons.

M. Delacroix, the chef and patron, has an excellent name for his food and hospitality. All the food, including his andouillettes and foie gras, are made on the premises. The inn was once an old Post halt and the decoration and furnishings remain in character: dark wood, rafters and flock wallpaper in the dining-room. Outside is a big garden where white tables are set ready for that cup of coffee or an apéritif. Flowers (from the garden, naturally) stand in vases on the red-clothed tables. 130f menu includes 'brochette de rognons d'agneau; canette aux fruits à l'aigre doux; cheese, dessert.

Upstairs, uneven floors lead to seven charming bedrooms (135–240f), all very clean and light; pretty chintzes, and glimpses of forest trees through the windows. We were much taken with it all and felt it could make a noteworthy *étape* – comments, please!

Map 6B   **VENDEUIL** (Aisne) 214 km SE of Calais; 16 km S of St-Quentin

02800
L'Auberge de Vendeuil

A modern hotel and restaurant. Although the Auberge actually stands on the busy N 44, it is classified as a Relais de Silence. Double

(HR)M
23.07.85.85
AE, DC, V

glazing and double walls effectively muffle traffic noise from the front. Across the route nationale are fields, the red roofs of the village houses (all post 1918), and gently rising, wooded hills: an almost dream-like scene into which the swiftly moving traffic hardly seems to intrude. At the back are woods, flowers and birdsong; and a small zoo and children's playground 2 km up a narrow forest road.

It's all been long discovered by the British: the restaurant is in its fifteenth year, and the hotel is five years old. Twenty-two bedrooms on two floors, each room named after a flower, with en suite bath, loo and wash-basin (250f). Only complaint is that the interior walls were not so sturdily built as the outer ones: we could only too clearly hear people talking downstairs when we retired for an early night. Large and elegantly equipped dining-room *au style rustique.* The restaurant won the coveted Gault-Millau listing in 1987, to add to the other trophies on the walls. M. Lefranc makes a charming host, taking the trouble to move around the tables and talk in excellent English to his guests.

Map 3C/4A | **VERMELLES** (Pas-de-Calais) 93 km SE of Calais; 9 km SE of Béthune; 10 km NW of Lens

---

62980
Le Socrate
(R)M
Rte Nationale
21.26.24.63
DC, EC, V

A charming restaurant on the N 43 between Béthune and Lens. Like the Chartreuse du Val St-Esprit at Gosnay, it is owned by the entrepreneurial M. Jean Constant, who opened the restaurant four years ago.

A large central fireplace deals with grills *au feu de charbon* (but not the real thing, I am sorry to say, being powered by gas). Over it all rises an unusual tent-shaped ceiling. Menus at 66f, 98f and 155f propose some delicious dishes, well worthy of Monsieur's estimable name.

Map 7B | **VERTES FEUILLES** (Aisne) 288 km SE of Calais

02600 | 10 km SW of Soissons on the N 2.

Le Retz
(R)L
Rte Nationale
23.96.01.42
Closed Mon.
p.m.; Tues.; 16/
8–2/9
V

Twenty-eight years ago this large house on the N 2 was the home of a wealthy farmer; farm buildings stand at the edge of green fields behind. Today it is an elegant and sophisticated restaurant, charmingly decorated with chintz curtains, and subdued wall-covering and carpets. Mme Lemoine, suitably stylish and polished, presides over the dining-room. Her son is in charge of the extensive wine list. Lost of flowers everywhere; Art Nouveau pictures; and pretty tablecloths on circular tables. Menu at 140f.

Map 5C | **VERVINS** (Aisne) 252 km SE of Calais

02140
(M) *Sat.*

24 km S of Avesnes; 49 km E of St-Quentin; 44km NW of Laon.

La Tour du Roy
(HR)L
23.98.00.11
Closed Sun.
p.m.; Mon.; 15–
1–15/2
All credit cards

A lovely hotel in the small town of Vervins. Here, in 1598, Henri IV was proclaimed King of France. The kitchen is presided over by Annie Desvignes, a lady chef of great renown, with a Michelin star to her credit. Her splendid menus (140f and 220f) include local products: lamb, game and cider from the Thiérache; and all the desserts are accompanied by fresh farm cream.

The building, an old, turreted manor-house, forms part of the ramparts that encircle the town. Part of it is built over the old town-gate. A marvelious view from the dining-room window looks straight down on to the old houses of the lower town. On the day we were there, a little travelling fair had set up stalls in the street below: the sights, and the sounds that drifted up, could have belonged to almost any century.

Until the 17th century, the building was a debtors' prison. The men were imprisoned in the cellar below the present kitchen. The women occupied a room in the tower, where the jailor, as one of the perks of his job, had the right to spend the night.

Reception rooms are luxurious and the bedrooms (150–350f) are charming. The 'honeymoon suite' (a little joke, we felt, on the part of M. Desvignes) is in the prison tower. It includes a bath for two, a musical seat on the lavatory and an imaginative (and, one hopes, romantic) bedroom up a circular staircase. M. Desvignes is very friendly and jolly and possesses an immense fund of knowledge about the surrounding countryside.

Arrowed for outstanding food and good bedrooms in an interesting tourist area, supported by friendly patron.

Map 6A

VIC-SUR-AISNE (Aisne) 280 km SE of Calais; 22 km E of Compiègne

---

 Wed.

From the N 31 between Compiègne and Soissons take the road signposted across the river Aisne to this large village. Nothing much of interest to see: a mediaeval château (now belonging to a local builder); some pleasure boats moored on the river below the bridge.

Lion d'Or
(HR)S
1 pl. du Général
de Gaulle
23.55.50.20
Closed Sun.
p.m.; Mon.
V

The Lion d'Or has been a restaurant for the last 45 years, 25 of them under the present owner (who speaks English). Could in no way be classified as a hotel: the two simple rooms to let across the enclosed courtyard are more like chambres d'hôte. They are decorated with family furniture; a surprisingly modern tiled bathroom in one, and wash-basin and bidet in the other (100–180f).

The house was once a little farm and the theme throughout the dining-room and small bar is taken from the old stables. Stall divisions stand here and there to separate the tables; there are horse collars and tack hanging on pegs beside the door. 82f menu includes 'mousse de foies de canard maison, rouget grondin à la provençale, plâteau de fromage, et desserts'. Other menus at 115f and 165f.

Map 7A	**VIEUX MOULIN** (Oise) 268 km SE of Calais

60350 — 10 km E of Compiègne by the D 937 and D 14.

➤ Auberge du Daguet
(R)M
44.85.60.72
Closed Thur.
p.m.; Wed.
All credit cards

What a find! In the heart of the Forest of Compiègne, in this charming 1730 village house that has always been a restaurant, Mme Lysseau presented us with one of the best – both service and cuisine – meals of our holiday. The dining-room is charming: red-tiled floor, white tablecloths and tapestry-covered chairs, deep-red ceiling and beams under which French families were quietly and seriously eating.

140f menu offered 'les escargots et leur julienne de racines, sorbet au vieux marc de champagne, paupiette de saumon à la cardinal, Brie de Meaux, profiteroles au chocolat'. Not able to contend that Sunday lunchtime with such a feast, we ordered compôte de lapéreau and salad and, as it turned out, embarked upon a lengthy lunch: prunes sautéd in brandy by our table as an aperitif; a portion of terrine of baby hare and one of chicken livers and prunes; bread accompanied by a reed box of local butter; salad; sweet biscuits and coffee. The bill – 68f. Mme has won many merits for her excellent classical cuisine; these prize-winning dishes are proudly included on the 140f menu.

A firm arrow for outstanding food in a delightful setting.

Map 7B	**VILLE-EN-TARDENOIS** (Marne) 246 km SE of Calais

51170 — 20 km S of Fismes, 20 km SW of Reims and 7 km from the A4, on the D 380.

Auberge du Postillon
R(M)
26.61.83.67
Closed Wed.;
Feb.

A small auberge on the main road, well recommended by locals. The village was rebuilt after the last war and, in spite of a certain amount of heavy traffic, it is a peaceful, rural spot, surrounded by great sweeps of farmland.

Monsieur and his restaurant were both, it seemed, very popular. All the tables outside were occupied by families lingering over coffee, and other people stopped to chat.

Menus 70f, 90f and 130f looked promising. On the 70f menu were la croustade champignon, andouillette de vin blanc aux herbes, cheese, dessert.

Hôtel de la Paix
(HR)S
26.61.81.45
Closed Mon.
AE, EC, V

M. Thery owns this little hotel round the corner from the Auberge du Postillon. Five simple bedrooms from 92f. Menus 60f and 100f. On the carte in the unpretentious and tidy restaurant were rognons de veau à la crème de cerfeuil (68f); terrine de foies de volaille (maison) et sa confiture (34f); cuisses de grenouilles au champagne (60f).

Map 7B	**VILLERS-AGRON** (Marne) 243 km SE of Calais; 26 km NE of Château-Thierry; 26 km SW of Reims

3 km from the A 4, exit Dormans; a large village on the D 25.

M. Xavier Ferry
(C)
23.71.60.67
Parking

A large château–farmhouse that was once the dwelling of the seigneurs de Condé. Five large bedrooms (160–180f, three with bath en suite) are furnished in excellent taste – did we, among French designs, recognise Laura Ashley and Habitat wallpaper? The young couple who own the farm speak good English and have lots of ideas about places to eat, things to do and towns to visit. Madame is a Parisienne and at first thought that she could 'never live here, deep in the country' but now, after six years of marriage, says that she would hate to return to a city. On request, she will provide a simple evening meal which she serves with style. We ate tomato salad, plenty of cold ham and beef, green salad, cheese, fresh raspberries from the garden (60f), and enjoyed a lengthy discussion about the ins and outs of farming in France today. Lots of room to park in the large, tidy farmyard, and tables and chairs on a terrace by the front door.

Map 7A

VILLERS-COTTERÊTS (Aisne) 283 km SE of Calais; 23 km SW of Soissons; 29 km SE of Compiègne

---

02600
(M) *Thur.*

A small town that grew up around its hunting lodge, built in the 13th century by Charles de Valois, surrounded by the great hardwood forest of Retz.

By the 16th century the original hunting lodge had become a vast château, the buildings greatly enlarged and embellished by François I and Henri II. It is now an old folks' home. The inner courtyard, which once formed a tennis court and was surrounded by the lodgings of the royal family, is today the peaceful precinct of citizens of the *troisième age*. Not a lot to see inside, but well worth the visit. The one elaborately decorated room on view was probably once the chapel; leading up to it are two magnificient staircases with richly moulded ceilings featuring the salamander, the capital 'F' for François I, and mythological scenes. This small tour starts at 8.30 a.m.: ask at the porter's lodge; how much you give in recompense is entirely up to you.

Villers-Cotterêts is the birthplace of the novelist Alexandre Dumas. There is a small museum devoted to his memory at 46 r. Alexandre Dumas, near the station. Apart from his Académie Française uniform, the exhibits are mostly first editions and manuscripts of his work. Open during the week from 2–6 p.m.

A few kilometres from Villers-Cotterêts, signposted off the D 32, is the village of Vez. Hard now to believe that this rural place was the capital of Valois long before Crépy. The remains of the once-great 13th-century château (which escaped the exacting restoration of Pierrefonds, although closely connected with that castle in history) stand, in all magnificence, on the wooded hillside.

Below, and just visible from the road, are the picturesque remains of a small abbey known as Lieu Restoré. Founded in 1131, it was ruined in the Hundred Years War and again during the Wars of Religion. Later the lovely church – a late and exquisite example of the Flamboyant Gothic – became a barn. In 1964 young M. Pottier, whose childhood dream had been to see the abbey restored, started work on the ruins with the help of friends: an ambitious project to which the State, eventually, added its support. The gable above the west door contains some of the most beautiful rose windows in France; in spite of its vicissitudes, it has remained almost intact for over eight centuries.

Le Commerce
(HR)M
17 r. du Général Mangin
23.96.19.97
Closed Sun. p.m.; Mon.; 15/ 1–15/2
V

A good hotel on a one-way street in the centre of the town. Park your car in the street behind the hotel, across the way from the château, and carry your bags across the small courtyard.

Bedrooms (85–120f) are simple and clean, but go for those at the back if you want a quiet night, free from traffic noise.

A large dining-room, well furnished with comfortable, tapestry-covered chairs and a big fireplace. Windows overlook the courtyard where a few white chairs and tables stand, ready for those balmy evenings. Menus at 70f and 90f. On the 90f menu,we ate 'surprise de la forêt (snails with mushrooms cooked *en cocotte*) and foies de veau aux baies de cassis. Very friendly and helpful patrons. All in all, a stop to be recommended.

Hôtel Regent
(H)M
26 r. du Général Mangin
23.96.01.46
AE, DC, Ec, V

An old coaching inn that stood on the route to Reims, Paris and the North, and traces its history back to the 16th century. Known until the mid 19th century as l'Auberge du Croix d'Or, it was used as stables for one hundred years until the family Peytavin-Thiebaut set about its restoration in 1968.

Eighteen bedrooms (190–265f). The one we saw was decorated in neo-Renaissance style: dark-red carpet and bedcovers, grey-painted panelling picked out in gold; a large and well-appointed bathroom. A worn, old staircase with timber set into the treads, leads to the upper floors. There is antique family furniture throughout and a big, open fireplace in the entrance hall: all beautifully in keeping with its historic past. Breakfast, 25.50f.

Map 7C   **VINAY** (Marne) 308 km SE of Calais; 7 km SW of Épernay

---

51200
Épernay

Hostellerie la Briqueterie
(H)L–M
Rte de Sézanne-Vinay
26.54.11.22

Follow the signs to Sézanne and you can't miss the Briqueterie.

A vast Swiss-chalet-style pile, set in a large garden and surrounded by vineyards, so a night's repose is guaranteed. The rooms are very comfortable and well equipped, as indeed they should be for 386–436f, and the young chef in the restaurant is improving all the time. With menus starting at 170f, it's far from cheap, but for those who want a certain degree of luxury it might well be the answer.

Map 5B   **WAMBAIX** (Nord) 158 km SE of Calais

59400
Cambrai
Ⓜ *Sun.*

9 km SE of Cambrai by the D 960 and D 142.

**M. et Mme
Becquet-Banse
et leurs enfants**
(C)
*16 r. de la
Dessous*
27.78.73.14

Les enfants are very much in evidence in this old village farmhouse, crawling or running everywhere and chattering non-stop – which is all right for some, not quite so peaceful for others.

I found Madame delightful. She is very interested in promoting tourism and has lots of brochures on the region. Our bedroom (100f) looked out on to a quiet road. The bed was comfortable, we had our own wash-basin and shared the noisy loo at the top of the stairs.

In the evening, Monsieur returned from the fields (he had given up work in a factory to get back to the land), and we all ate together at a long table in the kitchen (30f). The meal was hardly a gastronomic experience, but a jolly affair, accompanied by lots of advice on the places I should visit, and plenty of red wine. The little children (who kept resolutely awake until after we had gone to bed) were very pretty and amusing. Even the tiny ones fell into a pattern of enviable good manners when they said goodbye in the morning; and the eight-year-old hugged and kissed as though he had known us for years.

Map 1A   **WISSANT** (Pas-de-Calais) 17 km S of Calais

A few km after the astonishing coast road dips down into Escalles, it begins to call itself the Corniche de la Côte d'Opale, and continues its spectacular way to Wissant, confounding the North-of-France sceptics.

Five years ago I explored the village and wrote disparagingly. I don't think Wissant has ever forgiven me. On every subsequent visit, its skies have been leaden, its streets awash, its beach deserted, its inhabitants sulking indoors. It took a letter from a Mr Terry Thompson (*'I love the book but there is just one thing missing: no mention of Wissant, a lovely little place.'*) to make me try again, and this time, with a modicum of sunny illumination, I got a glimmering of understanding. But only a glimmering. Any resort that devotes its prime beach frontage to a shabby camping site and a couple of broken-down beach huts cannot be top of my pops. That said, there are definite signs that things Wissant-wise are looking up. Paint has recently been applied to surfaces that were peeling on my previous visit, smartish new apartment blocks are appearing. If your need is for a simple cheap beach stop very near the port, this could well be it. The sands are fine and extensive – I took a long walk by the water's edge, watching the windsurfers (for whom Wissant is a favourite base), enjoying the aspect of the enclosing arms of the two Caps, Blanc and Gris, with Kent across the waves.

Apart from the beach, not a lot goes on in the village; scattered about are a couple of *crêperies*, a Co-op, a *pharmacie*, a *boulangerie*, *friteries*, a Musée du Moulin, and a hotel well known for many years to the Brits:

Hôtel Normandy
(HR)M–S
21.35.90.11

The black and white bulk of Mr Davies' Hôtel Normandy dominates the centre of the town, but I am delighted to see that the even more dominating Watneys Red Barrel sign which put me off previously has gone. Inside is a well-stocked bar opening on to a very pleasant dining-room – red check cloths, ceiling beams – with views of the sea. The menus looked promising, at 65f, 85f and 105f, plus an unfortunate cover charge. I liked the sound of some of the items on the 105f version, which included regional dishes like an ice-cream flavoured with genièvre from nearby Houlle, but wondered if Mr Davies had read some of the translations like 'The gardener assorted platter'.

The bedrooms are modern and fair sized. Demi-pension for two people ranges from 386-355f.

Le Vivier
(R)S
21.35.93.61
Closed Wed.

An inviting little fish restaurant just opposite the Normandy. Sensibly they specialise in local fish, dished up on moderately priced menus, or singly: e.g.: a platterful of mussels costs 28f, a plâteau de fruits de mer 110f. I have not yet tried this one out myself, but look forward to doing so because it would seem to fill a surprising gap in the local market – unpretentious and fishy. Reports particularly welcome.

Map 2B

WISQUES (Pas-de-Calais) 42 km SE of Calais; 6 km SW of St-Omer

---

62500
St-Omer

A pleasant leafy village, high on a hill overlooking the lights of St-Omer at night. The Benedictine abbey of St Paul, known for its daily Gregorian chants, is set behind high walls.

➤ **La Sapinière**
(HR)S
21.95.14.59
Closed Sun.
p.m.; Mon.
o.o.s.; 2nd
week in Jan.
V
Parking

On the D 208e, the rte St-Omer, between the N 42 and the D 928 and only 2 km from the autoroute exit. It's a substantial white building, set in its own gardens, and recently repainted and freshened up, with green shutters and lattice; a great improvement all round in fact since its present owners, the Delbekes, took it over five years or so ago. They are still in the course of improving the rooms, gardens and general amenities, but already it is highly recommendable as a modestly-priced hotel that has retained its pleasantly old-fashioned character without becoming seedy.

The restaurant is well respected locally, and full of French families soon after midday. M. Delbeke uses vegetables from the Marais, local trout and any other fresh ingredients that come his way on bargain menus that start at 59f, including wine. Others at 85f, 95f, 140f and 160f are all interesting, but it was the cheapest version that I noticed on most plates, so at least give it a try.

The rooms are much more spacious than in more modern lodgeries, and excellent value at 80f to 180f; some have T.V. and baths.

M. Delbeke is an attentive and friendly host, welcoming many of his customers as old friends. The combination of his welcome, the convenient situation, the good cooking and comfortable rooms, and the quietness of the surrounding garden makes this a new arrow, much welcomed in an area where this kind of accommodation is rare.

La Sapinière, Wisques

'Pleasant ambience. All French at lunch, reasonable wine list and the chef seen actually cooking and not at his microwave.'

Map 2B	**ZOUAFQUES** (Pas-de-Calais) 36 km SE of Calais

62890
Tournehem-
sur-Hem

6 km N of Ardres on the N 43.

La Ferme de Wolphus
(C)
21.35.61.61

Well signposted from the route nationale. The friendly and helpful Mme Béhaghel runs a quail farm here and has recently converted three rooms into comfortable b. and b. accommodation.

She charges 210f for two people, which struck me as somewhat expensive, but the rooms do have their own showers and loo, the price includes a good breakfast and the situation is very convenient.

Le Cheval Noir
(R)S
21.35.60.29

The number of lorries regularly pulled up outside this Relais Routier on the nationale confirms the claim that this is the best eating-place in the district, and readers have been happy to stop here with their hungry families for a cheap fill-up.

48.50f buys three very substantial courses, and a carafe of plonk, which arrives almost as soon as you do.

Bruges

Bruges, Belgium

Venice of the North they say. Well, yes and no.

Yes for the obvious reasons – the canals and the antiquity, but yes too for a number of other twinnings that only occurred to me gradually. Foremost is the isolation of both these northern and southern gems. When you leave your car behind at the causeway entrance to Venice you leave the rest of Italy, the rest of Europe, behind too. Similarly with Bruges. Cross the ringroad and it's hard to remember that the other Belgium exists, or that the cross ferry link back home is a mere 10 km away. Both cities are figurative islands, fortified by history and fortune. Both have long been conscious of their privileged position and their uniqueness and have resisted all attempts to homogenise their individuality.

Because of their strategic position both cities have been fought over, subdued and annexed, but not for long. Both have enjoyed periods of supreme power and wealth, when the best craftsmen and materials in the world were put to excellent use in gilding their lilies. From their heterogeneous invaders they have assimilated a wealth of influences and treasures; by freaks of fortune two world wars have left them untouched and allowed us to appreciate their staggering inheritances.

One of the major joys of visiting Venice is to sit in its very heart, in St Mark's Square, confident that sooner or later the world will pass by; to sit in a café in the Markt is a similar experience, and an equal pleasure. Here are the hubs of the great cities from which all routes flow. Climb the belfries in either one, to gain stunning views of ancient roofs and snaking water. Alternatively there is the challenge of leaving the obvious behind to the other tourists, diving down quiet alleyways, walking along the lesser-known canals, arriving at unfamiliar squares. Echoing footsteps emphasise the tranquillity that comes from traffic-freedom.

Here the councillors of Bruges have been outstandingly clever, and how I salute them for their foresight. A few years ago they invested in vast underground car-parks and now the Zand and the Burg squares are open uncluttered spaces. Photographs show the incredible reincarnation from automobile jungles to pedestrian-friendly areas through which wander the unharrassed tourists, able to stand and stare. More and more streets are getting semi-pedestrianised, with more pavement and only cobbled access, so that there is less incentive to take a car into the centre of the city.

Both cities have two distinctive faces – of winter and summer. In winter the hotels, restaurants and museums are empty but so are the cafés which contribute much vivacity. In bad weather Bruges looks like Moscow, with its citizens furred, mufflered and booted, scurrying out of the biting wind, but in winter southerly Venice too can look devastatingly grey. In summer all is effervescence, the water sparkles enticingly, the chatter from the cafés orchestrates, but I'm told that if the heat gets ouf of hand, the canals begin to pong and the experience is not pleasant. Spring and autumn are undoubtedly the best times to visit.

Both are elegant, upmarket, not cheap cities, in which window shopping is a joy. Both, perhaps, have been made over-confident by their tourist potential and have an excessively high proportion of expensive restaurants and hotels, and in neither is it easy to find good cheap accommodation.

Here perhaps the similarities end. Unlike Venice, which of course is much larger, with many more canals, there is no water transport, as such, in Bruges. But an absolute must is a ride by motor-boat through the central canals. These are the core, the raison d'être for Bruges. Along them were built the first houses, many of them turning their backs on what is now the city, and facing the watery thoroughfare through which journeyed their provisions, their friends, their links with the outside world. The trip from any of the clearly marked stops lasts about half and hour and costs 110Bf. The driver will point out all the main attractions along the route, as will the well-informed drivers of the horse-driven cabs that ply for hire outside the belfry, at 650Bf. I suggest an early ride for early orientation, though the lofty belfry and the towers of St Salvador and Notre Dame make easy landmarks for the stranger.

Unlike Venice's sad record of decline and corruption, Bruges has been a competent administrator of its own heritage. The town planning and control has been admirably rigid and the amount of in-filling in the gorgeous mediaeval, 15th- and 16th-century houses has been remarkably sparse. Restoration is a continuous process and grants are awarded to householders prepared to paint their houses in their original colours, so that today Bruges is a vivid and accurate historical picturebook. Sometimes it looks as two-dimensional as a stage façade and sometimes like a children's game, with little toy houses carefully built up from coloured bricks.

The Tourist Offiice in the belfry building is a pleasure to visit. Light and airy in its pale arched brickwork, it is also extremely well run and its staff will direct patiently, book rooms efficiently and sell maps and guidebooks. (Perfect English is spoken of course, as everywhere else in this paradise for the lazy tourist.) I particularly recommend the purchase of the illustrated guide *Bruges, City of Art*, which suggests three walking tours around the city; to the classic tourist Bruges, to the area associated with the prosperous trading period, and to the 'unknown Bruges', all well documented and a fascinating way to see most of the treasures. Just to whet the appetite:

The market square is the natural start for any town, with interest attracted at once here by the 13th-century belfry, the mediaeval symbol of freedom, whose 366 steps lead to the famous 47-bell carillon and a panoramic view over the city. Try not to arrive there at the time when the bells are chiming! The wooden Halles date back to the same period and Bruges had a covered market on this spot even earlier, at the time when it was becoming one of the most popular and prosperous cities in Europe.

In the late 14th century, when a Burgundian king, Philip the Bold, was its ruler, Bruges became the centre of a sumptuous court. This golden age enabled the guilds and powerful merchants to build many of the elegant houses that give the city so much of its character. Look up at the roofs above the cafés in the Markt and find the guilds' symbols on the gables of the weaver's house, and the basket of fish on the fisherman's house. Cut through the pedestrianised Breidelstraat, to arrive at the glorious Burg, peacefully free of any traffic more frenetic than a horse and carriage.

For nearly two thousand years this has been the centre of Bruge's judicial, religious and administrative activities, as its surrounding architecture bears witness. Here is the uncontrived reverse of town planning – a hotchpotch of different motivations and styles which somehow contrives an effortless harmony.

For the earliest evidence, look for the little scale-model of the 9th-century Carolingian chapel, which used to stand where plane trees are now growing, opposite the town hall. Then cut diagonally across to the place of pilgrimage renowned through history, the Basilica of the Holy Blood; two superimposed oratories dramatically contrast in scale and character. The lower, St Basil's Chapel, is Romanesque, built as the Count's chapel, unique in West Flanders. The heavy door shuts out the light from the square and leaves you blinking in the dim light. Massive stumpy columns, blackened over the centuries, impressive in their stark simplicity, dominate. Wooden carvings of Ecce Homo and the Pièta, 14th-century masterpieces, are all the more striking in the severity of their surroundings.

The elegant 16th-century adjoining staircase leads to a very different prospect, the exuberant upper chapel, in Gothic style, where the relic of the Holy Blood is preserved. The gold and silver reliquary is the centrepiece of a mighty procession through the streets on Ascension Day.

Alongside the two chapels is one of the oldest (1376) and most beautiful Gothic town halls in Flanders. It's worth paying the fee to climb up to the first floor and see the magnificent painted wooden ceiling.

Then there's the Old Recorder's Hall (1534), the Renaissance representative; the Law Court (1727), the Classicist; and the Provost's House (1662), the Baroque. No-one nowadays mentions the modern building alongside the Holy Blood, but maybe future generations might be interested to see what the 20th-century architects had learned from their illustrious predecessors.

Walk under the arcade of the Blinde Ezelstraat to arrive at the most photographed canal in Bruges. To the left is the colonnaded fish market, open every morning except Sundays and Mondays.

From then on it's wander at will – right, perhaps, along the Dijver, where the cargo ships used to tie up, admiring the expensive lace in the shops lining the quays, or taking in a bit of culture in the Groeninghe Museum, rich in Memlings, Van Eycks, Heironymos Bosch, Breughels, and a flaying scene that brought on nightmares after the first time I was unwise enough to study it in detail.

The Hans Memling Museum is a bit further on, set in an old ward of the Hospital of St John, founded 1118, one of the oldest hospices in Europe. You can divert slightly to Notre Dame church to see the white marble Madonna with Child, one of the few Michelangelo works to be found outside Italy. Dominating the whole walk will be the brick tower of another famous Bruges landmark, St Saviour's Cathedral.

The extension of this walk along the canal will bring you to a favourite destination of artists and tourists, an oasis of green peace – the Béguinage (or Begijnhof on the signposts) a village within the city. Framed with whitewashed cottages dating back to the 13th century, the Béguinage in the Middle Ages was the religious retreat for young ladies of all classes who wished to lead a pious life, under the direction of the Grand Mistress, whose house can be seen in the far left corner. Nowadays the Benedictine nuns who live here have adopted the mediaeval dress of the original béguines.

Any one of the dozens of additional treasures – St Saviour's Cathedral with its amazing organ loft, the old Walplaats, where on a fine day you can see the lacemakers at their craft, the romantic Minnewater lake, the Groeninge Museum, the photogenic Bonifacius Bridge, the Tanners' House, the house of the Van de Buerze family, where the financial transactions conducted by the local merchants gave the word Bourse – Buerze – to the world's stock exchanges – would be of sufficient interest anywhere else to merit a lengthier study, but in Bruges the interest is all-pervasive and every aspect brings unique reward. Sit and study a guidebook by all means, but leave time to wander around and let your own eyes record the delights. In summer the main sights are floodlit and it's an unforgettable experience to drift along the canal on a balmy evening and let the history and art lesson flow by.

HOTELS AND RESTAURANTS

①Hotel de l'Orangerie
(HR)L
Kartuizerinnen-
str. 10
34.16.49
AE, DC, EC, V

The most luxurious hotel in Bruges, describing itself as 'already in the country' by virtue of its light and airy spaciousness and abundance of greenery, but in fact right in the centre, in an old creeper-covered house overlooking the principal canal.

You can take the very special breakfast (no lunch required) on a terrace overlooking the water.

The restoration has been achieved with great style and taste: the 19 rooms are lovely and if someone else were paying the bill, I have no doubt that this is where I would stay. But 3950–4550Bf!

②Die Swaene
(H)L
Steenhouwers-
dijk 1
34.27.98
AE, DC, EC, V

The Americans love this 15th-century patrician's house, with its bar à l'Anglaise, all oak and stained-glass windows; red plush, swags, chandeliers and four-poster beds feature in the bedrooms. A bit over the top perhaps but at least it's a change from the uniformly good taste (a bit boring?) of most other conversions.

It has a prime situation, very central, overlooking a tranquil canal. The service and buffet breakfast are both exceptionally good. 2600–3400Bf. A honeymoon suite is 5800Bf.

➤ Hotel ③Prinsenhof
(H)M–L
9 Ontvangerstr.
50

Small – just 16 rooms, but therefore benefiting from personal service; centrally situated, in yet another recently restored old house, designated Relais de Silence; the rooms have every possible comfort, and I would rate this among the best of the medium to high price range. 2600–3550Bf.

34.26.90
AE, DC, EC, V

'A small brand-new hotel (opened 1.8.86). They had one room left, out of I think 9 rooms. Spoke good English. Our twin-bedded room quite delightful, bowl of sweets on table, cotton wool in bathroom, wall-mounted hair-dryer etc. Beautifully decorated in pale blue. Very comfortable, very quiet and with parking outside. Excellent breakfast in pretty dining-room, ham, cheese as well as usual food. It is fairly expensive – £50 – but worth every penny.

'We were told to go just round the corner to have dinner at Die Broemjie (the little broom). Best meal I have ever had! Fresh blood orange juice, smoked salmon (huge portions) and steak had son in transports of gastronomic delight.' – Mrs J. L. Rankin.

➤ Pandhotel
(4)(H)M
Pandreitje 12
34.04.66
AE, DC, EC, V

Unbeatable in its category for location, style, size and welcome. It's in a quiet tree-lined square just off the main canal, and has recently been redecorated in discreet luxury. It also has a nice salon in which to rest the cobble-tired feet, and a sophisticated bar.

The bedrooms, all with bathrooms, are comfortable and stylish, without being over the top, and the patronne is efficient and helpful; 2200–2800Bf.

➤ Hotel Adornes
(5)(H)M
St Annarei
34.13.36
AE, DC, EC

Cheaper and also highly recommendable. I liked the calm atmosphere, the modest size, and the location, about five minutes' tranquil walk along the cobbled quays from the centre to a corner site overlooking one of the quieter canals.

The rooms are restored, like many others in the city, in modern style, all beige and brown, but are somehow more appealing than most. They cost from 1900–2900Bf.

(6)Hotel Bryghia
(H)M
4 Oosterlingen-plein
33.80.59
AE, DC, EC, V

An old brick house, overlooking one of the quieter peripheral canals, attractively decorated in the old style downstairs and, rather less happily, in the prevailing beige-modern in the bedrooms, which are none the less comfortable and well equipped. With private bathrooms, they cost 2170Bf.

(7)Ter Brughe
(H)M
Ooost Gistelhof 2
34.03.24

Another restored 15th-century building, with 20 comfortable bedrooms, and a pleasant breakfast room, overlooking a quiet canal. 2500Bf.

(8)Hotel Groeninghe
(H)M
Korte Vuldersstr. 29
34.07.96

A popular hotel, in a quiet street behind the cathedral. It was being redecorated when I was there, but the rooms that were finished looked comfortable and attractive. Good value at 1200Bf, or 1800Bf with bath.

Pandhotel Bruges.

Portimari , Bruges

► Portinari
⑨ (H)M
Zand 15
34.10.34
AE, DC, EC, V
Parking

An old building on the largest square in Bruges, recently converted into an extremely comfortable modern hotel. Rooms 2000–2500Bf. I couldn't fault it: my room looked out, via double glazing, on to the animation of the Zand, and I felt an invisible part of the city, smugly watching the Brugeois walking their dogs, hopping on buses, making assignations. In summer there are tables out on the terrace for even closer inspection.

The refurbishment has been carried out discreetly in light Scandinavian style in what emerged by the end of my trip as Bruges' favourite hotel colour scheme – beige and more beige. Good bathroom, lots of cupboard space, with everything working, including breakfast spot on ordered time. Alternatively there is a kind of buffet breakfast served in the pleasant dining-room, muralled with blow-ups of old Bruges, that makes lunch a non-event. Wade through pâtés, ham smoked and fresh, roast beef, salads savoury and sweet, all manner of Danish pastries and buns, yoghurts and fruit, with a boiled egg or two and you can save on the meal bills for the rest of the day. For bad weather there is a spacious lounge, and a first-floor secluded terrace for fine weather.

The Manager could not be more helpful or knowledgeable about the city. The Portinari has the big bonus of parking in the huge underground parking opposite and as everything in the town is within walking distance you can say goodbye to the car headache.

An arrow for comfort, position, helpfulness.

⑩ Hotel
Cordoeanier
(H)S
Cordoeanerstr.
18
33.90.51

Very central bed-and-breakfast hotel, with clean rooms at 1300–1800Bf.

⑪ Hotel de Barge
(H)S
Bargeweg 15
38.51.50

The weather in March, which had been bad, degenerated into downright malevolency on my last day and I funked walking through the driving snow to look at a boat. But I am told that the rooms on this converted Flemish barge are as spacious and comfortable as in many hotels, and it's certainly something different that might appeal to the kids, at a modest price – 1500–1600Bf with substantial breakfast.

In fact its only 500 metres from the station, so very conveniently situated.

⑫ Hotel de Pauw
(H)S
Sint
Gilliskerkhof 6
33.71.18

One of the more modestly priced guesthouses, about ten minutes' pleasant walk from the city centre. Rooms from 1220Bf.

➤ **Hotel Aragon**
⑬ (H)M
Naaldenstraat
24
33.80.59
EC, V
Parking

A recommendation from *FE4* recently checked out: *'We would like to extol the virtues of the Hotel Aragon. We had a large double room with a large bathroom and both were very well equipped (even a colour T.V. for the homesick!). M. and Mme Van Laere-Wulleman were most attentive and charming hosts and couldn't have been more helpful. They are obviously Brugge enthusiasts and treated us as very welcome house-guests. Hotel Aragon is very conveniently situated within two minutes of the Market, in a quite backwater. The breakfast buffet was beautifully presented and the orange juice was delicious. It knocked spots off anywhere else we stayed. The cost was 2650Bf b. and b. Please consider giving it an arrow.'* – R. E. Purnell.

I have, Dr Purnell, and here it is.

➤ **De Karmeliet**
⑭ (R)M–L
1 Jeruzalemstr.
33.82.59
Closed Sun.
p.m.; Mon
AE, DC, EC, V

Personally I would place this No. 1 Restaurant in Bruges, though I hasten to add it might not be everyone's choice. Geert Van Hecke has a prestigious pedigree behind him, having served with Alain Chapel, arguably the best chef in France, and at the Villa Lorraine, probably the best restaurant in Belgium. He has now brought his considerable expertise to this little converted monastery tucked away in a quiet back street, away from the tourist traps. It's all very low key, calm, and not out to impress. Geert is a cook not a showman. The food is the thing and of all the good meals I had in Bruges this was the one I enjoyed most.

The cooking can be elaborate – I had wonderful Breton langoustines wrapped in a cabbage leaf with a truffle-flecked sauce – or simple – a roast duckling served in the traditional way with turnips and onions.

If you like to spend your money on food rather than decor, this is the place, but be prepared for a ten to fifteen minute walk from the centre, and leave the stilettos behind. The 1600Bf menu is a bargain.

⑮ **'t Bourgoensche Cruyce**
(R)L
Wollestr. 41
33.79.26
Closed Sun.
lunch; Mon.
(from Oct. to
April); Tue.
(from 1/5–30/9,
Feb;
AE, V

The restaurant with the best setting in Bruges, overlooking the canal, and facing its rival the Duc de Bourgogne (whose restaurant was undergoing a crisis when I was there).

The decor inside is lush and plush; I would save it for a romantic candle-lit dinner with someone you wished to impress, and eat outside on the terrace for lunch.

The food is said to be lighter and 'moderne' these days but mine was as substantial and traditional as anywhere. You pay for the position and service but feel very smug being peered at by the tourists. Menus at 1400Bf, 1800Bf. Carte allow 2000–2500Bf.

⑯ **Den Braamberg**
(R)L
Pandreitje 11
33.73.70
Closed Sun.
p.m.; Tue.

A most reliable and satisfactory restaurant, very popular with the Brugeois. Solid bourgeois comfort in an elegant dining room, through whose plate-glass window you can watch François Bogaert prepare his skilful presentations of immaculately fresh fish, prime meat. Perfect service and good wine list.

The 'light' menu is the one I commend – 1700Bf for six courses!

Kardinaalshof, Bruges.

⑰**Kardinaalshof**
(R)L
St
Salvatorskerk-
hof 14
34.16.91
Closed Sun.
a.m.; Tues.; 15/
6–30/6

In the shadow of the cathedral, with an unexpectedly modern light and bright interior.

Jean Van de Vijver specialises in seafood. On his 1600Bf menu I ate asparagus with hot foie gras, a china-tea sorbet, sole with a lightly curried sauce and wild rice, and a pastry 'tulip' stuffed with strawberries in a raspberry sauce – all fresh and good. Stick to the menu if you can or the bill will get out of hand.

⑱**'t Pandreitje**
(R)M–L
Pandreitje 6
33.11.90
Closed Sun.;
Mon.; 1/3–24/3,
14/12–30/12
AE, DC, EC, V

Just opposite the Braamberg, an elegant little restaurant in a Louis XVI setting, with an English patronne. No fireworks, but good predictable Belgian food and very popular with the locals. Lunch menu 1050Bf, Dinner 1650Bf. Carte expensive.

➤ **Maximiliaan**
⑲**Van Oosterich**
(R)M
Wijngaardplein
17
33.47.23

Tourist restaurants usually spell tourist food at tourist prices. Therefore the M.V.O., one of Bruge's best-known restaurants, too picturesque one would think for its own good, at the entrance to the Beguijnhof, should be unrecommendable. But in fact it rises nobly above all the short-cut temptations and continues to offer, as it has done for many years, honest straightforward cooking – grills etc. – plus a few much appreciated and imaginative culinary touches – lots of herbs in the hollandaise.

Inside is dark and warm and cosy, ideal for a winter break, outside is flowery and summer fun. Of course I recommend it. 290Bf for lunch, dinner more.

➤ **De Visscherie**
⑳(R)M
8 Vismarkt
33.02.12
Closed Tues.;
22/3–31/3, 18/
11–15/12
AE, DC, EC, V

Very fishy. Opposite the fishmarket, the very place to try the Belgian waterzoi, served here enriched with half a lobster. Other simpler fish dishes equally good. There is a 98Bf menu but the 160Bf is better, e.g: 9 oysters, or fish pâté with sauce verte; monkfish with wild mushrooms, or salmon; cheese or fruit. There are a few meat dishes for the fish-allergic, like a feuilleté de ris de veau or beef au poivre. Good wine list.

Well known and popular, so best book. An arrow for the best fish restaurant and lots of atmosphere.

㉑**Den Gouden**
Harynck
(R)M
25 Groeninge
33.76.37
Closed Sun.;
Mon.; 11/7–7/8,
11/12–29/12
AE, DC, EC, V

Highly recommended by many locals, with the proviso that the service is appalling. It's in one of the main shopping areas and has recently been enlarged and smartened up.

Philippe Serruys' speciality is pastry, so go, perhaps, for his airy feuilletés, or keep it simple with a Flanders pigeon *nature*. At all costs leave room for one of his oustanding desserts, like a parfait flavoured with Ceylon tea – truly '*parfait*'.

At lunch there is a 1100Bf menu; otherwise its 1750Bf or 2500Bf including wine.

② Restaurant Andi
(R)S
Rosenhoedkai 7
33.70.89
Closed Mon.
o.o.s

A cheerful little bistro, facing the main canal, serving simple but good quality meals at around 225Bf.

③ Restaurant Malpertuis
(R)S
Eiermarkt 9
33.30.39
Closed Sun.;
Wed. o.o.s.

Popular with the tourists because of its unusual setting in the caves of a 16th-century convent in the heart of Bruges. Good for a not-too-expensive candle-lit supper. Say 800-1000Bf.

► Sint Joris
④ (R)S
Markt 29
33.30.62

The centre of the tourist beat will always be the market square, and there to serve them (this being commendably opportunist Belgium) there will always be tourist restaurants. This situation can often be the place to avoid for those who do not wish to be served rip-off food, surrounded by fellow foreigners. In Bruges, however, there is at least one honourable exception.

The Sint Joris is no fly-by-night. It has been in the same hands for years and is recognised by the locals as offering excellent steady value. The family who run it do not take advantage of their position to dish out the take-it-or-leave-it treatment; on the contrary, they are particularly friendly and welcoming. They do not stick to boringly safe food but are prepared to risk being original. There is a wide choice of menus or single dishes, all reasonably priced, as is the wine.

㉕ Bistro de Stove
(R)S
Kleine St Amandstr. 4
33.78.35
Closed Wed.

In a little alley just between the Eiermarkt and the Markt, a warm and cosy little bistro, good for a snack, drink, or modest meal at modest prices.

㉖ 't Bruges Beertje
Kemelstr. 5
33.96.16
Closed Wed.

It would be a crime to visit Bruges and not sample some of Belgium's renowned beers. They take their beers very seriously here and the patron of this old beer-house will 'diagnose' your taste from his range of 200 varieties.

A visit to this ancient, typically Belgian establishment, which could have come straight out of a *Secret Army* set, is an experience not to be missed. The locals use it regularly as as kind of parlour, and through the smokey fug always in progress are card games, which look as though they've been going on for ever.

From 4 p.m. to 1 a.m. there's non-stop diversion. Snacks too.

Two tea/coffee/snack ideas: **'t Koffie Boontje**, Hallestraat 4, a light and cheerful little coffee-house in a new development just off the Wollestraat, and **'t Fonteintje** in Simon Stevinplein, just off Zilverstraat, a tea-room/*brasserie* open from 11 a.m. to 11 p.m.

I had hoped to extend my range of hotels and restaurants to some of the attractive little tourist villages on the canals just outside the city of Bruges, but time and the weather did not permit. For those with longer than a few days to spare in the region, however, I can heartily recommend a trip by boat along the peaceful waterways, to Damme perhaps. Suggested restaurants, uninspected, are: **De Lieve and De Drie Zilveren Kannen** at Damme, and **Bruegel** (especially), **De Waterput**, and **Siphon** at Oostkerke.

Wine Hints from Jancis Robinson

HOW TO READ A WINE LIST

Wine lists in France, just like their counterparts in British restaurants, can be confusing – and sometimes even terrifying, with the only affordable bottles hidden below a stack of great names at even greater prices. There are certain ground rules in their layout, however.

The most basic of wines made in France are called *vins de table*, and may well be listed under this heading, to differentiate them from wines with some sort of geographical designation, either *Appellation Contrôlée* (AC or AOC) or, slightly more lowly, *Vins Délimités de Qualité Supérieure* (VDQS). The 'house wine' in many French restaurants is of the simpler *vin de table* sort and may be described as Vin de la Maison, or Vin du Patron, meaning 'our wine'. There are many branded table wines too, the sort that carry a brand name, and these should be listed under a special heading, *Vins de Marque*. There is also a newish breed of rather superior *vin de table* which is worth looking out for, and which may be listed under the heading *Vins de Table*, or the region where it was made, or under the general heading *Vins de Pays*. These are superior quality *vins de table* which are good enough to tag their provenance onto their name.

All other wines will usually be grouped under the heading of the region where they were made and, usually, split according to red wines (*rouges*) and whites (*blancs*). The following are the main wine regions of France, in the order in which they *usually* appear on a smart wine list (though there is, exasperatingly, no standard convention):

Bordeaux

France's biggest and best-known region for top-quality dryish reds, wines that we call claret. Most of such wines are called Château This or Château That, which will vary from about 60 francs a bottle to the earth and then some. Bordeaux's great white wines are sweet (*doux*) dessert wines from Sauternes, though there are now some good value dry (*sec*) wines too.

Bourgogne

We call this small, highly-priced region Brugundy. Its dry whites such as Montrachet are the greatest in the world; its reds can be lovely scented, smooth liquids, though there are some highly-priced disappointments.

Beaujolais/Mâconnais

This is the region just south of Burgundy proper that can offer some less expensive versions of Burgundy's white wines from the vineyards round Mâcon and some easy-drinking, gulpable reds from the vineyards of the Beaujolais area. Drink all these wines young.

Rhône

Mainly red wines and generally very good value. The whites can be quirky and heavy, but there has been a run of extremely good vintages of the meaty or spicy reds.

Loire

France's other great river is best known, rather neatly, for its white wines – all with lots of acidity and great with food. Most Loire wines are designed for early consumption.

Alsace

France's most overlooked wine region, perhaps because it is almost in Germany. Fragrant, dry whites named after the Germanic grape varieties from which they are made. (This practice, varietal naming, is still uncommon in France though it is gaining ground elsewhere throughout the wine world.)

Since French Entrée territory is so far from France's vine land, the visitor is offered a much more catholic selection of (French) wines than in wine regions further south. The French take chauvinism seriously and on a local scale. Remember that most dry white wines do not improve with age, so don't begrudge being asked to drink a very young vintage. Merely feel grateful that you can enjoy the wine while it's young and fresh. As for matching specific wines with food, I subscribe to the view that you should start by deciding what colour and weight you feel like drinking rather than following the choice dictated by the 'white with fish and red with meat' rule. If you want white with a rich meat dish, it makes sense to choose a full-bodied one such as white burgundy, while light-bodied, fairly tart reds like Beaujolais and Bourgueil make better fish partners than a rich Rhône would.

COMMON WINE TERMS – AN ALPHABETICAL GUIDE

The following are the words most likely to be encountered on labels and wine lists, with brief notes to help you towards the clues they give to what's inside the bottle.

Alsace – Wine region, see above.

Anjou – Loire source of lots of medium rosé and a bit of safe, unexciting dry white.

Appellation d'Origine Contrôlée – France's top 20 per cent of wine, named after the area where it is made.

Barsac – Sweet white Bordeaux. Part of Sauternes so all Barsac is Sauternes but not all Sauternes is Barsac.

Beaujolais – Light, juicy reds.

Beaune – Southern town in the Burgundy heartland. Any wine carrying this name alone will be expensive.

Blanc de Blancs – Sounds fancy but means very little. Literally, a white wine made of white grapes, unusual in a champagne but obvious in a still white.

Bordeaux – Wine region, see above.

Bourgogne – 'Burgundy', a wine region, see above.

Bourgueil (Pronounce 'Boor-gurr-yeh') – Light red from the middle Loire.

Brut – Extremely dry; applies particularly to sparkling wines.

Chablis – A much traduced name. True Chablis (and the only sort of Chablis you're likely to encounter in France) is steely-dry white burgundy from a village of the same name in the far north of the Burgundy region.

Champagne – Wine region, see below.

Château – Principally refers to Bordeaux wine estate, not necessarily possessing actual château. Because of the prestige of 'château', the title has become abused by dubious 'phantom châteaux' labels for very ordinary wines: *caveat emptor!*

Châteauneuf-du-Pape – Full-bodied spicy red from the southern Rhône.

Chenin (Blanc) – The white grape of the middle Loire, medium dry usually.

Corbières – Straightforward southern red.

Côte(s) de – 'Côte(s) de X' is usually better than a wine named simply 'X', as it means it comes from the (superior) hillsides above the lower ground of the X vineyards.

Coteaux de – Similar to 'Côte(s) de'.

Coteaux d'Ancenis – North Loire VDQS varietal whites. All dry except for Malvoisie.

Coteaux du Languedoc – Lightish southern red.

Coteaux du Layon – Small middle Loire area producing some excellent but many unexciting medium dry whites.

Coteaux du Tricastin – Lightish version of Côtes du Rhône.

Côtes de Provence – Appellation for the dry white, herby red and, principally, dry pink wines of Provence in south-east France.

Côtes du Rhône – This big appellation with some new-style dry whites but mainly lightish spicy reds like Châteauneuf is usually good value.

Crozes-Hermitage – Convenient, earlier-maturing but still quite concentrated version of (almost always red) Hermitage.

Cru – Means 'growth' literally, *Grand cru* means 'great growth' and really rather good. *Cru classé* means that the growth has been officially classified as up to some definite scratch, and most of the world's best clarets are *crus classés*.

Demi-sec – Literally, medium dry; more likely to mean sweet.

Domaine – Wine estate in Burgundy.

Doux – Sweet.

Entre-Deux-Mers – Dry, and rarely exciting, white from Bordeaux.

Fleurie – Single-village Beaujolais; superior.

Frappé – Served on crushed ice; e.g. *crème de menthe frappé.*

Gaillac – Inexpensive white and sometimes red from south-west France.

Glacé – Chilled; not the same as *frappé.*

Graves – Red and usually-dry white from a good-value area of Bordeaux.

Gewürztraminer – Perfumed grape grown in Alsace to produce France's most easily-recognisable white wine.

Haut – High or upper; topographical term. It happens that Haut-Médoc produces finer wine than the region's lower vineyards.

Hautes-Côtes de Beaune or *Nuits* – Affordable red and white burgundy from the slopes, high in altitude but not, for once, necessarily quality.

Hermitage – Long lived tannic red from the northern Rhône.

Juliénas – Single-village Beaujolais; superior.

Kir – Chilled dry white wine poured on to a little *crème de cassis* (q.v.). Splendid aperitif. Also Kir *royale* – made with champagne!

Loire – Wine region, see above.

Mâcon – Southern end of Burgundy, source of good-value whites and some unexciting reds.

Margaux – Médoc village producing scented clarets.

méthode champenoise – The Champagne region's way of putting bubbles into wine and usually the sign of a good one.

Meursault – Very respectable burgundy, almost all white.

Minervois – Better-than-average southern red.

Mis(e) bouteille au château – Bottled at the château (as opposed to in some merchant's cellars) and usually a sign of quality.

Moelleux – Medium sweet.

Monbazillac – Good-value country cousin to Sauternes.

Montrachet – Very great white burgundy.

Moulin-à-Vent – Single-village Beaujolais which, unusually, can be kept.

Mousseux – Sparkling.

Mouton-Cadet – Not a special property, but a commercial blend of claret.

Muscadet – Lean, dry white from the mouth of the Loire. Very tart.

Muscat – The grape whose wines, unusually, taste and smell grapey. Dry in Alsace; very sweet and strong from places like Rivesaltes, Frontignan and Beaumes de Venise.

Nouveau – 'New' wine; see *Primeur* (the more technical term) – popularised by Beaujolais shippers. Other regions have copied what some experts consider over-rated fad.

Nuits-St-Georges – Burgundy's second wine town. Bottles carrying this name are often expensive.

Pauillac – Bordeaux's most famous village, containing three of the five top châteaux. Very aristocratic claret.

Pétillant – Slightly sparkling wine.

Pineau – Unfermented grape juice fortified with grape alcohol: chilled, an interesting aperitif drink. *Pineau des Charentes* best known.

Pomerol – Soft, fruity claret. Similar to St Emilion.

Pommard – Soft, fruity red burgundy.

Pouilly-Fuissé – Famous appellation in the Mâcon region. Dry, white and sometimes overpriced.

Pouilly-Fumé – Much tarter than Pouilly-Fuissé, made from the Sauvignon grape (see below) in Loire.

Premières Côtes de Bordeaux – Inexpensive red and sweet white Bordeaux.

Primeur – Wine designed to be drunk within months of the vintage i.e. from November till Easter. Beaujolais Nouveau is a 'Primeur'.

Puligny-Montrachet – Steely white burgundy and often very good.

Riesling – Germany's famous grape produces great dry wine in Alsace.

Ste-Croix-du-Mont – Inexpensive sweet white bordeaux.

St Emilion – Soft, early-maturing claret from many little properties, most of which seem to be allowed to call themselves *crus classés*.

St Estèphe – Sometimes rather hard but noble claret.

St Julien – Another Médoc village housing many great châteaux.

Sancerre – Twin village to the Pouilly of Pouilly Fumé, and producing very similar wines.

Santenay – Light red burgundy.

Saumur – Town in the middle Loire giving its name to wines of all colours, degrees of sweetness and some very good sparkling wine too.

Sauvignon – Grape producing dry whites with lots of 'bite'.

Savigny-lès-Beaune – Village just outside Beaune responsible for some good-value 'proper' red burgundy.

Sec – Literally 'dry', but don't be fooled – usually a sweetish wine.

Supérieur(e) – as *Haut* (above), and not a qualitative term, an exception being in VDQS (q.v.).

Sylvaner – Alsace's 'everyday' light, dry white. Often the best wine you can buy by the glass in a French bar.

Touraine – An area in the middle Loire producing inexpensive Sauvignon and other wines.

VDQS – *Vin Délimité de Qualité Supérieure* (see above) – between AC and Vins de Pays.

Vin de Pays – Quality level at the top end of table wine. Many good-value inexpensive reds and some whites stating their region of origin on the label.

Vin de Pays des Marches de Bretagne – The only wine with an obviously Breton name. Light, tartish, usually white.

Vin de Table – The most basic sort of wine made in France. Very few excitements in this category. The blends with the name of a Burgundy merchant on the label are usually the most expensive.

Volnay – Soft red burgundy.

Xérès – ('ereth'): *vin de Xérès* = sherry.

WHAT TO BRING BACK

Provided you forgo any other liquor, and provided you make all
·the purchases in an ordinary (i.e. non-duty-free) shop, you may
bring back seven litres of wine to Britain without paying any
duty.

Nine 75cl bottles makes exactly this amount, as, of course, do
seven of the litre bottles so common in French supermarkets.
Ten 70cl bottles make so little more than seven litres that no
Customs official is likely to complain. The label will state a
bottle's capacity.

Excise duty is currently 78p on a 75cl bottle and 72p on a 70cl
bottle (plus 15% VAT of purchase price abroad), and it is largely
this that you are saving by importing your own wine. The extra
cost of transporting a bottle from Bordeaux to London as
opposed to Paris is negligible. Duty is the same on any bottle,
however, regardless of the value of the wine. This means that
savings are at their most dramatic – and most worth the effort –
for the least expensive wines. You can buy seven litres of *vin de
table* in France for around 50f, when the same amount of
equivalent quality wine in Britain would cost almost as many
pounds.

The corollary of all this is that you should bring back seven
litres of the most ordinary wine you find you enjoy drinking, if
your tastes and pocket are modest. Connoisseurs on the other
hand should confine themselves to bringing back the odd bottle
too obscure or rare to be found in this country. Many good
mature wines are cheaper here than there – though this of course
is dependent on the franc/sterling ratio.

HINTS ON CHAMPAGNE AND SPIRITS FROM JOHN DOXAT

Champagne

The only wine produced in the areas covered by this book is
happily the 'King of wines' – champagne. Doubtless, you will
drink other wines on your tour, but let us hope you will quaff
champagne in one of the towns – notably Reims, Épernay and Ay
– particularly associated with it. So let us briefly consider
champagne's background. Champagne is so zealously guarded a
name that the word itself is (within the E.E.C. at least) sufficient
guarantee of quality: an *appellation contrôlée* notation is not
required. (As from 1993, sparkling wines not qualifying as
champagne under rigorous French laws will be debarred from
bearing any indication that they are made by a 'champagne
method.')

We associate champagne exclusively with the unique sparkling wine. (There are excellent still (*natur*) champagne wines, but they are uncommon.) However, the vinous fame of the region far pre-dates the product we know: it was, in red and white wines, in historic competition with Burgundy. The Champagne wine-growers suffered a setback when the physician to Louis XIV opined – for venal reasons? – that Burgundies were best for his royal master. It was during the long reign (1653–1713) of this monarch, and into that of his successor, that there flourished Dom Pérignon, Cellar Master in the Abbey of Hautvilliers, near Épernay. Reputedly blind, almost as much legend as man, Dom Pérignon is said to have invented an effective way of sealing with cork a highly effervescent wine and strengthening the bottle. Both were vital to champagne's development into its present perfection. The Dom, immortalised in our own times by a very fine brand of premium champagne, did not invent sparkling wine. That had long been around, though secondary fermentation was little understood, and solid stoppers in poor bottles had such explosive results that sparkling wine was once called 'devil's wine'. The improved wine, credited to Dom Pérignon, found favour at the court of Louis XV – and never looked back.

For us, champagne is renowned not just for its superb natural bubbles, but for its grape-redolent dryness. Yet the original sparkling champagne was a sweet wine. For Tsarist Russia, a huge importer, it had to be almost sugary. Not until about a century ago did dry champagne catch on in England: an earlier experiment in importing it had been a failure. Then the Prince of Wales (Edward VII) praised a 1865 dry champagne and was publicised as drinking it. Smart Society aped his whim and the vogue for it quickly spread. This style became known as *gôut anglais*, or English Dry, and soon was dominant. Britain has been, and again is, the premier export market for champagne. When dry champagne was first called *brut* (the customary description today) I have been unable to discover – nor why. For *brut* translates as 'rough, coarse, raw' – everything champagne is not!

Champagne, chilled – but never to excess nor diluted with ice – is the supreme apéritif drink for many discerning folk. Champagne deserves respect – the habit of victorious sportsmen showering it on their admirers is frankly disgusting – yet it is not desecration to use non-vintage champagne in discreet mixes. I like a Kir Royale: a teaspoon of *crème de cassis* topped with the wine; a champagne *a- l'orange* (Buck's fizz): half-and-half fresh orange juice and NV champagne . . .

Champagne is for drinking. This is no place for explanations of production: you can get those from books. Or, much better, visit one of the great champagne houses: plan an itinerary to include that. Particulars from The Champagne Bureau, Crusader House, 14 Pall Mall, London, SW1Y 5LU. Tel: 01 839 1561.

Spirits

The great French spirit is brandy. Cognac, commercially the leader, must come from the closely controlled region of that name. Of various quality designations, the commonest is VSOP (very special old pale): it will be a cognac worth drinking neat. Remember, *champagne* in a cognac connotation, has absolutely no connection with the wine. It is a topographical term, *grande champagne* being the most prestigious cognac area: *fine champagne* is a blend of brandy from the two top cognac sub-divisions.

Armagnac has become better known lately outside France, and rightly so. As a brandy it has a much longer history than cognac: some connoisseurs rate old armagnac (the quality designations are roughly similar) above cognac.

Be cautious of French brandy without a cognac or armagnac title, regardless of how many meaningless 'stars' the label carries or even the magic word 'Napoleon' (which has no legal significance).

Little appreciated in Britain is the splendid 'apple brandy', Calvados, mainly associated with Normandy but also made in Brittany and the Marne. The best is Calvados *du Pays d'Auge*. Do taste well aged Calvados, but avoid any suspiciously cheap.

Contrary to popular belief, true Calvados is not distilled from cider – but an inferior imitation is: French cider *(cidre)* is excellent.

Though most French proprietary aperitifs, like Dubonnet, are fairly low in alcohol, the extremely popular Pernod/Ricard *pastis*-style brands are highly spirituous. *Eau-de-vie* is the generic term for all spirits, but colloquially tends to refer to, often rough, local distillates. An exception are the better *alcools blancs* (white spirits), which are not inexpensive, made from fresh fruits and not sweetened as *crèmes* are.

Liqueurs

Numerous travellers deem it worth allocating their allowance to bring back some of the famous French liqueurs (Bénédictine, Chartreuse, Cointreau, and so on) which are so costly in Britain. Compare 'duty free' prices with those in stores, which can vary markedly. There is a plethora of regional liqueurs, and numerous sickly *crèmes*, interesting to taste locally. The only *crème* generally meriting serious consideration as a liqueur is *crème de menthe* (preferably Cusenier), though the newish *crème de Grand Marnier* has been successful. *Crème de cassis* has a special function: see Kir in alphabetical list.

Glossary of cooking terms and dishes

(It would take another book to list comprehensively French cooking terms and dishes, but here are the ones most likely to be encountered.)

Aigre-doux	bittersweet
Aiguillette	thin slice (aiguille – needle)
Aile	wing
Aioli	garlic mayonnaise
Allemande (à l')	German style, i.e.: with sausages and sauerkraut
Amuse-gueules	appetisers
Anglaise (à l')	plain boiled. Crème Anglaise – egg and cream sauce
Andouille	large uncooked sausage, served cold after boiling
Andouillettes	ditto but made from smaller intestines, usually served hot after grilling
Anis	aniseed
Argenteuil	with asparagus
Assiette Anglaise	plate of cold meats
Baba au Rhum	yeast-based sponge macerated in rum
Baguette	long, thin loaf
Ballotine	boned, stuffed and rolled meat or poultry, usually cold
Béarnaise	sauce made from egg yolks, butter, tarragon, wine, shallots
Beurre blanc	sauce from Nantes, with butter, reduction of shallot-flavoured vinegar or wine
Béchamel	white sauce flavoured with infusion of herbs
Beignets	fritters
Bercy	sauce with white wine and shallots
Beurre noir	browned butter
Bigarade	with oranges
Billy By	mussel soup
Bisque	creamy shellfish soup
Blanquette	stew with thick, white creamy sauce, usually veal
Boeuf à la mode	braised beef
Bombe	ice-cream mould

Bonne femme	with root vegetables
Bordelais	Bordeaux-style, with red or white wine, marrow bone fat
Bouchée	mouthful, i.e. vol-au-vent
Boudin	sausage, white or black
Bourride	thick fish-soup
Braisé	braised
Brandade (de morue)	dried salt-cod pounded into a mousse
Broche	spit
Brochette	skewer
Brouillade	stew, using oil
Brouillé	scrambled
Brulé	burnt, i.e. crême brulée
Campagne	country style
Cannelle	cinnamon
Carbonnade	braised in beer
Cardinal	red-coloured sauce, e.g. with lobster, or in pâtisserie with redcurrant
Charcuterie	cold pork-butcher's meats
Charlotte	mould, as dessert lined with sponge-fingers, as savoury lined with vegetable
Chasseur	with mushrooms, shallots, wine
Chausson	pastry turnover
Chemise	covering, i.e. pastry
Chiffonade	thinly-cut, e.g. lettuce
Choron	tomato Béarnaise
Choucroute	Alsation stew with sauerkraut and sausages
Civet	stew
Clafoutis	batter dessert, usually with cherries
Clamart	with peas
Cocotte	covered casserole
Compôte	cooked fruit
Concassé	e.g. tomatoes concassées – skinned, chopped, juice extracted

Confit	preserved
Confiture	jam
Consommé	clear soup
Cou	neck
Coulis	juice, puree (of vegetables or fruit)
Cassolette or cassoulette	small pan
Cassoulet	rich stew with goose, pork and haricot beans
Cervelas	pork garlic sausage
Cervelles	brains
Chantilly	whipped sweetened cream
Cocque (à la)	e.g. oeufs – boiled eggs
Court-bouillon	aromatic liquor for cooking meat, fish, vegetables
Couscous	N. African dish with millet, chicken, vegetable variations
Crapaudine	involving fowl, particularly pigeon, trussed
Crécy	with carrots
Crème pâtissière	thick custard filling
Crêpe	pancake
Crépinette	little flat sausage, encased in caul
Croque Monsieur	toasted cheese-and-ham sandwich
Croustade	pastry or baked bread shell
Croûte	pastry crust
Croûton	cube of fried or toasted bread
Cru	raw
Crudités	raw vegetables
Demi-glâce	basic brown sauce
Doria	with cucumber
Émincé	thinly sliced
Étuvé	stewed, e.g. vegetables in butter
Entremets	sweets
Farci	stuffed
Fines herbes	parsley, thyme, bayleaf
Feuilléte	leaves of flaky pastry
Flamande	Flemish style, with beer
Flambé	flamed in spirit
Flamiche	flan
Florentine	with spinach
Flûte	thinnest bread loaf
Foie gras	goose liver
Fondu	melted

Fond (d'artichaut)	heart (of artichoke)
Forestière	with mushrooms, bacon and potatoes
Four (au)	baked in the oven
Fourré	stuffed, usually sweets
Fricandeau	veal, usually topside
Frais, fraîche	fresh and cool
Frangipane	almond-cream pâtisserie
Fricadelle	Swedish meat ball
Fricassé	(usually of veal) in creamy sauce
Frit	fried
Frites	chips
Friture	assorted small fish, fried in batter
Froid	cold
Fumé	smoked
Galantine	loaf-shaped chopped meat, fish or vegetable, set in natural jelly
Gallette	Breton pancake, flat cake
Garbure	thick country soup
Garni	garnished, usually with vegetables
Gaufre	waffle
Gelée	aspic
Gésier	gizzard
Gibier	game
Gigôt	leg
Glacé	iced
Gougère	choux pastry, large base
Goujons	fried strips, usually of fish
Graine	seed
Gratin	baked dish of vegetables cooked in cream and eggs
Gratinée	browned under grill
Grêcque (à la)	cold vegetables served in oil
Grenouilles	frogs; cuisses de grenouille – frogs' legs
Grillé	grilled
Gros sel	coarse salt
Hachis	minced or chopped
Haricot	slow cooked stew
Hochepot	hotpot
Hollandaise	sauce with egg, butter, lemon
Hongroise	Hungarian, i.e. spiced with paprika
Hors d'oeuvre	assorted starters
Huile	oil

Île flottante	floating island – soft meringue on egg-custard sauce
Indienne	Indian, i.e. with hot spices
Jambon	ham
Jardinière	from the garden, i.e. with vegetables
Jarret	shin, i.e. jarret de veau
Julienne	matchstick vegetables
Jus	natural juice
Lait	milk
Langue	tongue
Lard	bacon
Longe	loin
Macédoine	diced fruits or vegetables
Madeleine	small sponge cake
Magret	breast (of duck)
Maïs	sweetcorn
Maître d'hôtel	sauce with butter, lemon, parsley
Marchand de vin	sauce with red wine, shallot
Marengo	sauce with tomatoes, olive oil, white wine
Marinière	seamens' style, i.e. moules marinière (mussels in white wine)
Marmite	deep casserole
Matelote	fish stew, i.e. of eel
Médaillon	round slice
Mélange	mixture
Meunière	sauce with butter, lemon
Miel	honey
Mille feuille	flaky pastry, lit. 1,000 leaves
Mirepoix	cubed carrot, onion etc. used for sauces
Moëlle	beef marrow
Mornay	cheese sauce
Mouclade	mussel stew
Mousseline	Hollandaise sauce, lightened with egg whites
Moutarde	mustard
Nage (à la)	poached in flavoured liquor (fish)
Nature	plain
Navarin (d'agneau)	stew of lamb with spring vegetables
Noisette	nut-brown, burned butter

Noix de veau	nut of veal (leg)
Normande	Normandy style, with cream, apple, cider, Calvados
Nouilles	noodles
Onglet	beef cut from flank
Os	bone
Paillettes	straws (of pastry)
Panaché	mixed
Panade	flour crust
Papillote (en)	cooked in paper case
Parmentier	with potatoes
Pâté	paste, of meat or fish
Pâte	pastry
Pâte brisée	rich short crust pastry
Pâtisserie	pastries
Paupiettes	paper thin slice
Pavé	thick slice
Paysan	country style
Perigueux	with truffles
Persillade	chopped parsley and garlic topping
Petits fours	tiny cakes, sweetmeats
Petit pain	bread roll
Piperade	peppers, onions, tomatoes in scrambled egg
Poché	poached
Poêlé	fried
Poitrine	breast
Poivre	pepper
Pommade	paste
Potage	thick soup
Pot-au-four	broth with meat and vegetables
Potée	country soup with cabbage
Pralines	caramelised almonds
Primeurs	young veg
Printanièr(e)	garnished with early vegetables
Profiteroles	choux pastry balls
Provençale	with garlic, tomatoes, olive oil, peppers
Purée	mashed and sieved
Quenelle	pounded fish or meat, bound with egg, poached
Queue	tail
Quiche	pastry flan, i.e. quiche Lorraine – egg, bacon, cream
Râble	saddle, i.e. rable de lièvre
Ragout	stew

Ramequin	little pot
Rapé	grated
Ratatouille	provencale stew of onions garlic, peppers, tomatoes
Ravigote	highly seasoned white sauce
Rémoulade	mayonnaise with gherkins capers, herbs and shallot
Rillettes	potted shredded meat, usually fat pork or goose
Riz	rice
Robert	sauce with mustard, vinegar, onion
Roquefort	ewe's milk blue cheese
Rossini	garnished with foie gras and truffle
Rôti	roast
Rouelle	nugget
Rouille	hot garlicky sauce for soupe de poisson
Roulade	roll
Roux	sauce base – flour and butter
Sabayon	sweet fluffy sauce, with eggs and wine
Safran	saffron
Sagou	sago
St-Germain	with peas
Salade niçoise	with tunny, anchovies, tomatoes, beans, black olives
Salé	salted
Salmis	dish of game or fowl, with red wine
Sang	blood
Santé	lit. healthy, i.e. with spinach and potato
Salpicon	meat, fowl, vegetables, chopped fine, bound with sauce and used as fillings
Saucisse	fresh sausage
Saucisson	dried sausage
Sauté	cooked in fat in open pan
Sauvage	wild
Savarin	ring of yeast-sponge, soaked in syrup and liquor
Sel	salt
Selle	saddle
Selon	according to, e.g. selon grosseur (according to size)

Smitane	with sour cream, white wine, onion
Soissons	with dried white beans
Sorbet	water ice
Soubise	with creamed onions
Soufflé	puffed, i.e. mixed with egg white and baked
Sucre	sugar (sucré – sugared)
Suprême	fillet of poultry breast or fish
Tartare	raw minced beef, flavoured with onion etc. and bound with raw egg
Tartare (sauce)	mayonnaise with capers, herbs, onions
Tarte Tatin	upside down apple pie
Terrine	pottery dish/baked minced, chopped meat, veg., chicken, fish or fruit
Thé	tea
Tiède	luke warm
Timbale	steamed mould
Tisane	infusion
Tourte	pie
Tranche	thick slice
Truffes	truffles
Tuile	tile, i.e. thin biscuit
Vacherin	meringue confection
Vallée d'Auge	with cream, apple, Calvados
Vapeur (au)	steamed
Velouté	white sauce, bouillon-flavoured
Véronique	with grapes
Vert(e)	green, e.g. sauce verte with herbs
Vessie	pigs bladder
Vichyssoise	chilled creamy leek and potato soup
Vierge	prime olive oil
Vinaigre	vinegar (lit. bitter wine)
Vinaigrette	wine vinegar and oil dressing
Volaille	poultry
Vol-au-vent	puff-pastry case
Xérès	sherry
Yaourt	yoghurt

FISH – Les Poissons, SHELLFISH – Les Coquillages

Anchois	anchovy	*Langouste*	spring lobster,
Anguille	eel		or crawfish
Araignée de mer	spider crab	*Langoustine*	Dublin Bay prawn
Bar	sea bass	*Lieu*	ling
Barbue	brill	*Limand*	lemon sole
Baudroie	monkfish, anglerfish	*Lotte de mer*	monkfish
Belon	oyster – flat shelled	*Loup de mer*	sea bass
Bigorneau	winkle	*Maquereau*	mackerel
Blanchaille	whitebait	*Merlan*	whiting
Brochet	pike	*Morue*	salt cod
Cabillaud	cod	*Moule*	mussel
Calamar	squid	*Mulet*	grey mullet
Carrelet	plaice	*Ombre*	grayling
Chapon de mer	scorpion fish	*Oursin*	sea urchin
Claire	oyster	*Palourde*	clam
Coquille	scallop	*Pétoncle*	small scallop
St-Jacques		*Plie*	plaice
Crabe	crab	*Portugaise*	oyster
Crevette grise	shrimp	*Poulpe*	octopus
Crevette rose	prawn	*Praire*	oyster
Daurade	sea bream	*Raie*	skate
Écrevisse	crayfish	*Rascasse*	scorpion-fish
Éperlan	smelt	*Rouget*	red mullet
Espadon	swordfish	*St-Pierre*	John Dory
Etrille	baby crab	*Saumon*	Salmon
Favouille	spider crab	*Saumonette*	rock salmon
Flétan	halibut	*Seiche*	squid
Fruits de mer	seafood	*Sole*	sole
Grondin	red gurnet	*Soupion*	inkfish
Hareng	herring	*Thon*	tunny
Homard	lobster	*Tortue*	turtle
Huitre	oyster	*Tourteau*	large crab
Julienne	ling	*Truite*	trout
Laitance	soft herring-roe	*Turbot*	turbot
Lamproie	lamprey	*Turbotin*	chicken turbot

FRUITS – Les Fruits, VEGETABLES – Les Légumes, NUTS – Les Noix
HERBS – Les Herbes, SPICES – Les Épices

Ail	garlic	*Basilic*	basil
Algue	seaweed	*Betterave*	beetroot
Amande	almond	*Blette*	Swiss chard
Ananas	pineapple	*Brugnon*	nectarine
Aneth	dill	*Cassis*	blackcurrant
Abricot	apricot	*Céléri*	celery
Arachide	peanut	*Céléri-rave*	celeriac
Artichaut	globe artichoke	*Cêpe*	edible fungus
Asperge	asparagus	*Cerfeuil*	chervil
Avocat	avocado	*Cérise*	cherry
Banane	banana	*Champignon*	mushroom

Chanterelle	edible fungus	Morille	dark brown crinkly
Chatâigne	chestnut		edible fungus
Chicorée	endive	Mûre	blackberry
Chou	cabbage	Muscade	nutmeg
Choufleur	cauliflower	Myrtille	bilberry, blueberry
Choux de Bruxelles	Brussels sprouts	Navet	turnip
Ciboulette	chive	Noisette	hazelnut
Citron	lemmon	Oignon	onion
Citron vert	lime	Oseille	sorrel
Coing	quince	Palmier	palm
Concombre	cucumber	Pamplemousse	grapefruit
Coriandre	coriander	Panais	parsnip
Cornichon	gherkin	Passe-Pierre	seaweed
Courge	pumpkin	Pastèque	water melon
Courgette	courgette	Pêche	peach
Cresson	watercress	Persil	parsley
Échalote	shallot	Petit pois	pea
Endive	chicory	Piment doux	sweet pepper
Épinard	spinach	Pissenlit	dandelion
Escarole	salad leaves	Pistache	pistachio
Estragon	tarragon	Pleurote	edible fungi
Fenouil	fennel	Poire	pear
Fève	broad bean	Poireau	leek
Flageolet	dried bean	Poivre	pepper
Fraise	strawberry	Poivron	green, red and yellow
Framboise	raspberry		peppers
Genièvre	juniper	Pomme	apple
Gingembre	ginger	Pomme-de-terre	potato
Girofle	clove	Prune	plum
Girolle	edible fungus	Pruneau	prune
Grenade	pomegranate	Quetsch	small dark plum
Griotte	bitter red cherry	Radis	radish
Groseille	gooseberry	Raifort	horseradish
Groseille noire	blackcurrant	Raisin	grape
Groseille rouge	redcurrant	Reine Claude	greengage
Haricot	dried white bean	Romarin	rosemary
Haricot vert	French bean	Safran	saffron
Laitue	lettuce	Salsifis	salsify
Mandarine	tangerine, mandarin	Thym	thyme
Mangetout	sugar pea	Tilleul	lime blossom
Marron	chestnut	Tomate	tomato
Menthe	mint	Topinambour	Jerusalem artichoke
Mirabelle	tiny gold plum	Truffe	truffle

MEAT – Les Viandes

Le Boeuf	Beef	Faux Filet	sirloin steak
Charolais	is the best	Filet	fillet
Chateaubriand	double fillet steak	L'Agneau	Lamb
Contrefilet	sirloin	Pré-Salé	is the best
Entrecôte	rib steak	Carré	neck cutlets

Côte	chump chop	*Les Abats*	Offal
Épaule	shoulder	*Foie*	liver
Gigot	leg	*Foie gras*	goose liver
Le Porc	Pork	*Cervelles*	brains
Jambon	ham	*Langue*	tongue
Jambon cru	raw smoked ham	*Ris*	sweetbreads
Porcelet	suckling pig	*Rognons*	kidneys
		Tripes	tripe
Le Veau	Veal		
Escalope	thin slice cut from fillet		

POULTRY – Volaille, GAME – Gibier

Abatis	giblets	*Lièvre*	hare
Bécasse	woodcock	*Oie*	goose
Bécassine	snipe	*Perdreau*	partridge
Caille	quail	*Pigeon*	pigeon
Canard	duck	*Pintade*	guineafowl
Caneton	duckling	*Pluvier*	plover
Chapon	capon	*Poularde*	chicken (boiling)
Chevreuil	roe deer	*Poulet*	chicken (roasting)
Dinde	young hen turkey	*Poussin*	spring chicken
Dindon	turkey	*Sanglier*	wild boar
Dindonneau	young turkey	*Sarcelle*	teal
Faisan	pheasant	*Venaison*	venison
Grive	thrush		

Index